DISGRACEFUL CONDUCT OF A CRUEL KIND

The true story of a Politically Motivated Court Martial

by

Robert Kyriakides

Text © Robert Kyriakides

Cover design © Richard Kyriakides

World Rights Reserved

No part of this book may be reproduced or utilised in any form by any means without prior permission in writing of the copyright owner.

Published by Dorian Press

DEDICATION

This book is dedicated to the memory of Major Frank Edmunds and all those who served in the intelligence services of the British military during the Second World War and the aftermath of it

CHAPTER 1
The Secret File

What is disgraceful conduct of a cruel kind? You will not find that crime in any of the standard law books, but it was and still is a crime in the British Army and in the Royal Navy to commit "disgraceful conduct of a cruel, indecent or unnatural kind". This crime has its origins in the old naval Articles of War but is still contained in current legislation. It is a convenient crime to prosecute behaviour that the authorities disapprove of because it is flexible and uncertain in scope. What is 'disgraceful' is a subjective test, judged by the standards of the day. For example, a homosexual relationship would have been judged to be disgraceful seventy-five years ago, but not today. Totalitarian states delight in such inchoate definitions of crime.

In 1948 three men, all former soldiers working at the interrogation department in the British Zone in Germany at the Combined Services Detailed Intelligence Centre (CSDIC) near Hanover, were charged with having committed disgraceful conduct of a cruel kind. The three had been conducting severe interrogations of two former SS officers at the British controlled prison at Bad Nenndorf. The SS men complained of brutal treatment and the interrogators were charged before a court martial.

When we talk of the fog of war, we usually mean the uncertainty and lack of clarity which hinders those who must make decisions in the course of a war but there is also a great fog that settles on the decisions and events after a war has ended. That fog is terribly convenient to those who have conducted the war, for it frequently obscures or exaggerates the truth and the events that happened in war.

In May 1945 Germany was defeated and occupied by the Allies, who divided Germany into four zones; the zones were controlled by Britain, the USA, France, and the Soviet Union. The Allies were intent on pursuing war criminals and preventing any repetition of the evils of fascism by 'de-Nazifying' Germany. Many Germans were imprisoned and then interrogated as part of this process. Some were tried for war crimes. Some were hanged.

One of the three former soldiers charged with disgraceful conduct of a cruel kind was Frank Edmunds. I first met Major Frank Edmunds in January 1988 forty years after the court martial. Frank asked me to prepare his will – a mundane task but an important one. He used his honorary rank of 'Major'.

He presented, as the doctors say, as a fit wiry bachelor of nearly four score years, living with some small private means, modestly, in Cannes, in the South of France. His eyes sparkled and were bright. He was always immaculately dressed and extremely polite, but tenacious. He was one of the politesse men I had known.

He spoke perfect English with an accent that is impossible to place; it was not any English accent that I knew. It had a German inflection and a slight tone of French, a genuine trans-European voice. His grammar was perfect. He was at pains to impress upon me that he was British and regarded himself as British, and although he spent long periods in the South of France, he regarded these islands as his home.

Frank was gay. He never told me directly that he was gay, but it was not difficult to deduce. Frank did not make an exhibition of his sexuality. He never discussed his sexuality or referred to it or mentioned it, but when one of my young male staff would attend our meetings Frank might later mention that so and so was a very nice boy and extremely helpful and pleasant. His eyes lit up when any young man entered the room. "Such a nice boy", was Frank's usual comment made discreetly after the 'boy' had left the room.

I learnt quickly that Frank was practical; before engaging me, he had enquired about my age. He told me that he came from a family whose members lived long lives and he wanted to be sure that his lawyer would live longer than him. I was thirty-seven years younger than Frank, and he felt the odds were good that I would survive him. I did survive him, even though Frank did his best to live as long as he could and died when he was ninety-seven.

Frank belonged to that relatively rare class of client that likes to constantly change wills. Some clients change their wills because of some perceived slight or insult, or better to control their offspring, rather like the classic 'will rattler' of the Victorian era, but for Frank revising a will was a matter of logical fine tuning. I later learned that he had pre-paid for his funeral and corresponded with the funeral director so much that the director had a very fat file.

He retained all his connections with England and kept a flat in London but lived for long periods in Nice in the South of France, which then was an old-fashioned thing to do, but Frank had always been old-fashioned. He would regularly be in touch with me to discuss ideas and make requests for advice about the changes he had in mind, although I suspect that part of the reason for his long correspondence and regular meetings was that he liked me.

As I took instructions and got to know him (and you must know your clients very well to do your best for them) I did not realise for many years that this elderly friendly man had spent the war gathering secrets and questioning high ranking Nazis as an Intelligence Officer in the British Army. He kept secrets because he was sworn to keep them, and he kept them throughout his long life.

He was taught interrogation and then developed interrogation techniques which enabled him to prise the truth out of those he interrogated. First, he questioned captured enemy soldiers and later civilians after the war ended. His approach to me, when asking for advice, was logical and well thought out. He wanted to leave no stone unturned and no contingency undiscussed. The information he obtained saved lives and was one small piece of a massive jigsaw that comprised the Allied war effort. He had interrogated those we would today call insurgents and terrorists as well as the vanquished and captured German generals.

Frank was born in Nuremberg in 1912, which made him German by birth and he was Jewish by religion. Nuremberg was and is a vibrant trading centre in Bavaria. It was the home of great Nazi rallies in the 1930s and after the war the Allies conducted war trials in the Nuremberg Palace of Justice from 1945 to 1949. When Frank was a young man his parents left Nuremberg to avoid the persecution that the Jews suffered in those times. Hitler published a decree in Nuremberg in 1935 that deprived Jews of their German citizenship, so the family left for Britain and settled in Wembley in North London where the family became naturalised British citizens. It was as well that they did come to Britain because Frank was two things that the Nazis detested. He was a Jew and he was gay.

The fact that the Germans killed many millions of Jews is well known to history. Perhaps less well known is that the Nazis suppressed homosexuals violently, incarcerating more than a hundred thousand of them; they were forced to wear pink triangles in the concentration camps. The SS led by Himmler, took the view that "we must exterminate these people root and branch". Germany was not the only European country that oppressed gays in those days. In some parts of Europe homosexuals were experimented upon, in order to find a cure for homosexuality. In Britain gay men were regularly prosecuted for relationships with other gay men even if they were conducted in private. Sex between consenting men in private was a criminal offence until 1967 and for many years after that gay men were treated with opprobrium.

When war was declared in 1939 Frank joined the British Army mainly serving with other men; there must have been other gay men in the army, but had Frank formed relationships with them he would have been imprisoned and disgraced, which is not quite as bad a fate as that decreed by Himmler, but nevertheless a serious consequence for a young man trying to serve his adopted country in a war against the country of his birth. He, like many others in those times, repressed his desires by working hard, diligently, and long hours. His work distracted him.

It must be hard if you are surrounded by people and you find that there is one with whom you wish to make a relationship, but you know that cannot be. Sometimes relationships can be started by looks across a crowded room, developed by talking and socialising until they blossom into love and love's expression, sex, but that was not to be for Frank for many years. The war Britain was fighting was ostensibly a fight for freedom, but freedom was not defined to include freedom for gay people to enjoy loving relationships.

Frank had a very sharp logical mind and could understand the most complex of legal concepts. During our long chats about his will, he told me that he was an Intelligence Officer of the British Army. He had served his country, Britain. I told him that my own father, a N.C.O., had been seconded to Intelligence, but then spent four years as a prisoner of war, carrying a copy of the Geneva Convention and drawing the attention of the German authorities to its provisions, so that his men would be safer and better treated by the Germans.

This must have struck a chord with Frank because Frank then told me, in general terms, about his court martial. He had served his country, Britain, well but afterwards his country had accused him of terrible crimes and put him on trial which he said was the most extraordinary and longest court martial in British military history. He called it a political court martial. Frank was not prone to exaggeration.

Frank told me that he had a file of papers and one day I would have them; their contents were top-secret, but I could do with them as I wished, but only after his death. I could publish his file or turn it into a book, but only after he had died.

He gave me the file in 1995 asking me not to read it until he died, but I told him that I would find it too tempting to look at and it would be better, if he wanted to keep things secret, for him to look after the file for me and I handed it back to him. Lawyers are used to keeping many secrets but not, usually, secrets of state.

So it was that Frank thereafter kept the file under his bed, reminding me whenever we met that the file was mine and I would have it when I undertook my duties as his executor when the time came. When I visited him in France, he delighted in showing me the file, a red cover with elastic bands around it to prevent the yellowing contents inside from spilling out. The contents were mine, he said, to be divulged, but only if I thought fit, after he had died. If I wanted to throw the file in the dustbin, he said, that would be fine by him.

In early November 2009 I got news that Frank had died in the South of France. I felt a brief sadness, but sadness is not really what you feel for long when a friend dies at the age of ninety-seven having become increasingly infirm and a shadow of the lively vibrant seventy-seven-year-old whom I first met. The paraphernalia of very old age in modern times, the gradual erosion of strength and mental agility usually leaves living beings as shells of their former selves. Death is a fitting ending to these decays.

It took me a month before I could bring myself to read Frank's file. There were a few missing pages, but the vast bulk of his manuscript was intact, but yellowed with age, mostly typed by him on flimsy A4 sized paper in 1984. It tells a story, a true story, of extraordinary events with extraordinary people and at the centre of it all I read the story of an intelligence officer poorly treated by an ungrateful nation that he served. It interested me. I did further research, looking at the trial transcripts of what must have been the longest and most elaborate court martial conducted by the British Army at the end of the Second World War.

CHAPTER 2

Frank Goes to War, Interrogating Generals and Hitler's Will

I learned that when war broke out Frank joined the army. After serving for about two years in 1940-41 as a wireless operator in the ranks of the Royal Corps of Signals, Frank was detached for special duties which involved using his three languages – French, English and German – and then served for a period anonymously under Colonel Lewis Gielgud (brother of Sir John Gielgud). Frank spoke German and French fluently so it was natural that he would work for the intelligence services of the army.

On 16 February 1942 Frank was invited to an interview at Orchard Court, in Portman Square in the Baker Street part of London's West End with Major Maurice Buckmaster. Orchard Court was the Headquarters of the Special Operations Executive. Special Operations Executive 'ran' agents such as Violette Szabo and Odette Churchill in enemy occupied Europe. Frank was commissioned in the field and launched into his future career as an intelligence officer. After a series of intelligence courses, in London and at Oxford and Cambridge, he was posted to the Combined Services Detailed Interrogation Centre (CSDIC) in March 1943. At Cambridge Frank was trained in the art of interrogation; he was taught that not only was torture not permitted but it was self-defeating because under torture the information that a prisoner gives will almost certainly be useless.

At the end of 1943, with the rank of Staff Captain, Frank became an interrogation officer for operational and long-range interrogation. Many German military prisoners of war passed through his hands. They ranged from private soldiers to SS members and generals. Frank had to tease out useful intelligence from all of them including men who had guarded Hitler's Chancellery, those who had been employed at the Auschwitz Concentration Camp, and officers of special intelligence value or technical knowledge who knew about fortifications, V1 sites, gun emplacements, ammunition dumps on the invasion coasts and the prospective landing beaches, detailed long range information on V1 and V2 weapons more than a year before these weapons were employed by the Germans: Frank managed to obtain the layout of the German's V weapon research station at Peenemunde which enabled the subsequent successful RAF raids on it. Finally, Frank was entrusted with the interrogations of some captured German generals during the closing stages of the war. Some of these interrogations clarified many until then unknown or obscure matters and provided valuable information which was used by historians and other experts who wrote books on the subject often using verbatim texts taken from Frank's reports of his interrogations.

Of the many 'generals' interrogations which Frank carried out, intelligence information obtained from two of his 'star' generals was particularly important. Frank questioned these generals, Blumentritt, (who planned the invasion of Poland) and von Manteuffel (who served in the Afrika Corps under Rommel and on the Eastern Front) and this is what he learned from his interrogation of them.

Frank discovered that after the successful evacuation of the bulk of the British Expeditionary Forces at Dunkirk, Hitler gave orders, through his generals Halder and Brauchitsch, for Field Marshal von Rundstedt, the Commander in Chief in the West to make the necessary preparations and carry out Operation Sea Lion for the invasion of England. Von Rundstedt did not take the orders seriously according to his own statements and assessments at the time and was convinced that Hitler was never in earnest about the invasion, because he was obsessed with the idea of making peace with England, for which he had appealed on 19 July 1940 in his Reichstag Speech.

Rundstedt decided, according to Frank, to take little interest in the task which had been entrusted to him and left matters entirely in the hands of his adjutant Blumentritt. General Blumentritt went ahead with preparations to invade England, followed by exercises, but when eventually his detailed report reached Berlin, the whole operation, Hitler's phantom adventure, as Rundstedt and Blumentritt thought of it, was called off.

Frank learned that the plan that Blumentritt devised was to make landings in England on a broad front between Dover and Land's End from bases on the Belgian and French coasts, between Antwerp and Brest. Bridgeheads were to be set up on the English coast followed by a forward thrust to London and the West. All the German generals agreed that the capacity and resources of the German Navy were inadequate and could not compete with the powerful Royal Navy. Furthermore, that the best opportunity, the time of the Dunkirk evacuation, had been missed.

Frank interrogated General Hasso Von Manteuffel who was one of the youngest German generals. He had become the most effective tank general who had excelled himself through his ingenious ideas and new methods of tank warfare on the Russian Front. He divided his forces into small mobile groups and broke in behind the rear of the advancing Russians with sudden ripostes which often brought the Russian advance to a halt.

Hitler got to hear about this, and he was very interested to hear more of Manteuffel's new methods. He invited Manteuffel to visit him frequently at his East Prussian HQ and Manteuffel spent Christmas 1943 at Hitler's headquarters.

Manteuffel co-operated fully with Frank and gave a wealth of technical information which Frank reports was most appreciated by MI6, the Director of the Royal Armoured Corps Major General Raymond Briggs and the British Tank Experimental Station at Ascot.

Amongst Manteuffel's information were details about the waterproofing of tanks, which had enabled the German Tank Units to cross Russian rivers without suffering damage. The greatest 'coup' however, was achieved with detailed information including photographs of an entirely new tank, details of which were completely unknown to the Allies at the time and could not be obtained otherwise. Photographs of the new tank were recovered by Frank personally from the loft of the house of *Freifrau* von Manteuffel and her mother in Stade near Hamburg. Frank reports that Manteuffel maintained that he was not a Nazi or a Hitlerite.

Frank's interrogation of Manteuffel had been 'soft'. It had been friendly interrogation without making threats and without the use of force, just as he had been taught at Cambridge. I imagine that by his appearance Manteuffel would have thought of Frank as English, a typical Englishman, protestant and without any Jewish 'taint'. Frank had worked his way into Manteuffel's mind and not only got the information that lodged there but also the plans of the new German tank that Manteuffel had hidden in his attic. Months later Frank received a personal note of thanks for his work from Major General Briggs, which he kept as a memento.

In the course of his work Frank discovered and studied Hitler's last will and testament which Hitler made before he committed suicide. Hitler made his will on 29 April 1945, the day before he committed suicide. Frank knew that the will existed from two of the prisoners he interrogated, Colonel von Below and Major Freytag von Loringhoven, who were amongst the closest of Hitler's entourage and who were also present at the time when the will was dictated by Hitler to one of his secretaries, Frau Junge, shortly after Hitler's marriage to Eva Braun.

In the course of interrogating Heinz Lorenz, alias Georges Thiers, Frank found, sewn up in Lorenz's clothes, two copies of the triplicate set of Hitler's will. Lorenz was an official of the *Deutsche Nazhrichtenbureau* (Press Service) working at the Propaganda Ministry. Lorenz frequently reported to Hitler's bunker, delivering news. Some of the information delivered to Hitler by Lorenz made Hitler decide to include provisions in his will, disgracing Himmler and Goering, who without Hitler's knowledge were trying to negotiate surrender. The Himmler negotiations with Count Bernadotte of Sweden had been leaked and reported by Reuters.

Frank discovered that Colonel Nicklaus von Below was the very last person to leave the Hitler Bunker before Hitler's death. Von Below was Hitler's Luftwaffe aide-de-camp. General Krebs and Major Freytag von Loringhoven were other late leavers of the bunker. Frank obtained the information about Hitler's will from these sources, which also helped to throw light upon the last days and hours of Hitler's life, and all of which he passed on in the form of Memoranda to Intelligence Division at Bad Oeynhausen, from where presumably the information found its way to Professor Trevor Roper, a young officer at the time and a friend of Dick White, the future head of MI5 and MI6. Professor Trevor Roper reproduced much of this information in his book, *The Last Days of Hitler*, but without acknowledgment to the work that Frank Edmunds carried out in obtaining this information.

Hitler's will was made in triplicate, and each of the three documents were separately addressed to Grand Admiral Doenitz, to Field Marshal Schoerner (then Commander of an army group in Bohemia) and the Nazi Party Archives in Munich. None of the documents reached their destination. All three documents were recovered by the British.

The will was signed by Hitler in the presence of his faithful Martin Bormann, Joseph Goebbels (who followed Hitler, with his wife and children, to commit suicide), General Hans Krebs and General Wilhelm Burgdorf, who was Hitler's personal aide-de-camp.

The first part of the will deals with generalities, stating that it is untrue that Hitler or anybody else in Germany wanted or started the war in 1939; that it was all provoked by politicians either of Jewish stock or working for Jewish interests. It provided that in spite of all the setbacks after six years of war, the war would go down in history as the most glorious and heroic manifestation of a people's will. Hitler would never forsake the capital of Germany. Since his forces were too small to withstand the enemy's attack, he wished to share the fate that millions of others had accepted and to remain in Berlin. Further, "*I will not fall into the hands of an enemy who requires a new spectacle, exhibited by the Jews to divert hysterical masses. I have, therefore decided to remain in Berlin and there to choose death voluntarily when I believe that the residence of the Fuehrer and Chancellor can no longer be held...*"

The second part is more of a political testament and deals with recriminations and new appointments. "I expel from the Party the former *Reichs* Marshal Hermann Goering and withdraw from him all the rights conferred upon him by the decree of 29 June 1941 and my Reichstag speech of 1 September 1939. In his place I appoint Grand Admiral Doenitz as Reichs President and Supreme Commander of the Armed Forces."

The next paragraph dealt with "the other traitor" Himmler. "Before my death I expel from the Party and from all his Offices the former *Reichsführer* SS and *Reichs* Minister of the Interior Heinrich Himmler."

Hitler appointed in his place Gauleiter Karl Hanke and Gauleiter Paul Giesler as *Reichsführer* SS and Chief of the Police and *Reichs* Minister of the Interior, respectively. Apart from Doenitz as the new Reichs President and Supreme Commander of the Armed Forces, Hitler's other proposed appointments to a new phantom Government were Goebbels as Reichs Chancellor; Bormann as Party Chancellor; Seyss Inquart – the Quisling and oppressor of the Netherlands – as Foreign Minister. Ribbentrop and Speer were quietly dropped and not mentioned at all.

The final and personal part of Hitler's will deals with his personal belongings "as far as they are worth anything", which he left to the Party and the State. The paintings "bought" by him over the years and "never assembled for private purposes" were to go to a picture gallery to be established in his home town of Linz in Austria. "As executor I appoint my most faithful Party Comrade Martin Bormann".

Frank learned that Hitler could have escaped Berlin but chose not to do so. Hitler did not accept the offer of a woman test pilot, Hanna Reitsch. She flew into Berlin with her companion Ritter von Greim on 26 April 1945, went to Hitler's Bunker and offered to fly him out of Berlin and to Berchtesgaden. She left – with Greim – on 29 April, the day before Hitler committed suicide. She managed to get out of Berlin and fly to Austria, where she was captured by the Americans. Frank met Hanna Reitsch whilst staying at Colonel Phelps' Secret Intelligence Camp Oberussel near Frankfurt. He found her to be a remarkable woman.

Other important information that Frank obtained was set out by him in eleven reports of his interrogation of a prisoner called Kopkow. These gave details of the organisation of the German Intelligence Service, the Gestapo, of German counter espionage against Russia and the efficiency of the British Intelligence Service compared with the German and Russian Intelligence Services.

CHAPTER 3

Post War Interrogations and CSDIC at Bad Nenndorf

In November 1945, a special section was formed under Frank's command to deal with information about economic and political conditions in the Soviet Occupation Zone of Germany, information which was not available or obtainable directly from the Soviets. The establishment of this new section was undertaken by the Combined Services Detailed Intelligence Centre (CSDIC) because a steady stream of Germans escaping from the Soviet Zone of Germany arrived in the British Zone and they all had to be interrogated for possible war crimes and to obtain information about the Soviet activities in East Germany.

To house the intelligence unit and its prisoners Frank went to Bad Nenndorf, near Hanover where he requisitioned a hotel building, the *Deister Haus*, and built a camp around it to house these escaping Germans until they could be interrogated and charged with war crimes or released as necessary. Frank chose Bad Nenndorf, a small German spa town near Hanover in Lower Saxony. It was strategically situated in the British Occupation Zone, not far from Field Marshal Montgomery's H.Q. at Bad Oeynhausen, and not far from Air Chief Marshal Sholto Douglas' R.A.F. base at Wunstorf, Lueneburg, where the official German surrender took place and subsequently an important prisoner of war camp was established where its most important prisoner at the time was the most outstanding German military leader Field Marshal Fritz Erich von Manstein né Lewinski. It was not far from the Royal Navy's establishments at Hamburg and Wilhelmshaven, and not far from the main American Intelligence Centres in and around Frankfurt am Main.

A part of Bad Nenndorf was wired off from the remaining German civilian part of the town for the CSDIC Camp and comprised excellent facilities for housing the several hundred strong of all ranks of the CSDIC unit and provided suitable segregation of the prisoners in the large converted 'Bath House'.

The old-fashioned hotel was converted into the main Intelligence Headquarters in which also the Commanding Officers and Senior Interrogation Officers' Offices were located. The building, which Frank chose and shared with his colleague Majors Cochrane and Rowe for their respective Sections' Offices, was a recently built block, said to have been used during the Hitler era as a special hotel, where meetings were arranged between selected, elite and beautiful Aryan Fräuleins and young privileged SS men for the purpose of producing '*Hitler Kinder*' who were taken to be brought up by the Reich.

In the beginning the flow of people into CSDIC was moderate and as they were interrogated and released, new people took their place. Many Germans arrived at Bad

Nenndorf voluntarily because they knew that was their route to denazification and a normal life. Frank's workload was moderate at first, but then Soviet agents began flooding the Western Zone. This was when the importance of this aspect of CSDIC's work increased rapidly. Some of the people who presented themselves to CSDIC were spies who pretended voluntarily to give information of subversive activities. Frank obtained a lot of information about the Soviet activities in the British Zone. There was then a great deal of Soviet activity in the British Zone.

This Soviet activity was kept secret from the public in Britain. On 15 January 1946, the London Evening News reported that the activities of 'Red Agents' in Germany had been brought to light by the efforts of British investigators. Frank was one of them.

In January 1946 Frank drafted Special Interrogation Reports 10 and 11 setting out information from a German of the Diplomatic Corps, who had made the most startling revelations to Frank, which sounded quite fantastic at the time. It gave a complete and accurate description of the Russian post-war programme and intentions. It was clear that the Soviets planned to control the whole of Europe and the reports set out in detail the steps which they would take to accomplish the establishment of communist satellites in those parts of Western Europe which were at present under democratic governments. Frank Edmunds was involved in the gathering of information about this Soviet plan to push on from Russian occupied Berlin and East Germany and together with the Communist East German Army, invade the West and trigger off a Third World War.

His report about this was the most important document produced by Frank at CSDIC. This case was the only case investigated by Frank, in which his Commanding Officer, Colonel Stephens, played a part by interviewing the informant personally after Frank had sent Stephens the completed report. Stephens added a postscript saying that in his personal opinion the information in Frank's report about the Soviet threat was entirely reliable.

The report was flown to the United Kingdom by Major Hall, the Commanding Officer's personal assistant, and was put before Ernest Bevin, the Foreign Secretary, within twenty-four hours of publication. General Brooks of MI6 is said to have expressed the view that it was the most important intelligence report in 1946.

By this time CSDIC had become CSDIC (WEA) in the typical way that armies make alphabet soup out of their various branches. Later CSDIC became DIC74, but for the sake of convenience I shall refer to the organisation as CSDIC. CSDIC only dealt with military prisoners of war but when CSDIC (WEA) was formed Frank had also to deal with political prisoners, saboteurs, and spies. The treatment given to military prisoners of war during interrogations was very much left to the discretion of interrogation officers, subject to the requirement that such treatment had to conform to the rules of the Geneva and Hague Conventions, whereas cases within the category of criminal spies and political prisoners were not entitled to be accorded the treatment required to be given to prisoners of war under international treaties.

Frank said that it was generally recognised and accepted in intelligence circles dealing with all types of prisoners that in urgent operational matters an interrogation would be allowed to continue until the prisoner of war 'broke'. A person being interrogated 'broke' when he told the truth. Frank was taught that threats of violence to the prisoner and to his family could be used provided they were never carried out. Mr Preisswerk of the Swiss Protecting Power ruled that threats could be used provided they were not carried out and in fact stressed that the Swiss Red Cross regarded threats during interrogations as justifiable *ruses de guerre*.

There were no restrictions as to the length of interrogations. Frank learned this from Brigadier General Crockatt under whom Frank had served during the war. Subsequently Frank had carried out during the war, with the Brigadier's full knowledge and approval, a fourteen-hour interrogation of a prisoner of war in respect of twenty-one timebombs, which were said to have been planted by the Germans at Cherbourg before they evacuated the town. At CSDIC Frank was also involved in a long nine-hour interrogation working with Major Maurer from the Swiss Federal Police. Very long interrogations were not usual, but they happened and were regarded as an important tool for the interrogators.

Frank said that none of the CSDIC interrogators were ever given written instructions or guidance about the techniques of interrogating a prisoner. To lay down interrogation techniques in writing is a difficult task, because so much depends on the character of the individual interrogator and on that of the prisoner. CSDIC had to evolve its own systems of interrogation based on trial and error, building on what they had been taught and had already learned in the field. It was a cardinal rule at CSDIC that physical violence was forbidden. This was not only on moral grounds, but also because striking, or otherwise ill-treating a prisoner shows that the interrogator has lost control and may induce the prisoner to give an untrue answer which he thinks may please the interrogator.

The interrogators' aim was to induce the prisoner to cooperate and tell the truth by patient and painstaking means. It was commonly said that an interrogator who resorted to physical violence was a bad interrogator and useless for CSDIC purposes. Despite often considerable difficulties, the accuracy and scope of CSDIC reports were such that they often revealed that reports issued by other agencies were completely inaccurate. Other agencies, to hide their lack of interrogation skills, sometimes concluded, and then falsely claimed, that the information had been extracted by CSDIC interrogators using brutal methods. These rumours were also spread by prisoners after they had left CSDIC: prisoners who had given a lot of information often felt ashamed and uneasy afterwards and sought to salve their own consciences by inventing stories of ill-treatment during interrogations.

Frank was taught at the Cambridge School of Interrogation that the first step in interrogation is to make a quick assessment of a prisoner's personality and a quick appreciation of the approach that will give the interrogating officer the mental and moral ascendancy; that strict discipline was to be observed and maintained throughout and that no insolence on the part of the prisoner was to be tolerated even if this involved getting tough. I suppose that is exactly what lawyers must do when faced with a witness that they must cross-examine.

Cambridge also stressed that prisoners must be kept mentally attentive throughout the interview and that in extreme cases, if a man was refractory and the interrogator believed that he might be withholding information, threats might be used, but these threats must never be carried out.

Frank was careful to note that without wishing to make the slightest form of criticism or reflection of probably the most successful intelligence officer he knew, his own Commanding Officer Colonel Stephens, there was a point on which Frank disagreed with him. Frank would always use the soft methods as taught at Cambridge and almost always used no other methods. He rarely found it necessary to use severe interrogation. Frank was famous for his soft methods of interrogation of leading Nazis, who were hardly famous for their humanity or soft methods when it came to interrogating those unlucky enough to fall into their hands. It must be hard to be an interrogator. It must be especially hard when you are told that there is good reason to believe that a successful interrogation will save lives and an unsuccessful interrogation will mean that blood will be spilled because the responsibility for finding out the truth to save lives rests solely with the interrogator.

In 1940 when Frank was trained at Cambridge in the art of interrogation, he was taught that not only was torture not permitted but it was self-defeating because under torture the information that a prisoner gives will almost certainly be useless. Eighty years on, torture is often used in interrogations by nations that had previously refused to use it. The refusal to use torture was on practical grounds not humanitarian reasons, because the object of interrogation, like cross-examination, is to elicit the truth.

Frank was a literal, fussy person, as you will see. He followed rules almost slavishly and he found it quite wrong that others did not. That may have been the German influence in his early years and the fact that when his parents came to England they were, like most immigrants of the time, anxious to follow the laws of their adopted country in all respects. In Frank's view rules were there to be obeyed; that was his training and his instinctive belief. You can see the way in which Frank and those of his generation approached the rules of interrogation more so many years ago. We have progressed since then, but progress is a matter of movement, not necessarily in the right direction.

In recent years prisoners kept in Iraq, Afghanistan, and at Guantanamo have claimed that if the security services discovered that a prisoner had certain knowledge of the location of a terrible bomb, it would be justified, in the interests of saving life, to undertake any means including torture of the prisoner and his family, to discover the bomb and save life. This was not the rule in the British Army in 1946.

Many countries have committed torture or colluded with it or aided and abetted torture by co-operating in the rendition of suspects to jurisdictions where torture is permitted. Legally, torture is prohibited by International Law and the law of most civilised nations. International Law is only enforced against the weaker nations, not against the super powers. Frank would have argued that torture is illegal and against regulations and he was a stickler for observing regulations, but also torture would be useless and serve no purpose. Severe interrogation in an effort to break down the prisoner was the only means available to an interrogator who must not harm a hair on the prisoner's head. If you tortured a suspect the information you would get would be disinformation and that would be useless to you. The object was to get the truth.

In April 1946 Frank would conduct his last and what seemed at the time to be his most important interrogations. CSDIC received credible evidence of a threat to British lives; they learned that there would be an insurgency of fanatical former Nazis against the British occupying the British Zone, and if the insurrection or insurgency could not be stopped many lives would be lost.

A German named Michael came to CSDIC and Frank quartered Michael in the Deister Haus, where Frank would interrogate him. On 25 March 1946 Michael told Frank that he had overheard a conversation at his previous camp, Nienburg, which showed that one of the prisoners was the leader and the other a co-member of an illegal underground organisation, which was going to strike against the British authorities in the British Army of the Rhine on 20 April 1946, Hitler's birthday, irrespective of whether the two men were free to lead the uprising. Michael did not at that time know the names of the two men who would, if free, lead the uprising but he knew that they were among British prisoners.

Frank's suspicion fell on two senior ex-SS men: Rudolf Oebsger-Roeder, the supposed leader of the insurrection and Horst Mahnke. Upon interrogation, Michael was sure that Oebsger-Roeder had talked to Mahnke about a certain 'organisation' of a subversive nature. Michael claimed that Oebsger-Roeder was the leader of an organisation called *Freiheit Bewegung* (Freedom Movement) which was about 500-strong in the Hanover area; its aim was to organise resistance against the British. It had Russian arms and equipment in hidden ammunition dumps, and they were to strike on Hitler's birthday, 20 April 1946, against British troops and British installations; even if the attempt failed, the finding of Russian arms would cause a desired conflict between the British and Russians.

Frank took this intelligence seriously. In his opinion Michael had spoken the truth. He passed the information to the Intelligence Bureau at Bad Oeynhausen. Following urgent discussions with the Intelligence Bureau, Michael was taken to a prisoner of war camp, where he picked out from amongst sixty prisoners the alleged leader of the *Freiheit Bewegung*, Rudolf Oebsger-Roeder, whose name he did not know. On the Intelligence Bureau's instructions, Oebsger-Roeder was transferred to CSDIC for immediate investigation on 25 March 1946.

Following Michael's detailed statement of the circumstances of the conversations overheard, and from information gathered from an interrogation report prepared at the camp, it became clear that the other prisoner with whom Oebsger-Roeder had discussed the armed uprising, was Horst Mahnke. Mahnke's whereabouts were located by the Intelligence Bureau. They asked CSDIC to conduct an investigation of Oebsger-Roeder and Mahnke. Frank heard from American intelligence officers that they too had received warnings about a likely uprising on Hitler's birthday, and that Oebsger-Roeder and Mahnke were likely to be involved in the plot.

British Intelligence code named the plot 'ROME'. Frank was due for demobilisation in April 1946, but Colonel Stephens asked Frank to stay on to conclude the investigation into ROME. Frank, despite being quite exhausted having worked continuously for several years as an intelligence interrogator, agreed to a two month deferment.

Frank checked with a German informer who worked for the Americans, known under the code name '*Hirschfeld*'. Hirschfeld told Frank that Mahnke had admitted to the American authorities that he was involved in the *Freiheit Bewegung*. Immediately following Oebsger-Roeder's arrival at CSDIC on 25 March 1946 a further study of the case and the Bad

Nenndorf interrogation report showed Mahnke had admitted being part of the Freedom Movement. Frank drafted a plan of action, which he discussed with Colonel Stephens, who approved it.

The plan was that Mahnke was to be transferred to CSDIC as soon as possible, and that Frank would begin with the joint investigation of Oebsger-Roeder and Mahnke immediately after Mahnke's arrival. Some preliminary interrogations of Oebsger-Roeder were to take place before Mahnke's arrival, but the main investigation was to commence after Mahnke's arrival. The reason for this was the belief that confrontation and other top-secret intelligence methods (this was the use of what were then highly advanced secret microphones in the cells of prisoners) might enable Frank to obtain the necessary results more easily and more quickly.

Mahnke was found in the American Zone. The American Case Officer of Mahnke's at US Forces European High Command was Bruce Smith of the Federal Bureau of Investigation in Frankfurt and he proved to be extremely helpful. He was not at all surprised when Frank told him of the suspicions; the information which had been obtained from Michael corroborated the American agent's findings. Bruce Smith informed Frank that he was personally convinced that his informer Hirschfeld, who he said was a very excellent man, had been right on many other occasions, and that in fact Bruce Smith believed that Mahnke was very much involved in the underground movement and that it would strike against the British on 20 April 1946. Smith tried to arrange for Frank to meet Hirschfeld but, unfortunately, they could not find him. Mahnke was immediately transferred to CSDIC, where he arrived in the evening of 11 April 1946.

Colonel Stephens told Frank it was vital that Frank discover the truth about the uprising at least three to four days before 20 April, to enable them to take effective countermeasures.

Information from another source, a Mr Huelsen, was to the effect that he also had reason to believe that both Oebsger-Roeder and Mahnke were involved. Bruce Smith of the FBI said that in the FBI's opinion the threat was genuine and that he considered the threat from a British point of view of vital and urgent importance; Frank's personal opinion, based on the background information, and also after seeing the prisoners and learning about their Nazi and SS and Intelligence Service background, was that this was a real threat. The men were former SS officers, fully committed Nazis; their full wartime titles SS *Obersturmbannführer* Rudolf Oebsger-Roeder and *Hauptsturmführer* Dr Horst Mahnke.

So it was that Frank's department received intelligence that a bomb was ticking in the form of an uprising and would detonate on 20 April 1946. On 11 April 1946 Oebsger-Roeder and Mahnke were in custody at the CSDIC. Frank's orders were to discover whether there would be an uprising and give the authorities ideally at least four days' notice of the details by the evening of 16 April so that they could prevent the uprising and save lives.

We know now that there was no uprising against the British forces in Germany on Hitler's birthday in 1946. Whether there was ever going to be one or whether the discovery of a plot about an uprising and Frank Edmunds' subsequent interrogations of the two former SS men prevented the uprising we shall probably never know.

These days many blame the events of World War II and the war itself on Adolf Hitler. Of course, Hitler bore responsibility, but he could not have achieved what he achieved in terms of death, destruction and genocide, without the active support of a majority of the German people. Hitler had created a system of checks and balances and counterbalances governed by threats, terror and instability to maintain control and ensure his orders were carried out. He created various competing organisations and the largest and most powerful of these was the *Schutzstaffel* (the Protective Echelon), commonly known as the SS. According to the Judgment at Nuremberg most war crimes were committed by members of the SS, who enjoyed privileges, wealth and power if they supported Hitler and did or exceeded his bidding. The SS led the genocide against the Jews, Gypsies, Poles, and Slavs and led the killing and torture of groups such as homosexuals, clerics and freemasons. This organisation was declared a criminal organisation after the war. Frank needed to interrogate two senior SS men, Rudolf Oebsger-Roeder and Horst Mahnke, to see what he could find out about the planned uprising.

At the beginning of the Allied occupation of Germany and Austria immediately after the war ended most authorities in the Allies expected subversive activity in Germany on a large scale, but these fears proved to be unfounded and organised movements against the Allies were rare. Nevertheless, a great deal of underground activity went on and attempts were made to reconstitute the Nazi organisation and prepare to take power when the time was ripe. As members of these fledging movements like the *Freiheit Bewegung* were discovered and arrested, they were passed to CSDIC where a long and patient investigation led to the complete unmasking of the movements and to the arrest of most of their leading members.

The British military were very worried about a threat of an uprising on Hitler's birthday. Squadron Leader Wigglesworth and Captain Dawson kept pressing Frank for information. They had already warned all the Field Security Sections in the British Zone of

Germany and particularly in the Hanover area not to relax during the Easter period. In 1946 Easter Day fell on 20 April. All Frank could do was to assure them that he and his team were doing their utmost to discover the truth and were sparing no effort.

Frank must have had some interesting personal conflicts as he gathered intelligence. He was a Jew, interrogating people who had been intimately involved in murdering hundreds and thousands of his fellow Jews. He was a gay man interrogating men who would have, at the height of their power, snuffed out the life of a gay man with as much compunction as they would have stepped on a fly. Frank must have seen inside the minds of men who had become immune to their own depravities. It must have been a heavy burden to bear, to not only get inside the ugly minds of these people, but also to have the responsibility of ensuring that they would not kill or damage others.

Frank prepared his plan of action with the help of his assistants Captain Oliver 'Dick' Langham and Captain Van Rije. Oliver Langham was, like Frank, a German-born Jewish Intelligence officer who had worked closely with Frank for several years. Van Rije was Dutch and commissioned in the British Army after he escaped from the Netherlands. Frank decided to take charge of and to personally conduct the interrogations. Langham and Van Rije were the best officers he had available for what he expected would be a difficult and lengthy task ahead. By deciding to conduct the interrogations personally, Frank had the full responsibility for the ROME case, as far as the army was concerned.

Frank's plan of action was based on using severe interrogations. He would conduct long interrogations of Oebsger-Roeder and Mahnke individually as follows:

(a) Frank, Langham and Van Rije would work in relay.
(b) The interrogations would be the severest possible.
(c) They would threaten violence and harm to the prisoners and their families if they did not speak the truth.
(d) Frank would arrange a confrontation between the suspects and the informer Michael to see if any information came from this.
(e) If this plan of action did not reveal the truth, Frank and his team would conduct further intensive interrogations.

SS Obersturmbannführer Oebsger-Roeder was, like virtually all members of the SS, known to British Intelligence. Oebsger-Roeder was born in Berlin in October 1913; he joined the NSDAP[1] in May 1937, the SS in December 1937, worked in the RSHA[23] (*Reichs*

---

[1] The abbreviations for the full name of the Nazi Party, whose full name was Nationalsozialistische

Sicherheits Haupt Amt) Amt VII and became a member of the *Sicherheitsdienst*, (foreign intelligence) also known as the S.D.

Oebsger-Roeder was thought to be a "harmless Foreign Office Official dealing with ideological research" and "likely to be a useful tool for the political education of the German nation". This view of Oebsger-Roeder proved to be completely false. Oebsger-Roeder was a very clever and very dangerous Nazi and SS Officer, who had had plenty of intelligence experience during the war. He was an excellent liar and fooled other people who were tasked with profiling him. Oebsger-Roeder's statements to the previous interrogator were soon proved to be complete lies. He was active and important in his Nazi SS and SD work. He was arrogant and full of fight.

Mahnke had a similar background but was not as strong a personality as Oebsger-Roeder.

Deutsche Arbeiterpartei.

[2] Reich Security Main Office.

CHAPTER 4

The Interrogations

The interrogations started and lasted for many hours, with a view to putting the suspects under as much mental stress and pressure as possible. Frank and his team did make threats against the prisoners' lives and their families as part of a sustained effort to extract information by mental pressure. During this time Oebsger-Roeder held up occasionally, as Frank thought, feigning exhaustion but Mahnke undoubtedly showed signs of fatigue and sank to his knees from sheer exhaustion and he had to be revived by a drink of water, supplied by the sentries who were summoned by the officer doing the interrogation for this purpose. Frank was trying to 'break' the prisoners – to force them to tell the truth.

Frank reported each interrogation session in writing. His reports of the interrogations were worded using expressions such as "break the prisoner" "collapse" and "revive" because they were intended for consumption by intelligence sources who knew what these expressions meant. They were not intended for consumption by people who were outside intelligence circles or the general public.

The final interrogation of Oebsger-Roeder ended at 0500 hours on 16 April 1946. Frank by then had concluded that no useful purpose would be served to continue with further interrogations. When Mahnke's interrogations ended Franke reached the view that Mahnke's mind was so badly affected by the intensive interrogations that he would rather make false statements to avoid further interrogations. Mahnke had written a note which said, *"please shoot me"* and *"I can't stand it any longer"*.

Long hours of severe interrogations had not revealed any plot for an uprising. Oebsger-Roeder and Mahnke vigorously denied that there was any uprising planned. Frank reached the view that they were telling the truth about this. He ended the ROME investigation and reported his findings of his interrogations in effect that there was no evidence of a planned uprising. He included Mahnke's note in his report which was sent to Major General Lethbridge, Brigadier General Shoesmith, the Commander in Chief of MI5 and numerous departments in the War Office.

These were the times when Frank worked late into the night and the responsibilities must have weighed heavy on him. He was not concerned about Mahnke's note. Solitary confinement with the threat of death hanging over his head if something happened on 20 April had affected Mahnke. Frank had seen many similar notes over the course of his career and like most intelligence officers was immune to these and other hysterical outbursts from people he interrogated. The important point about the note, as far as Frank was concerned, was that it showed Frank that it would be purposeless to continue the interrogations. The prisoners were ready to make up stories to please the interrogators and that would be entirely counterproductive.

Neither Mahnke nor Oebsger-Roeder complained about their treatment to Frank or the other interrogators. They were visited in the course of their incarceration by intelligence officers, various duty officers, Orderly Prison Control officers, a German doctor, a British medical officer, senior NCOs, the Senior Intelligence Officer and the Commanding Officer when they visited the prison (as they frequently did) but never complained about ill treatment.[4]

Frank informed Squadron Leader Wigglesworth of the Intelligence Bureau at Bad Oeynhausen of the negative outcome of the investigation and told him that he was getting a draft report ready for the following afternoon, 17 Apr 1946, and that there was nothing further Frank could do because no useful purpose would be served in further interrogations until additional enquiries had been made by Intelligence about some of the information disclosed and some of the people mentioned by Oebsger-Roeder and Mahnke.

Squadron Leader Wigglesworth said that he would send Captain Dawson to visit Frank the following day, 17 April at 1400, for Captain Dawson to extract whatever information he could from Frank's Draft Report. He also said, notwithstanding the negative outcome of the investigation, that he would arrange for a signal to be sent out to all military authorities to warn them to be in a position to take immediate counter measures if necessary, on 20 April 1946.

Captain Dawson duly turned up at CSDIC on 17 April, but through a misunderstanding, he went to see Major Rowe in respect of Operation Nursery. The misunderstanding was discovered by his superior officer Squadron Leader Wigglesworth on his return to Bad Oeynhausen and he ordered Captain Dawson to return the following day, 18th April, to see Frank regarding the ROME case. The misunderstanding and subsequent instructions were put in writing by Squadron Leader Wigglesworth and recorded on their files.

Frank was informed – around Easter – by his second-in-command Captain Alan Teare, that he had received word from the medical officer that Mahnke was suffering from pleurisy. The medical officer recommended the prisoner's immediate transfer to hospital. As

---

[4] The complaint culture was not as prevalent then, but both the Germans and the British took their obligations under the Third Geneva Convention for Prisoners of War seriously.

a result of this message, Frank agreed to Mahnke's speedy transfer to hospital where his pleurisy would be treated.

It was agreed with the Intelligence Division that since they had seen the Draft Report on 18 April 1946 and extracted what information they desired that there was no further urgency for the actual publication of the official report, which helped the Editorial Section, who were under considerable pressure at the time. As a result, the official report was only published on 2 May 1946.

Frank clearly felt that he had done everything that was permitted by the regulations to find out whether there would be an uprising on Hitler's birthday in 1946. It is also clear that Frank felt that the regulations were designed to get useful reliable information and that torture would not produce information that was reliable.

Frank stayed in the army for two months after these interrogations but must have been anxious to rebuild his life, just like many hundreds of thousands of service men were, in 1946. The interrogation work had taken its toll on Frank's mental health. By the time he left the unit on 28 June 1946 he was exhausted from the responsibility of his work and had to spend some time in hospital recovering. I have written that Frank's work imposed a great strain upon him. That is an understatement. In fact, Frank found the pressure of conscientiously interrogating war criminals and spies and other undesirables so overwhelming that as soon as his leave started, he suffered a mental breakdown. He was exhausted from his work and from the responsibilities that his work entailed. Although official, technical, and final responsibility for his work, actions and decisions rested with his Commanding Officer, Colonel Stephens, all of Frank's recommendations and proposals were 'rubber stamped' by Colonel Stephens, so Frank was very aware that the true responsibility for his decisions and actions was truly his and his alone.

Before he left the army, he told Colonel Stephens that he considered it unfair on his future successor Captain Teare to carry the burden of Frank's work. As a result, a Major Beith was also appointed to help Captain Teare after Frank left.

Frank was officially released from the army and military duty on the expiration of his official leave, with effect from 12 September 1946. He had already spent some of his leave in hospital. He returned to England in August 1946 and began his efforts to re-establish his plastics business in Manchester, which he had had to close down over six years earlier when joining the army.

I suspect that there was another factor that contributed to Frank's breakdown; at this time Frank, having spent the war mainly in the company of fine young men, many of whom he led, had begun to recognise his own sexuality more clearly. In 1946 there was no way in which he could 'come out'; homosexuality was a criminal offence and not a matter or tendency that could be raised or spoken about except to other gay men. He had not at that time found a way to cope with his own sexuality nor were there the support mechanisms in place for someone who was, according to the mores of the time, so different.

Frank must have felt very alone. No doubt he wished to establish relationships with some of the fine young men that he knew but dared not. Gay soldiers were persecuted and tried as criminals in the Second World War in all the allied armies. This must have created difficulty for Frank, who almost certainly repressed his feelings and drowned his instincts and desires by undertaking a massive workload. Also, he must have known that there was a regulation prohibiting disgraceful conduct of a cruel kind but also of an indecent or unnatural kind, a regulation directly aimed at homosexuals.

CHAPTER 5

An Honourable Member Intervenes

On his return to the United Kingdom and civilian life, Frank found very different political conditions in post-war and peacetime Britain. A new Labour government was installed under Prime Minister Clement Attlee and Frank felt, as with many others of that time, that the electorate in voting in the new Labour government had betrayed Winston Churchill. The some in the new government, Frank wrote, *"certain leftish elements ... looked with disfavour upon certain aspects of work in which I was engaged at CSDIC"*. It was also not surprising for him to learn that many months' criticism both from British and German politicians went on against CSDIC calling for CSDIC to be disbanded. The Chief Intelligence Division did not want to lose the services of Colonel Stephens, who was only on loan to the Intelligence Division, and since CSDIC had proved its value time and time again these attacks were not successful in disbanding CSDIC and CSDIC continued its work at Bad Nenndorf.

Amongst the Germans the very secrecy that surrounded the CSDIC at Bad Nenndorf, coupled with false horror stories invented by former inmates, many of whom Frank regarded as "the lowest criminal types", led to a feeling of revulsion of the unit in Germany and of shame in Britain. In recent years there have been rallies held at Bad Nenndorf by neo-Nazis, complaining about what they called the British torture camp run by CSDIC.

The Commander in Chief of the British Army on the Rhine (B.A.O.R.) then was Sir Sholto Douglas, who was a very ambitious and politically motivated man. Frank thought Sholto was looking for opportunities to appease and please important members of the newly formed Labour Government. The opportunity presented itself when Oebsger-Roeder and Mahnke complained to a British Member of Parliament, Mr R. R. Stokes M.P. for Ipswich, when Stokes toured the British Zone of Germany. The complaints were of mental and physical cruelty having been meted out to them whilst at CSDIC at Bad Nenndorf.

As a result of the complaints (which were made many months after the alleged incidents) a Court of Inquiry was set up. Non-commissioned officers were interviewed by the Court of Inquiry and as a result, three people would have their lives profoundly affected – Dick Langham, Frank's junior officer, an Allied Intelligence Officer, Kees Van Rije of the Netherlands and Frank himself.

Mr Stokes, (described in 1950 by an article[5] in the socialist review as "one of Mr Bevan's left wingers") had always taken an interest in humanitarian matters. In 1945 he

---

[5] http://www.marxists.org/history/etol/writers/challinor/1951/03/labour.html

spoke up for the Sudeten Germans. Mr Stokes objected to the Czechoslovak practice of imprisoning Sudeten Germans and described them as 'slaves' for the Czechs. Clearly, he was a humanitarian but seemed to fail to understand the whole context. The Sudeten Germans he spoke to described themselves as Social Democrats and by implication 'good Germans'. It would be hard to find any German after the war that would not characterise themselves thus. [6]

Stokes always admitted that his sympathies were on the side of the prisoner, and that is not a bad thing. Someone should always be on the side of the underdog, to see fair play. Of course, the underdogs in this case had been top dogs, just a few short years earlier, and busied themselves with oppression and executing millions of people that it regarded at *untermensch*[7] and thereby deserving of what they got.

On 25 January 1947 Stokes inspected the unit. He had been given carte blanche by the Commander in Chief to see everything in the unit, which was unprecedented, for up until that date only persons connected with Intelligence had been admitted to the Bad Nenndorf Camp. The Chief Intelligence Division left it to Colonel Stephens to show Stokes round. He was shown everything, including the prison, secret devices, and case files.

The prison was in a poor condition, which mirrored the terrible conditions that existed throughout Germany (and to a significantly lesser extent in Britain) at that time. The heating was not working due to the lack of coal and since this was in the middle of a severe winter, prisoners were living in conditions of considerable hardship and discomfort, although Colonel Stephens did his best through the issue of extra blankets to alleviate the situation where there was no coal to be found in Germany. No doubt, the impression all this made upon Stokes was not favourable. Complaints regarding the condition of prisoners arriving at outside agencies, particularly the German Internee Hospital at Rothenberg increased Mr Stokes' impressions and views were aggravated following his visit to the Rothenberg Internee Hospital, where he met Mahnke amongst other ex-CSDIC Prisoners.

The hospital was staffed by Nazi-orientated Germans, who were extremely anti-British. Most patients were in automatic arrest categories under the Allies' rules but were regarded in Rothenberg as patriots and victims of British persecution. Except where patients incurred personal disfavour, they were kept at the Rothenberg Hospital much longer than necessary. Many thought that the place had become a rest home for Nazis. Stokes interviewed

---

[6] My Mother lived in the Sudetenland when the Germans moved in, in 1938. At the age of ten she was required to work, without wages, for a German family as a cleaner. Her sisters worked as slave labour in factories in Germany from 1938 until 1945. I do not suggest that two wrongs make a right, but that Mr Stokes may well have been misled by some of the Sudeten Germans.

[7] "Under Man" coined by Nietzsche to describe the common man and used in Nazi Germany as a term of contempt implying that such people had no rights and were akin to slaves.

some of the patients including Mahnke and Oebsger-Roeder and heard their accounts of their treatment at CSDIC. It became evident to Stokes that both men had been severely beaten up at CSDIC by warders.

Following his return to the United Kingdom Mr Stokes, then not a member of the government, made a speech in the House of Commons[8].

> *I come now to an unsavoury case. I always find that if I bump into M.I.5 I find something dirty. Of course, the real truth of the matter is that practically no man is capable of having authority over any other, unless he is under the closest supervision. I refer to a camp at Bad Nenndorf, in Germany, which must be under my right hon. Friend's control in some way. I turned up there the other day and I thought there was something funny going on. It had been rumoured that it was third degree, but I am satisfied that there was no third degree of the body, though indeed there was of the mind. I do not complain of that. I understand that in cross-examining some of these fellows it may be necessary to indulge in forms of verbal persecution which we do not like, but there is no physical torture, starvation, or ill-treatment of that kind.*
>
> *Of course, the day I arrived was the very worst that had happened and would never happen again. The temperature was 12 degrees below zero. I was shown round the men's cells. There were 65 of them, mostly in solitary confinement. The temperature inside the cells was 10 degrees below. When I complained the commandant said, "There is no coal, so I have given them seven blankets instead." That was perfectly true; they had seven blankets each, but it is outrageous that human beings, whatever their faults, should be so treated. It is true that some of them were murderers, but even if a man is a murderer you have no right to treat him as other than a human being while he is kept in detention.*
>
> *The women were worse. There were only four of them and they were all said to be very hard cases. I asked to see them, and I saw three. After I had seen the third, I was so fed up I did not see the fourth. The first was a child of 18. That child had been held incommunicado for the best part of three and a half months without being allowed to communicate with her parents or with anybody outside. She saw her fellow prisoners once a day for an hour and that is all.*

---

[8] You can read the whole of Mr Stokes' speech at
http://hansard.millbanksystems.com/commons/1947/mar/24/german-prisoners-of-war#S5CV0435P0_19470324_HOC_505

I was so ashamed of it that when the door of the cell was shut, I turned to the commandant and said, "Goodness gracious, the British Empire will not fall if you allow a child like this out to mix among her fellow human beings." The commandant said, "Wait until you see her case," and I did so. The second child of nineteen had not been in quite so long, but her case was similar. The third was a girl of twenty-five who was married to a German who was in another part of the prison.

Let me tell the House, as an example, what the child had done. She was picked up at Koenigsberg by a Russian officer and raped. She lived with him for some weeks, and then she was told that if she took a message over to a certain Herr Schmidt in Schleswig-Holstein, she would on her return be repatriated to her parents. She was picked up by the security police somewhere in Schleswig-Holstein and sent to a place of civilian detention for inquiry. That is the dreadful woman on whom the whole fate of the British Empire hangs, and in order to make sure that nothing dreadful happens, this wretched child is kept in solitary confinement for three and half months. It is not really the fault of the camp commandant. I do not blame him as much as I blame the Military Control. My right hon. Friend should see to it that he has generals in charge of Intelligence in Germany who are up to their job. I would lay him money, if that were not an improper thing to do in the House, that the general in charge, who is responsible for that camp has not been near the camp since August of last year. If so, it is a disgrace, and he ought to be sacked.

Within a week of this speech a Court of Inquiry was established to investigate the conditions at CSDIC. Prior to the court assembling Major General Bishop, Deputy Chief of Staff (Executive) inspected the prison and informed Colonel Stephens that in his opinion prisoners at Bad Nenndorf were better cared for at CSDIC than those at the Chief Intelligence Centre.

It is significant that Mr Stokes did not in this speech allege that there had been physical third degree or torture but concentrated his anger on people being imprisoned in the camp and its conditions.

In January 1947 when Stokes visited Germany, Germany was broken. The winter was exceptionally bitter and cold. Coal production had been virtually stopped by the war and had not restarted. Many coal mines had been bombed and there was no fuel oil to be had. In Berlin 150 people died as a result of a combination of cold and lack of food. At the same time England was undergoing a spell of exceptionally cold weather, coal supplies were short, and many people were also suffering from cold. This is what war does; it is easier for war to destroy these things than for peace to fix them.

While Frank was in Manchester trying to rebuild his plastics business and unknown to him, a Court of Inquiry consisting of Brigadier Britten, Mr Miller, Deputy Inspector General Public Safety Branch CCG[9] and an official of legal division CCG started its sittings on 5 April 1947, continuing throughout the Easter holidays because the Commander in Chief wished to have its findings by 8 April 1947.

This insistence on speed seemed obvious. If the findings of the Court of Inquiry were favourable the Commander in Chief could deal strongly with attacks upon his senior officers. Should the findings be unfavourable he could take action to protect these same officers before enquiries from London would force his hand. The Court of Inquiry found it unable to comply with this timetable and continued its sittings throughout the following week.

At first it heard evidence regarding the general administration of the unit. On conclusion of this part of the evidence Brigadier Britten assured Colonel Stephens that they had entirely satisfied themselves and that he had absolutely nothing to worry about. They then heard individual evidence from prisoners regarding specific allegations of ill treatment.

This evidence was heard without the officers against whom the allegations were made being present and when they themselves were called no indication whatsoever was given as to the nature and details of allegations made against them. The Secretary to the Court of Inquiry (a qualified lawyer) drew attention to the court that the proceedings were irregular and unfair, but the court took no notice of what he advised; the Court of Inquiry had been given a completely free hand by the Commander in Chief regarding the manner in which they intended to hear evidence.

On 16 April 1947, while Frank was in Manchester trying to rebuild his business, Colonel Dalby of HQ Intelligence Division delivered a letter from Major General Lethbridge to Colonel Stephens. The letter said that following inquiries recently held at Bad Nenndorf, the Commander in Chief had ordered that Colonel Stephens, Lieutenant Colonel Short and Medical Officer Captain Smith were suspended and must leave Bad Nenndorf forthwith. Command of the unit was handed over to Lieutenant Colonel D. E. F. Waight M.C., who arrived on the same day.

In the course of the same day verbal orders were received from the Headquarters of the Intelligence Division that five officers were also to be suspended: Captain Van Rije,

---

[9]Control Commission Germany

Captain Langham, a Captain Brezcicki, a Mr Oakey, and a Mr Spiller. This order was confirmed in writing the following day. On 18 April 1947 all of those officers were interviewed by Major General Lethbridge.

During the interview, Major General Lethbridge professed ignorance regarding the exact legal position of the Court of Inquiry, and whether it had completed its work or whether it had simply adjourned sine die, and whether it had produced any findings. He claimed that he realised that officers had had no opportunity to clear themselves of any allegations made. He stated that the Commander in Chief had ordered a new "judicial inquiry" that is "a proper Court of Inquiry adhering to all the Rules of Procedure as laid down in the Army Act".

Towards the end of April 1947, the new Court of Inquiry made its first appearance at Bad Nenndorf, when Mr Hayward, Assistant Inspector General, Special Inquiry Bureau, Safety Branch[10], and his chief Assistant Mr Timmerman came to see the new Commanding Officer at CSDIC, Lieutenant Colonel Waight and Major Kettler (the acting Senior Intelligence Officer. They explained that they would tour all Intelligence Centres in the Zone collecting whatever complaints there might be against CSDIC. On completion of this tour, they would start at CSDIC – which by then had been renamed DIC[11].

In the meantime, feelings amongst the officers at DIC had become very strong in view of what they felt was the high-handed action taken against officers of the unit; so much so that on 9 May 1947 Brigadier Maynell of the Commander in Chief's staff was sent to DIC to 'explain' the position. He addressed all officers.

He praised the work of the unit fulsomely, and spoke of how it had assisted Mr Bevin, the Foreign Secretary, in making foreign policy. He said that the Commander in Chief had ordered the inquiries "to cover himself against professional humanitarians such as Mr Stokes." The first Court of Inquiry found the job too big to complete, allegedly because they were unable to deal properly with "some of the biggest crooks in Europe" who were many of the prisoners who had come through CSDIC.

When tackled on the serious irregularities that had occurred during the first Court of Inquiry, he replied that he could not answer since he was not a legal man but as far as he could see, the more Court of Inquiry irregularities that occurred the better for the officers involved in the long run. Apparently, he regretted this remark later, as after the talk he asked Major Kettler not to be quoted on this.

---

[10] An investigative bureau which has in its title the word 'safety' sound rather chillingly Orwellian.
[11] Detailed Interrogation Centre.

The Brigadier stated that should the present inquiry show that further action against certain officers was indicated, he could give the assurance on behalf of the Commander in Chief that these officers would be given "more than usual facilities for defence".

A Public Safety Investigation (in other words a police investigation, as the so-called investigation turned out to be) began at CSDIC in the middle of May. Attempts had been made by certain officers to obtain legal assistance and in the case of civil servants, to have an observer present from the Society of Civil Servants. Mr Hayward stated that he would not accept this and that he would refuse to question anybody represented by lawyers or Trade Union officials.

The investigations, consisting of four Public Safety officials and three or four other officers sat at CSDIC until the beginning of June, interrogating officers and Oebsger-Roeder and Mahnke. All the investigators worked separately and not as a court.

The trend of their questioning made it appear that they had instructions to pin the responsibility for any irregularities on officers within CSDIC. There was a bias, possibly due to instructions, against certain officers, partly personal, partly on nationality grounds. Captain Van Rije was a Dutch national, and Captain Brezcicki was a Polish national.[12] Their method of investigation did not accord with the promises made by Brigadier Maynell and certainly were not in accordance with the army's Rules of Procedure. Many witnesses were threatened into giving evidence. The chillingly named Public Safety Investigation accepted certain evidence without checking its reliability or accuracy, leaving it to the officers implicated and concerned to disprove allegations made against them.[13]

The investigation at DIC was completed at the beginning of June 1947.

On 17 June 1947 Mr Hayward visited DIC and in the presence of witnesses told Lieutenant Colonel Waight that pursuant to his report filed the previous day in Mr Hayward's opinion there was no case for prosecuting any intelligence officer.

During the latter half of June 1947 both Captain Van Rije and Captain Langham wrote to Major General Lethbridge, drawing attention to the fact that the assurance he had given had not been kept and asking for an explanation of the delay in the investigation. The

---

[12] Frank Edmunds would have also (in my view) been perceived as a foreigner; his English was slightly accented; he was Jewish and probably considered in the same way, as a foreigner, as was the other officers mentioned here. Oliver Langham, as the prosecution told the court martial, was born in Munich and I guess must have spoken with a German accent. I suspect there was more than a strong element of bias against 'foreigners' in the choice of who should be prosecuted.
[13] Frank has already described how carefully he and his officers checked and double-checked information obtained from interrogation of Nazis, but this investigation did not cross check at all.

replies received were extremely non-committal and were signed by a Colonel Dalby of HQ Intelligence Division.

On 1 July 1947 Mr Oakey, Mr Spiller and Captain Brezcicki were de-suspended. No indication was given regarding the action (if any) contemplated against the other suspended officers.

During the weekend of 20 July 1947 Colonel Stephens, Lt Colonel Short and Captain Smith were placed under arrest. They were not permitted to communicate with any person within the unit.

On 25 July 1947 Lt Colonel Waight phoned Brigadier Maynell to enquire what action was contemplated against Captains Langham and Van Rije. He was informed that the matter was in the hands of the Judge Advocate General Branch[14] and that a decision would be taken within two to three days. When nothing was heard by 29 July 1947 Lt Colonel Waight phoned again. This time he was informed by Brigadier Maynell that the matter was still under consideration and that further telephone calls would be pointless. Brigadier Maynell curtly refused to see Captains Van Rije and Langham. These events were later confirmed by Brigadier Maynell in writing.

In the meantime, Public Safety officials appeared periodically and removed files and interviewed men.

On 20 September 1947 Captain Van Rije wrote to Lt. Colonel Waight complaining of the unsatisfactory state of affairs regarding his case, asking for legal advice. This letter was forwarded to HQ Intelligence Division. There was no reply. On 25 Sept 1947 Captains Van Rije and Langham – after 162 days' suspension – were placed under close arrest on four holding charges for Van Rije and three holding charges for Langham. The charges gave the impression of having been very hastily framed.

CSDIC throughout its existence experienced considerable unpopularity due to the personality of Colonel Stephens. The counterintelligence work of CSDIC that Stephens supervised sat uncomfortably against the strong beliefs of many leading left-wing socialists who characterised the German people as a peace-loving nation who had been misled by a small group of madmen and that they now wished for nothing more than to co-operate with Socialist Britain. The socialists also fervently believed that the Soviet Union wished to be

---

[14] The Judge Advocate General (as a department) at this time acted as both prosecutor and as a judge at courts martial. This inequity was remedied after Frank's court martial. It is noteworthy that Frank never comments on the inequity of a single department providing both a prosecutor and a judge. This probably indicates the confidence in which he held regulations and systems. However, it was a fundamental flaw in all British courts martial at this time.

friends with Britain, that it had no aggressive intentions towards Britain and that Britain's future required a policy of co-operation with the Soviet Union.

Stokes' mention of CSDIC in the House of Commons and his attack on Major General Lethbridge required the matter to be urgently dealt with by the Commander in Chief. Frank thought it reasonable to assume that at that time Sir Sholto Douglas had already decided to enter public life as a socialist and that he, therefore, could not afford to alienate an important socialist M.P. such as Stokes. The sudden urgency of the Court of Inquiry combined with the Commander in Chief's condoning of the clearly irregular investigation tends to show that there was some truth in Frank's opinion.

Despite the fact that the Court of Inquiry never completed its work, action was taken on its findings (or were they recommendations?), namely the suspension and removal of some officers. Major General Lethbridge either intentionally or through ignorance misled officers into believing that they would be given a fair hearing in accordance with the Rules of Procedure.

The Public Safety Inquiry would certainly be correct if it found that the prison was, due to the shortage of coal, very unsatisfactory during the bitterly cold winter,[15] and that the medical care taken of prisoners supervised by the medical officer was unsatisfactory; and that excesses did occur within the prison. It went further than that. It concentrated its criticisms on interrogation officers.

Because the Public Safety Inquiry failed to follow the Rules of Procedure, it was impossible for the officers to get a fair hearing before it. The Public Safety Inquiry did decide that there were no rotten apples in the barrel, except those that came from foreign parts who spoke with foreign accents and in the case of two of them, were Jews.

It seems strange that to produce mere holding charges against two junior officers should take well over three months from the date of the receipt of Mr Hayward's completed report. To Frank's mind this suggested 'cooking' evidence.[16] I take the view that it was more likely that there were discussions by the prosecuting authorities as to whether the three should be charged at all, and only when those discussions were ended did the prosecution decide that they had better get on with the case, hence the hastily formulated charges.

There is no doubt that the allegations against Colonel Stephens and the other officers had a political flavour. It may be surmised that the courts martial which were to follow were

---

[15] The winter was the coldest in Germany in living memory. The country had almost no fuel.
[16] Today three months might sound like a reasonable period to frame charges. In 1947 justice moved more swiftly than today and normally the charges would have been framed much more quickly. Holding charges could have been framed in a matter of a few hours or days.

probably only ordered by the Commander in Chief to obtain scapegoats for something for which he and Major General Lethbridge might have held ultimate responsible.

Small events can only be properly understood when looked at through the spectacles of the then Zeitgeist. It is right and proper that allegations of mistreatment are investigated, and guilty perpetrators punished, but in this case the investigation was motivated not just by humanitarian beliefs but in some quarters by a belief that it was time to throw our national lot in with Stalin, rather than our other allies, the USA and France. The investigation that was carried out was not forensic and was incomplete. There was a natural bias to believe the complainants, instead of a bias towards finding the truth, whatever that may be. There seems also to have been a bias against people who spoke with foreign accents; there was no concept of 'diversity'; prejudice against foreigners prevailed.

I could almost touch Frank's bitterness towards the inquiry and the army when reading his notes; such bitterness is natural; many accused consider the investigators as their enemy. Frank's feeling must have been made sharper by the way he had spent his war sifting facts from speculation, separating truth from lies, examining evidence, corroborating, cross checking and reaching what he genuinely believed to be accurate conclusions. He must have found the process of investigation to which he was subjected very similar to investigations conducted by Nazis during the war or by the Soviets before it, where the conclusion was determined before the investigation was established. Frank had been trained not to reach any conclusion until the end of the investigation, rather than twisting the facts to fit a particular narrative.

On 1 September 1947 Frank was contacted by Assistant Inspector General Hayward who informed him that he was investigating on behalf of the Commander in Chief (BAOR) Sir Sholto Douglas certain matters in conjunction with the investigation that Frank had carried out at CSDIC of two prisoners Oebsger-Roeder and Mahnke in April 1946. The contact was unexpected for Frank had not known about the inquiries that had taken place.

Frank told Mr Hayward that he could not speak to him about these matters until he had obtained the necessary and proper clearance from the Deputy Director of Military Intelligence, which was the only way that Frank could talk to Mr Hayward without breaching the Official Secrets Act. Mr Hayward was very annoyed by the stance Frank took, but without proper clearance Frank would be breaking the law. Eventually, clearance came through and when it did Frank answered Mr Hayward's questions and a written statement on 27 Sept 1947.

In the course of being questioned Frank learned from Mr Hayward, to his surprise and amazement, that it had come to light that some prisoners and especially Mahnke had been severely beaten up by a number of non-commissioned officers and prison warders, who had admitted to having carried out these assaults.

Frank made it clear to Mr Hayward then that he had never heard of these or any other similar assaults being committed at the Bad Nenndorf Camp and that such activities, which were strictly forbidden by the Commanding Officer, were entirely against all principles of intelligence methods that Frank had been trained in.

Frank assumed that the matter was over and heard nothing further until 30 October 1947 when he was told to contact a police officer at Scotland Yard. He left Manchester and went to London. When he got to Scotland Yard, he was formally recalled to the army against his will. An official letter, signed by Major Denton of Army Group 23 was handed to him and he was arrested there and then on holding charges, jointly with Captains Van Rije and Langham, alleging cruelty to two Nazis, Oebsger-Roeder and Mahnke.

After strenuous efforts Frank insisted on talking to the War Office. He obtained through Colonel Robertson of Army Group 3 temporary release until 2 p.m. on 3 November (three days later, taking into account a Saturday and Sunday), which permitted him to establish contact with his solicitors Markby Stewart & Wadeson[17] and make temporary arrangements regarding his business and personal affairs.

The initial holding charges alleged disgraceful conduct of a cruel kind between 11 and 20 April 1946. The dates indicated to Frank that the intention of the prosecution was to allege that mental and physical cruelty had been inflicted by the intelligence officers during the interrogations.

After an overnight stay, in what Frank called disgracefully filthy conditions in the officers' quarters at Chelsea Barracks (not those in Kings Road) Frank was flown under double escort and close arrest to Bueckeburg in Germany and from there taken to 50 R.H.U. Bielefeld, where he remained under open arrest – joining his former junior officers Van Rije and Langham – until his transfer to 125 Transit Camp Hanover for the Summary of Evidence:

SUMMARY OF EVIDENCE 18/19 Nov 1947: Top Secret.
in the case of:–
WS/Captain T/Major Frank Edward Edmunds, Intelligence Corps
WS/Lt T/Captain Kees Ignatius Van Rije, Royal Pioneer Corps

---

[17] This firm is now merged into CMS Cameron McKenna LLP.

WS/LtQ Richard Oliver Langham, Royal Armoured Corps
Mr. J.C.G. Arthur, Interpreters Group CCG, is duly sworn as Interpreter.
The evidence of the witnesses is taken on oath at the request of the accused.
The Summary of Evidence is taken in the presence of the three accused officers by; Lt. Colonel Campbell, JAG (Judge Advocate General) according to Rules of Procedure 4 (c) (d) (e) and (f) but first it was noted:–
Major Edmunds makes the following objection to these proceedings:–
"The authorities who ordered my recall to the forces have exceeded the powers of recall conferred upon them and, in exercising their discretion, have acted on wrong principle. I therefore submit that my recall to the forces is unlawful.
The jurisdiction of this tribunal is dependent upon my recall being lawful. Such recall being in my submission unlawful, I submit that this tribunal has no jurisdiction in this case, so far as I am concerned.
It must be clearly understood that I do not submit voluntarily to the jurisdiction of this tribunal. I appear here today by compulsion and under protest."
Mr Hayward made a sworn statement:
"I know Major Edmunds. I now recognise him. On 1 Sept 47 in the office of JAG[18] in London I saw Major Edmunds and told him of my name and office and explained that I had been directed to carry out an investigation into various matters connected with the DIC at Bad Nenndorf. He told me that he was unable to discuss such matters as they were secret, until he had received the necessary permission to do so. We later saw Lord Russell and a senior Officer from the War Office, the Deputy Director of Military Intelligence, who gave Major Edmunds the necessary permission. Major Edmunds then informed me that he would be pleased to give me any information I wished with regard to matters at Bad Nenndorf but he felt that if I wanted a written statement he should have time to consider the matter as he had been brought to JAG's office without any prior knowledge of what was required of him. I agreed that before he should reduce anything to writing he should duly consider it. I had with me two case files referring to Oebsger-Roeder and Mahnke. I showed Major Edmunds the files. I now produce these files – Exhibits D and E. In Exhibit D I referred to a document marked IIB headed 'Proposed Plan of Action' and Major Edmunds said

---

[18] Judge Advocate General.

that that was drawn up by him in conference with other Officers. I think he also said that he had discussed the plan with Lt Colonel Short.

I then referred to the documents numbered '22A', '21A', '20A', '19A' and '18A', and said that these appeared to show that Oebsger-Roeder had been under interrogation continuously from 1430 hours on 15 April 1946 until 0505 hours on 16 April 1946. Major Edmunds agreed that that it was so, pointing out that the circumstances of the case of Oebsger Roeder and Mahnke were very serious. In the case of Exhibit E I referred to the document 6B, in which there was a similar proposed plan of action, and to documents '14A', '12A' and '13', which indicated that Mahnke was under continuous interrogation on 13 April 1946 from 1350 hours until 2145 hours. Major Edmunds indicated to me that the documents to which I referred in Exhibits D and E were prepared by him and his Colleagues, Captain Van Rije and Captain Langham in the normal course of their duties and they were distributed in the usual way.

Major Edmunds informed me that he had daily conferences with Lt Colonel Short on all matters appertaining to the interrogation of those persons being dealt with by his section and that Lt Colonel Short was kept advised at all stages of the case. I left Major Edmunds with the understanding that we should meet later if he was willing to make a written statement. I did not see Major Edmunds again but in due course received from him a letter dated 27 September 1947 enclosing the statement which we had previously discussed. I produce the letter and statement – Exhibits F and G".

All the accused declined to cross-examine this witness.

Mr J. Timmerman's duly sworn statement read:

"I know Captains van Rije and Langham. I now recognise them both. On 20th May 1947 at Bad Nenndorf I interviewed Captain Langham. I told Captain Langham that I was there as one of Mr Hayward's Assistants and that Mr Hayward had been detailed by the Commander-in-Chief to conduct an investigation into the affairs of the DIC at Bad Nenndorf, also that in the course of that investigation certain information had come to our attention which appeared to require an explanation.

I then cautioned him, explaining to him that he did not have to give me a statement or in fact talk to me at all. Captain Langham said that he was quite willing to make a statement and we started a statement on the understanding that he could stop at any time. Captain Langham dictated a statement to me, which I typed. In the *course of taking the statement reference was made to certain prison records and files. Exhibit E was referred to. We went through the whole file. In particular I drew his attention to folios 6B and 8B to 14B inclusive. After I had finished typing the statement I gave it to Captain Langham who read through it. He then added in his own handwriting, 'I have read through the above statement of five and one half pages and certify that it is the truth'. He then signed it. I countersigned it. I now produce the statement – Exhibit H.*

On 22 May I interviewed Captain Van Rije. I informed him that I was one of a team of Officers, working under Mr Hayward who had been appointed to conduct an inquiry into the affairs of the DIC. I further informed him that in the course of the investigation certain information had been obtained which I would give him, and that in this connection he might wish to make a statement. I then cautioned him. He then made a statement, which I took down in longhand and later typed in my billet. I gave the typed statement to Captain Van Rije the next day. Later he returned the statement to me and said, 'I have read this statement and find it true'. He then signed and dated it in my presence. I now produce the statement, Exhibit I.

During the time that Captain Van Rije was making the statement I showed him various files. Exhibit E was one of the files I showed him. We referred particularly to Folios 6B and 8B-14B inclusive."

Cross-examined by Captain Langham, Mr Timmerman said:

"I told you that you were not obliged to make any statement and that you could refuse to answer any questions. I can say that you gave me an answer to any question that I put.

Major Edmunds and Captain Van Rije declined to cross-examine this witness but having been cautioned in accordance with Rule of Procedure 4(e) each said on oath: *"In my submission no prime facie case has been made out against me."*

No doubt what they said had been composed by their lawyers. At this stage of a case saying any more than this would have given the prosecution more ammunition to fire at the accused when it came to trial. Almost always lawyers advise clients not to say anything. The accused followed the advice that they had received.

Then three charged men were returned under escort, to Bielefeld. Whilst at Bielefeld, it was not difficult for Frank, in spite of official restrictions, to be brought right up to date with the situation, with which he was unfamiliar, by Van Rije and Langham. They agreed on joint representation solicitors and defence counsel, who was yet to be nominated. In view of what Frank regarded as his moral responsibility[19] Frank undertook to take care of the financial arrangements, however difficult, knowing that many of his friends would come to his assistance.

Partly closed and partly open arrest conditions did not prevent them from communicating. The Bielefeld Officers, C.O. and Adjutant especially, were most friendly towards the three prisoners but were not amused when they heard that Frank had marched his closed arrest junior officers out of the camp, with the sentries duly presenting arms. Restrictions were tightened up as a result. Van Rije embroidered handkerchiefs as a memento of their stay at Bielefeld, which he gave to Frank and to Langham. It was common in those days for soldiers to do embroidery for colleagues they held in high esteem.

Frank was released from arrest without prejudice to re-arrest on 21 November 1947 so that he could return to the United Kingdom to attend to his business and prepare the defence of his brother officers and himself. The only restriction imposed upon him was not to communicate any matters concerning the charges against him except to his legal team.

---

[19] Here Frank is referring to his moral responsibility as being the immediate officer in charge of these captains. Frank was not a wealthy man.

CHAPTER 6
The Legal Team

Frank's solicitors, Messrs. Markby Stewart & Wadeson were a very old established reputable firm in the City of London and one of their senior partners, Mr Fullerton, had been looking after Frank's legal affairs.

Since the case was a very difficult one which required a younger energetic man, who would be willing and able to move freely around Britain, Ireland, and Germany to take statements from witnesses and eventually attend the court martial, which looked like lasting a long time, Frank agreed with Mr Fullerton that one of their bright young solicitors, David Goy, should handle the case.

Mr Goy, a married man with a family, was a remarkable person in Frank's opinion. He spared no effort to investigate. Markby Stewart & Wadeson, realising Frank's financial situation, were reasonable with their charges, Frank thought, considering that David Goy worked almost full time on the case for many months. Mr Goy and Frank became firm friends in the course of the case.

Mr Fullerton did not remain inactive either and from behind his city desk he helped matters behind the scenes and through his contacts with Members of Parliament and other personalities, especially his friend, Sir Patrick Hannon M.P.

The three that the legal team were defending were charged with serious offences. If they were found guilty, they would have to spend many years in prison. There was no limit to the length of the prison sentence that a court martial could impose. Mr Goy was gathering evidence to build the defence. He and Mr Fullerton needed to find a barrister to deal with the advocacy at trial. There was evidence that showed that Mahnke and Oebsger-Roeder had been beaten up at Bad Nenndorf, and that they had suffered mental distress in the interrogations. The accused needed a trial lawyer who would present their case and deal with the case the prosecution presented, and cross-examine prosecution witnesses. The case would attract massive publicity: British officers were accused, in effect, of behaving like Nazis to Nazis. The court martial would be assiduously reported and there was an important political element, as the case has been brought as a result of pressure from left-wing members of Parliament. The British Army was on trial.

One of the most important tasks for a solicitor is to select and engage counsel. In a serious case they would need leading counsel, especially recognised barristers who had achieved the title of 'King's Counsel' – today Queen's Counsel. King's Counsel were recognised by the Crown to be excellent barristers. They had special privileges and usually charged the highest fees. One of the best of the time was Derek Curtis-Bennett, K.C. He was asked if he would take the case. He said that he would like to see Frank, before deciding.

Frank met Derek Curtis-Bennett K.C. in the bedroom of his Kensington Home; he had become ill after being vaccinated for a forthcoming trip to the Far East where he had been engaged to defend an accused in a murder trial. He was wearing his pyjamas and sat with Frank in his lounge to discuss the case.

Frank explained the main points of the prosecution case and his defence. The problem was that Mr Curtis-Bennett had already a number of important briefs on his hands, including the murder case in the Far East, which would keep him away for some time and also there was the problem that as a leading King's Counsel his fees were quite out of Frank's reach. Curtis-Bennett liked Frank. He could see that the case involved important matters of law and politics and that Frank had been badly treated. The K.C. agreed there and then to take on the case to defend Frank and both junior officers. He offered to defend the three officers without any remuneration, other than his out-of-pocket expenses. It was an incredibly generous offer as it was expected that the trial would last more than ten days in court and that more than twenty days would have to be spent in preparation.

Curtis-Bennett had, like his father, been very successful at the bar. He was outraged by what he learned from Frank. He had seen enough cases in which the British establishment had made scapegoats of those who had served faithfully but were without connection, like Frank. He was, no doubt, influenced by the fact that his late father, a very eminent King's Counsel of his day, had also been an officer in Military Intelligence.

Derek Curtis-Bennett was well known as a brilliant advocate. When seeing and hearing him perform in court, one would not have suspected that he was a bundle of nerves, who had butterflies in his tummy before every appearance and chain smoked like a chimney.[20]

King's Counsel would need help with the case from junior counsel. Junior counsel would assist in analysing the evidence and deal with the advocacy when Curtis-Bennett was away on other cases. Mr Malcom Norris was chosen as junior counsel.

Frank believed that the Commander in Chief, Sir Sholto Douglas, had made up his mind to show good faith to the Labour Party and its ideas by producing three scapegoats in

[20] Frederick Henry Curtis-Bennett K C was known as Derek to his friends. He defended William Joyce (Lord Haw Haw) John Christie and Karl Fuchs, all unsuccessfully. He died in August 1956, some reports say, of alcoholism, but in 1954 he gave a lecture, 'Alcoholism and the Law', to the Society for the Study of Addiction. He was a brilliant barrister and his closing speech in this court martial ranks as one of the most powerful in English legal history.

the form of British intelligence officers, all of whom were not quite British in their backgrounds.

Sir Charles Russell, solicitor for Colonel Stephens, asked that Frank's legal team join forces in subpoenaing various important personages, including Sir Sholto Douglas, Major General Lethbridge and others. This would have turned the politically inspired prosecution into a blatant political trial. Frank and his team decided that they did not wish to turn this into a trial which examined the political motives of the prosecution. They would rely on defending the case against them on the facts.

Russell also wished to combine and to call some highly placed American officers as witnesses, including officers whom Colonel Stephens had assisted with the establishment of an 'American CSDIC' near Frankfurt, staffed by American officers, some of whom Frank had initiated and trained in the CSDIC methods of interrogation. The legal team decided to leave the Americans out of their list of prospective witnesses. Three of the American officers, Colonel Phelps, Lt Colonel Webster and Mr Enno R Hobbing, with whom Frank had cooperated on some cases, and who had read about the cases in the German press came voluntarily forward and offered to give evidence for the defence. Frank passed Colonel Phelps and Lt Colonel Webster's letters over to Colonel Stephens as they were relevant to his defence.

Being at liberty now to contact potential witnesses, Frank helped his solicitors by tracking down and then interviewing and obtaining statements from ex-officers, NCOs and warders. These statements were sifted by David Goy and then passed over to Derek Curtis-Bennett in his final brief. By the end of January 1948, the defence was ready.[21]

---

[21] The work was completed in less than three months; a similar trial today might take a year's preparation. I am not sure that today's preparation would be any better than that which occurred in 1948.

CHAPTER 7
The Start of The Court Martial

It was decided that the court martial should start in Hanover, Germany, where many witnesses were based and after the witnesses in Germany had been heard, the court martial would move to London. In early March Frank travelled from Manchester to Hanover to be tried on charges of disgraceful conduct of a cruel kind.

When Frank arrived in Hanover for the start of the court martial the legal team heard that the charges against Captain Van Rije had been dropped. The Dutch Government had strenuously objected to one of the nationals being tried. Charges against Lt Colonel Short had also been dropped, after he agreed to give evidence for the prosecution. Separate charges were being formulated against Colonel Stephens and Captain Smith (the medical officer) and separate courts martial would be held for each of them. The defence needed to know exactly what case they faced. It seemed that because the charges against Captain Van Rije and Lt Colonel Short were withdrawn, the prosecution were not relying on allegations of mental cruelty during interrogations. This seemed to be confirmed by a letter from Judge Advocate General to that effect, dated 22 January 1948, which the legal team received.

The case was of growing interest to the press.

COURT MARTIAL HANOVER 2 MARCH 1948.

Extracts from Daily Telegraph of 26 Feb 1948

"Court Martial of 2 Officers. A General Court Martial is to be held at 125 Transit Camp Hanover next Tuesday, to try two British Officers accused of irregularities at a camp at Bad Nenndorf. They are Major F. E. Edmunds, Intelligence Corps and Captain R.O. Langham, Royal Armoured Corps. The case was referred to in the House of Commons on Tuesday by Mr R.R. Stokes[22], Socialist M.P. for Ipswich in a question to Mr Shinwell, Secretary for War. He asked, 'when the Courts Martial on the Officers concerned with third degree methods employed at Bad Nenndorf will be completed and when he proposes to publish a statement of fact'. Mr Shinwell replied that he could not publish any statement while the matter was still sub-judice."

Joint charges against Captain Langham and Frank, in their real names, were publicly read out in open court, which Frank considered a most irregular act, contrary to all the security regulations to the effect that intelligence officers' true names must not be divulged.[23]

---

[22] Mr Stokes was taking advantage of the fact that statements made in the House of Commons are protected from libel by Parliamentary privilege. There was no purpose in Mr Stokes asking such a question, except for publicity and political purposes.

[23] This would be tantamount today to providing the real names of intelligence officers who had

The charge sheet was dated 1 March 1948 and was signed by Lieutenant Colonel on behalf of General Officer Commanding in Chief, British Army of the Rhine. Frank was accused, along with Langham, of causing Mahnke to be submitted to brutal treatment on 18 April 1947, and Oebsger-Roeder to be submitted to brutal treatment on 19 April 1946, being disgraceful conduct of a cruel kind.

The officers who were trying the case were all senior to Frank and none of them had any experience in intelligence work. The President of the Court was Brigadier W E Underhill. The members were Lt Colonels D.C. McCormack, Royal Tank Regiment and CHR Wynne of the Royal Artillery, and Majors Slater (5th Royal Inniskilling Dragoon Guards), Ditchfield (Royal Artillery), Thelwell (Sherwood Foresters) and Sheen (Worcestershire Regiment). These were famous and established regiments of the British Army. Their faces were immobile throughout the court martial. They comprised the jury.

Brigadier Underhill and his members were advised on the law by G L Stirling, King's Counsel, who held the position of Deputy Judge Advocate. Langham and Frank were being prosecuted by Lt Colonel Campbell K.C., another of His Majesty's Counsel. Frank sat with Dick Langham and looked at the legal team. Derek Curtis-Bennett was there, having chain-smoked the early morning away, a bundle of nerves, but now looking calm and confident. His junior counsel was Malcolm Norris, a sharp and hardworking lawyer. David Goy was also there, sitting behind counsel papers with notebook at hand. The proceedings were started, and it soon became clear that only Dick Langham was being tried. Frank's name was not mentioned at all.

Frank had been charged and brought to court because he was going to be tried. However, only Dick Langham's name was mentioned. When they got to court the defence knew that the case against Van Rije had been dropped, but now the case seemed to be just against Langham. Why did the prosecution not refer to Frank? Was he not on trial too?

The reason became clear as the prosecution droned on. Whilst the court was in session a note was handed, in the middle of the opening of the case, to Mr Stirling, the Deputy Judge Advocate General, whose job was to advise the court martial on matters of law. It was from Sir Richard McCreery, the then General Officer Commanding the Rhine Army, the contents of which was read out by Mr Stirling. The note stated that the charges against Frank were not to be proceeded with, in view of a recent High Court decision[24]. On 28 February 1948 three senior judges sitting as judges of the High Court (the Lord Chief Justice with Lords Denning

---

interrogated suspected terrorists in open court; it would not be done.
[24] R v Governor of Wormwood Scrubs, ex parte Boydell.

and Humphries) granted an application of a writ of habeas corpus by one ex-Captain Boydell. Mr Boydell left the army in December 1945 but was arrested a year later, tried by court martial and convicted of fraud charges and sentenced to two years imprisonment. The Court of Appeal ruled that as Mr Boydell was no longer in the army and not receiving pay, his arrest and court martial was illegal, he was being illegally detained, and his conviction must be quashed.

At the first opportunity Curtis-Bennett leapt to his feet. He asked the court either to try Frank Edmunds or to dismiss the charges against him. He complained that Frank had been charged with Langham but now the court was simply ignoring the charge, as though it never existed having been ordered not to try Frank. This was not a technical matter, but as Curtis-Bennett resoundingly proclaimed a matter of the law of England. *"There are only two ends to the matter, either he is convicted, or he is acquitted—natural justice demands it"*. He insisted that the trial against both Major Edmunds and Captain Langham should proceed, since charges had been read out and promulgated on 1 March 1948 and were not officially rescinded. Mr Curtis-Bennett therefore asked the court to acquit Major Edmunds formally of the charges.

Curtis-Bennett's point was important. Frank wanted to be found not guilty. Simply not proceeding with the charges against him left his reputation blemished and could open the way for other charges, under the common law, or under international law as a war crime. An acquittal would mean that Frank could not be tried again for these matters. For Frank, those technical details were not of overriding importance. He wanted to have his name cleared. That was what mattered to him.

The Judge Advocate advised the court that it had no jurisdiction to try Frank and that meant that it had no jurisdiction to acquit Frank. After an adjournment to consider Curtis-Bennett's objection, the President rejected Curtis-Bennett's application to acquit Frank. Curtis-Bennett protested that the refusal meant that *"the principles of natural law have been infringed in one of the most extraordinary cases in the history of British law. Court Martial proceedings could not be taken against a man three months after he had left the Army. I will take appropriate action against Mr Shinwell, the Secretary for War in the Civil Courts in due course,*[25]" he said, *"meanwhile I demand that the stigma be removed."* That was bluster. If the court had no jurisdiction to try Frank it could not proceed one way or another, as Curtis-Bennett knew, but Curtis-Bennett also knew that the case was being assiduously reported and

---

[25] Barristers often make threats of this nature but rarely are they ever acted upon.

the more protests of Frank's innocence the better. Stirling correctly ruled that the court martial was unable to bring Major Edmunds before it and was, therefore, unable to acquit or discharge him.[26]

Curtis-Bennett had lost the first skirmish in the case. He had bustled and argued and like all good advocates feigned anger at injustice but had not succeeded in persuading the court. Even if he had persuaded the court to find Frank not guilty, Frank would not have been satisfied with that. He knew that the only way to clear his name would be if Dick Langham were to be found not guilty. After months of preparation and worry and expense, Frank would not be tried. He wanted to be tried and acquitted. He needed to clear his name. He also was aware that if he were not tried in the court martial other criminal charges could be lodged against him under the common law.

The charges were then read out to Dick Langham who pleaded not guilty to each of them. Curtis-Bennett then rose to his feet and sought to have the charges against Dick Langham dismissed on the grounds that it was a defence that these offences had been condoned or pardoned by higher authority, and not proceeding with the trial against Frank constituted condoning of the charges, which comprised a complete defence under military law. The prosecutor, Mr Campbell, stood up and said he did not agree. Not trying Frank because the court had no jurisdiction was not the same as condoning or pardoning him. Stirling advised the court that Campbell was right and again the court adjourned to consider the argument. Ten minutes later, the President announced that the court rejected Curtis-Bennett's plea. Curtis-Bennett had lost the second skirmish.

Campbell then made an application that parts of the case be heard *in-camera* – that means parts of the case would be held in a closed court to which members of the public would be excluded. Holding cases *in-camera* is an anathema to almost all British lawyers and these lawyers were no exception. Clearly, some secret matters should be heard *in-camera* but the power to hold parts of the case *in-camera* should be used very sparingly; it was the first topic upon which everyone was agreed.

The court then sat *in-camera*. When I looked through Frank's papers, I found that I had to augment them by looking at the files of the case at the National Archives. The files were marked 'Closed until 2024' but the rules had been relaxed since that marker had been placed on the files and I was able to see most of what happened when the court sat *in-camera* and I can now report it in this book.

---

[26] In my view Mr Stirling was right; I suspect that Curtis-Bennett was simply grandstanding.

Brigadier Page was called. He gave evidence that CSDIC was formed to gain intelligence from the German armed forces, civilians, refugees and government departments. The techniques used included stool pigeons, direct interrogation and secret microphones. These methods were top-secret then, although I imagine they were well known and used by the Nazis in their interrogations. Among the information that CSDIC obtained was that about the V1, the V2, German atomic research, beams used by German bombers in 1940 and acoustic mines, all of which Page spoke about.

The President sought guidance from Brigadier Page as to which matters in this trial should be dealt with *in-camera*. Page suggested that six matters should be heard in a closed court:

1. The three-way approach – stool pigeons, direct questioning and microphones.
2. Where CSDIC were situated, their methods of operation and the results obtained.
3. The co-ordinated functions and methods of CSDIC .
4. The intelligence results received by CSDIC and the information obtained.
5. The direction to CSDIC to obtain information of Russian methods of interrogation.
6. The presence, whether in CSDIC or elsewhere, of Russian deserters.

Curtis-Bennett, never one to stay quiet on these occasions, asked an innocent sounding question about whether there would be any objection to naming people who worked at CSDIC. The answer came, no objection, but Curtis-Bennett then asked about the practice of CSDIC using false names when they interrogated people, as part of their interrogation techniques. Page got quite confused with this questioning and was unable to say whether it was wrong for the aliases that were used to now be exposed in public court. The President understood and decided that the court would suppress *noms de guerre*. The court then resumed to sitting in open court.

Having dealt with all preliminary matters, such as excluding the prosecution of Frank and all that flowed from it and having ruled on what the court would hear *in-camera*, Colonel Campbell opened his case for the prosecution.

Campbell started by telling the court that Langham was born in Munich in 1921, left Germany in 1934, became a British subject in 1936 and joined the army in 1940. In late 1944 he was commissioned and then trained in intelligence, joining CSDIC at Bad Nenndorf. Campbell explained the layout of Bad Nenndorf and the fact that the prisoners were looked after by the administration of the camp but questioned by the intelligence staff, of which Langham was one. Langham was posted to Edmunds' unit as was Van Rije.

Campbell then talked about Mahnke: his immediate superior was Dr Six, who in turn reported to Heydrich (later Kaltenbrunner) who reported direct to Himmler. Like Oebsger-Roeder, Mahnke was in the SS. These were not men of good character; they may have served punishment but CSDIC was not a place of punishment. Campbell proceeded to explain that during the interrogation Mahnke had collapsed on a number of occasions.

Curtis-Bennett, hesitating to interrupt an opening speech because it is considered bad manners to do so by barristers, jumped to his feet as soon as he heard that Mahnke had collapsed several times during interrogation. Curtis-Bennett had prepared his defence on the basis that the methods of interrogation did not amount to cruelty and had taken the precaution of getting written confirmation from the prosecution that this was the case. Curtis-Bennett needed to know whether that no longer constituted the prosecution's case, in which event Curtis-Bennett was unprepared, or if the prosecution were to abide by what was in writing, then it was wrong for Campbell to raise any issue about the interrogations.

Campbell replied that the cruelty comprising the beatings up, not the interrogations. The Judge Advocate intervened to say that the court should have all the facts before it, but Curtis-Bennett persisted in his objections. He was trying to establish in the minds of the court martial that severe interrogations which were not violent but included threats of violence was not disgraceful, cruel or brutal conduct, but accepted practice both under the law of England and under international law. The President ruled that the court would listen to the whole story as background even though some parts may not be relevant to the charge of cruelty.

Notwithstanding the ruling Curtis-Bennett did not accept the court's ruling and argued that the background was not relevant to charges of cruelty. He continued to argue with the Advocate General until he secured an admission that the prosecution were making no allegations of impropriety about the earlier interrogations which he received, not from the prosecution but from the Advocate General. At times Curtis-Bennett must have felt that he was facing two prosecutors. It would have been better for the defence if the severity of the interrogations had been agreed not to be referred to in the trial. Curtis-Bennett had lost the third skirmish of the day.

Campbell continued to outline the prosecution's case. He said that a conversation took place either on Maundy Thursday 17 April or Good Friday 18 April between Frank and Company Sergeant Major Mathers. After that conversation Mathers, either alone or with others, assaulted Oebsger-Roeder and Mahnke. What Oebsger-Roeder and Mahnke had to say about the beatings would be corroborated by Mathers and other witnesses. Mahnke was tripped, naked, made to run around, pushed violently from one soldier to another, kicked and punched all over his body for hours, he said. Oebsger-Roeder was made to run from one end of his cell to another continuously with his arms raised above his head and as he ran, he was beaten, punched; he was made to stand on tip toe and then had his legs pushed, so he fell over onto the hard cell floor.

When Langham saw Mahnke naked, beaten and exhausted he said, according to Campbell, *"You aren't dead yet. Do you wish to confess?"* When Langham saw Oebsger-Roeder he said, "Now let's hope you've had enough of this. Make your confession." Mahnke, said Campbell, was so badly injured that he had to stay in hospital for six months and now, after the beatings, has to walk with a stick because he limps.

Campbell ended his opening speech having set out what he expected to prove; the alleged conversation between Mathers and Frank formed the basis of the case, even though the rules against hearsay prevented Campbell stating what was said in that conversation. By the end of the first day Curtis-Bennett had made a lot of noise, a lot of sound and fury but the prosecution had achieved all that it set out to achieve.

Most English courts start at 10.30 a.m. in the morning and end at about 4.30 p.m. in the afternoon with a lunch adjournment of about an hour. This court martial started at 10.00 a.m. and ended at about 4.15 p.m. The court martial continued on 2 March 1948. Frank Edmunds remained not as a defendant in the court martial, but a shadow defendant whose reputation and freedom would ultimately depend upon the verdict brought in against his junior officer, Oliver Langham. A defendant in the shadows has no opportunity to defend himself.

Before he withdrew from the court martial, Frank made the following statement:

"In view of the High Court's decision (in favour of Ex-Captain T.A. Boydell) and now the new situation, whereby it has been stated that all charges against me have been dropped, I would refer to the Manual of Military Law, Page 147 (Power of Courts of Law) (v) 'Actions for damages' against members of courts martial and individual officers, which states : 'It is a general rule of law that magistrates and others, who, acting without jurisdiction, or in excess of their jurisdiction, violate the personal rights of any person by causing his arrest, imprisonment, or otherwise, are liable to an action for damages. It is now recognised that the same general rule applies to officers where a person's common law rights are infringed. Members of a court martial who try a person not subject to military law or for an act which is not an offence cognisable by them, or who pass a sentence which they have no power to pass, and the Officer who confirms the proceedings are all liable to an action at the

suit of the person so aggrieved. So too are individual officers who transgress the bounds of their lawful authority.'

I would like to state here and now that it is not my desire unless my legal advisers should decide otherwise to claim for damages beyond a refund of all expenses incurred in the preparation of my defence provided a matter of far greater importance and interest can be achieved, i.e. my complete exoneration publicly in such terms agreeable to us. Every endeavour should be made to air publicly a number of points which have greatly aggrieved me, i.e. the matters in connection with the actual allegation, the unfair 'investigations' by Public Safety[27] (Messrs Hayward & Company), abuse and infringement by Judge Advocate General of the Official Secrets Act, causing my name to appear in the daily press. The seriousness of this latter flagrant abuse is evidently not realised except by those who know about the Top-Secret work in which I was engaged."

At the request of defence counsel, Derek Curtis-Bennett, Frank then withdrew from the court martial, so that he could be used as a witness for the defence later in the trial.

The court martial proceeded – incredibly to Frank – solely against the most junior officer in the case – Captain Richard Oliver Langham.

Frank remained at the Hanover Transit Camp for some more days at the request of Counsel, though well away from the court martial proceedings, to be available for consultations.

---

[27] It seems very un-British to call an agency 'Public Safety'. The phrase has an Orwellian *1984* tone to it.

CHAPTER 8

Prosecution Witnesses

Oebsger-Roeder was due to give evidence first, and Campbell would have prepared his case accordingly. When he arrived in court on the second day Campbell was told that Oebsger-Roeder had run away. He was no longer there to give evidence. Apparently Oebsger-Roeder left a message to the effect that he did not want to give evidence but would let alone what had passed and did not want to talk about it. Oebsger-Roeder had escaped. This meant that unless the missing former SS officer could be found, captured, and brought to court the only evidence of mistreatment that Campbell could bring before the court was that relating to Mahnke. The case would be weakened by more than half because to a large extent the evidence of Oebsger-Roeder and Mahnke corroborated each other.

Campbell was furious. He ordered that top priority be given to finding Oebsger-Roeder and bringing him to court, while he continued with the case. Instead of calling Oebsger-Roeder Campbell called the other SS man, Mahnke, while the army sent out search parties for Oebsger-Roeder.

Frank did not see his first enemy, Mahnke, give evidence because Curtis-Bennett had kept Frank out of the court room. The former SS man called himself Dr Horst Mahnke and claimed to be an assistant professor of cultural philosophy and the history of thought at the University of Berlin and an advisor to the German Foreign Office. He gave his evidence through an interpreter, and none of the lawyers spoke German well enough to be able to understand his evidence until it was interpreted, although Langham was fluent in his native language and understood German perfectly.

After the 'capitulation', as Mahnke called the Nazi defeat, he settled in Hanover with his family and was arrested on 28 January 1946. At first he was in American custody and was transferred to Bad Nenndorf on 11 April 1946.

Mahnke told how he was interrogated by three officers in a cell, one major and two captains, one of whom he identified as Dick Langham, who was in court and the others as Major Edmunds and Captain Van Rije. Van Rije was not in Germany; Frank Edmunds was outside the court, waiting for updates when the adjournments came and no doubt fretting. Mahnke said that at about 1600 hours Captain Van Rije was relieved by a major. At this time, he did not know this major's name and could not say for certain now that he was present in the court room.

This major remained in the interrogation cell until about midnight. During the evening he was joined by Captain Langham. The major, said Mahnke, did the talking, telling him that accomplices had been caught, they knew about the plan and that he should make a confession. He said that the major gave him a detailed dissertation about secret service, its traditions, achievements and successes, and that he had to make a full confession, or he would be shot; then added that shooting would be too good for a swine like him – SS swine should be hanged not shot. The major told him that his family had been arrested and that if he did not confess the same methods would be applied to his wife. The interrogation that day lasted fifteen to twenty minutes.

Mahnke then described lengthy interrogations on the following day, 13 April 1946, at which he was ordered to stand to attention by Frank during the interrogations for hours at an end. He was not offered a chair and eventually had to prop himself up against the wall or lie on the cell floor. The interrogation was mainly about Mahnke's connections and contacts in the British Zone in Germany but it did not prove to reveal much to Frank and his team. On one occasion Mahnke said that Langham rolled up his sleeves and assumed a boxing stance, waiting for an order from the major to hit him, an order which never came. After ten or so hours of interrogation Mahnke was taken back to his cell and given some blankets. Mahnke slept on the floor because there was no bed.

The prosecution needed Mahnke to identify those who had been guarding him. There were a number of guards: Company Sergeant Major Mathers, Sgt Lewis, Sgt Thomas, Sgt Sore, and Sgt Brant.

The prosecution then brought some of those who had guarded him into the court for Mahnke to say whether he knew them. Company Sergeant Major Mathers was identified as someone who could have been the sergeant major. Mahnke did not know his name or nickname. Sgt Lewis was identified, under his nick name 'the Panther'. Mahnke knew Sgt Thomas by his nickname 'Robert Taylor', Sgt Brant by 'Henry the Eighth' and Sgt Sore as 'Bloodshot Eye'.

Having identified or recognised all of these guards, Mahnke went on to describe the events of 18 April 1946. He was stripped naked, made to run around with his arms outstretched, punched, pulled, pressed against the wall, had his hair pulled, and struck all manner of blows from ten in the morning until six in the afternoon, with only short periods of relief when the guards were changed or when meals were served. He was beaten with fists and struck in the sexual organs. He fell to the floor and was revived several times. Every ten or fifteen minutes he lost consciousness and was brought to his senses with one or more bowls of water. He could not remember whether Thomas (Robert Taylor) took part in the beatings, but he remembers him giving instructions. Mahnke had the impression that Thomas was in charge. Langham was duty officer when the evening meal was served and saw Mahnke, Mahnke said, naked and bleeding from his treatment by the guards as Mahnke went to collect his food.

Langham spoke to him in German, "*Well, you aren't yet dead. Do you want to make a confession?*" Mahnke refused to say anything and Langham took him the three or four metres back to his cell. He claimed that when in the cell, he was forced to eat by a sentry. After his meal the treatment continued until the evening round, which was between nine and quarter to ten. At this time Langham came round again because Mahnke saw him standing in the doorway. Before he came the sentries were ordered out of the cell. *"Langham could see I was bleeding,"* he said. Langham asked again if Mahnke would like to make a confession, in German. Mahnke replied to the effect that he would in conscience blame himself if he lied to prevent further ill treatment.

This curious turn of phrase prompted the Judge Advocate to ask if Langham was a "German Scholar" to which Langham replied he was. The Judge Advocate asked whether he was satisfied with the translation the interpreter was rendering. Langham said he was, apart from a few small errors. In effect, the court accepted Mahnke was saying he would not incriminate himself by lying to escape brutal treatment.

A short time after Langham left, Mahnke said, a number of guards came, and the treatment started all over again. This time Mahnke was made to run naked into a rope in the corridor and into a washroom round the corner by Robert Taylor and his sentries. He was kicked, pushed over and against furniture. He was forced to take a cold shower for fifteen minutes and when he tried to leave the shower, he was forced back into it "with fists". He was moved from cell to cell by Robert Taylor and Henry the Eighth and other guards, unable to rest. In the shower basin with cold water turned on again he was beaten with mops and brooms. A table was thrown on him. Mahnke then described how the soldiers gave him pencil and paper, urged him to write and he did write, giving the paper to the soldiers, who later brought another piece of paper, upon which he wrote again and the process was repeated with a third piece of paper.

The following morning Mahnke was taken to be interviewed by Captain Langham. Langham asked him to read his writing on the papers out loud. Mahnke only remembered reading the first piece of paper upon which he wrote and the interpreter translated:

"To the interrogating officer. I can't stand this anymore. I will speak the truth for the last time that I have not belonged to any resistance movements and do not know that Roeder has done either. If I am asked like this again I will incriminate Roeder and

myself by untruths because I can't stand this anymore. So help me God, I cannot do otherwise."

Mahnke had signed the paper.

The same process followed for a second note that Mahnke wrote;

"To the interrogation officer. I can't stand this any longer and say in addition to what I wrote originally. First Roeder made a statement to me at the camp. He had not previously spoken to me on this matter, nor did he do so later. When I was travelling with him he did not speak to people about resistance. Secondly, I had intended setting up a news service /intelligence service with Leipold. Apart from that I spoke to no one else about it on my journey. My primary interest was in East Prussia, I must make these statements which do not conform to the truth because I am in despair and I do not know what I can do to help myself. Please shoot me dead as I am innocent and know nothing about Roeder. So help me God."

Mahnke had signed it and then the last note was translated:

"I am supposed to write more so I will have to go on telling lies which I hope God may forgive me. With Hilpert and Aust I was going to start a 'news' or 'intelligence' service. I visited them for this purpose. Hilpert could not leave his farm and with Aust there were women so no discussion could take place. I spoke to no one in Hamburg about such things. There are no contacts there which could incriminate me. Now please leave me in peace otherwise I shall go mad."

Mahnke initialled this document.

The translations were perfected after prompting and correcting by Curtis-Bennett. Langham confirmed that he was satisfied with these translations.

Reading these communications more than seventy years after they were written I get an impression that although Mahnke was beaten, he was not so badly beaten that he did not have his wits about him, writing quite clearly that he was only confessing because he was being treated in a bad way and even then Mahnke refused to confess to anything at all. An SS officer appealing to God to forgive him for telling lies is a nice touch. I would imagine SS officers had more serious sins for which they should appeal to God for forgiveness.

Mahnke went on to say that Langham had told him that they had received information about an uprising on Adolf Hitler's birthday, 20 April, and if a single hair on a British soldier's head were harmed then what Mahnke had experienced so far would be as child's play compared to what he would experience in the future. Mahnke stayed in a cell for four days and on Easter Monday he was taken to hospital. He had wounds which had become infected. He was seen by a doctor taken to hospital and remained in hospital until 3 or 4 September.

Mahnke's evidence had finished. He was then cross-examined by Curtis-Bennett. It is always difficult to cross-examine someone whose native language is not English. There can be misunderstandings, even with the best of interpreters, and the court had two interpreters to assist. The use of interpreters gives a witness who knows English time to think of an answer without appearing evasive. It can also be unfair on the witness who might not get the exact meaning of a question through the interpreter. Finally, for both witness and advocate the interpreter's intervention can make it harder to bring out the right impression of honesty or dishonesty in the witness. Cross-examining through an interpreter makes it harder for the court to form a true picture of the demeanour of the witness.

Curtis-Bennett established that the interrogation officers knew that the interrogation had reached a stage where Mahnke no longer had self-control and was prepared to lie, and that there was no point in beating him up when he was already at a state where he was prepared to lie. He asked Mahnke about this. The question was discussed by the court and translated, giving Mahnke plenty of time to think of an answer. He said, *"from a purely technical point of view the whole of my treatment at Bad Nenndorf was incomprehensible."*

Curtis-Bennett established that Mahnke was a member of the SS and the SD[28] and from May 1939 an honorary leader of the SS:

A. My work was with the University and the Foreign Office. I was in the service of the Sicherheitsdienst (SD) of the Reichsführer of the SS (Himmler) and could not leave this service although I had no functions. There were, amongst the SS, several leaders who, though in the SS, had no function to perform. They were so-called honorary leaders. From 1939 onwards I was one of these honorary leaders.

Q. During the time after 1939 did you remain subject to the discipline of the SS?

A. What do you mean by discipline?

Q. During the time after 1939 did you remain under the control of the SS?

A. I wish to answer the question as follows: during the time I was under the honorary discipline of the SS, that is I was supposed to and did act in accordance with the principles of the SS. I never received official orders from the SS.

Q. Did you at any time sign a declaration of secrecy?

---

[28] Sicherheitsdienst (Security Service). The SD was the intelligence agency of the SS and the Nazi Party in Nazi Germany. The organisation was the first Nazi Party intelligence organization to be established.

A. When I joined the SD, I had to sign a statement that I should keep secret anything I saw and any reports I made. When I joined the service of the Foreign Office, I signed a similar document for this service.

Curtis-Bennett suggested that when Langham did his round at 9 pm, Mahnke was clothed and any wounds would be covered by the clothing and not be visible to Langham. Mahnke denied that. Mahnke said that he did not complain to the prison authorities about his treatment because he had no opportunity so to do.

Curtis-Bennett hammered away at this point, and Mahnke then said he could not complain because when he spoke his voice was drowned out by invective and he could not make himself heard. When Curtis-Bennett suggested that his evidence about Langham assuming a fighting pose was untrue, Mahnke denied that and asked whether counsel wished to employ the methods of invective used at Nenndorf or whether this was a court of law. Langham assisted in the accurate translation of Mahnke's rhetorical question.

Mahnke said he was insulted by being accused of not telling the truth. Curtis-Bennett cross-examined him about inconsistencies between the written summary complaint that Mahnke had made and his evidence in court; in court Mahnke had claimed that his hair was pulled, and he was burnt with cigarette butts, neither of which was mentioned in the summary report. When Curtis-Bennett suggested that Mahnke was inventing this, Mahnke begged the court to protect him from these "insults". Unflustered by this complaint Curtis-Bennett ploughed on relentlessly. He established that Mahnke did not recognise Frank, who was not in court at that stage, and then asked how he could identify Frank as the major who had interrogated him. He resorted to claiming that other people had told him the major's name was Edmunds. Curtis-Bennett threw out some more questions.

It was five past five. It had been a long day. The court adjourned. The proceedings were fully reported in the British press.

The next morning Curtis-Bennett continued to cross-examine Mahnke. Overnight he must have been poring over the notes of the day's cross-examination, looking for gaps, inconsistencies and lies, so when he resumed his questions Mahnke found that the barrister was in a quarrelsome mood. Words were dissected for their meanings, the interpretation of other words and phrases were challenged by Langham, sometimes leaving the Advocate General thoroughly confused as the court sat impassively hoping no doubt that they would understand the points that Curtis-Bennett was trying to bring out. In fact, Curtis-Bennett was merely trying to show that Mahnke was a skilled and inveterate liar.

It is a good idea, in cross-examination, to stop sooner, rather than later, leaving the court with the impression of the witness that you want the court to form. Curtis-Bennett sat down.

Campbell re-examined Mahnke politely, calling him "Doctor Mahnke" and establishing that Doctor Mahnke was under no restraint now, and as free as any other German. The court put some questions through the Advocate General, establishing that the very cold conditions in Bad Nenndorf had caused Mahnke's health to break down. By 11.30 Mahnke's ordeal in the witness box was over, and Dr Heinz Buttner was called, Oebsger-Roeder still not having been captured.

Dr Buttner was a Doctor of Medicine, the principle medical doctor at the hospital to which internees at Bad Nenndorf were sent. He remembered Mahnke, saying that when he arrived at the hospital his condition was so bad that he might be expected to die. He complained of suffering and on the right knee was a small infected wound with bad bruising on his legs and abrasions on his body, which Curtis-Bennett established were superficial on the shoulders and forearms.

I do not know how the British Army found Oebsger-Roeder but find him they did. They arrested him and brought him to court, keeping guard on him to ensure that he did not escape. One thing was clear: Oebsger-Roeder did not want to give evidence in court. I can only speculate on his reasons, but they were likely to be connected with a desire to keep dark his SS past and his activities working as an SS officer. He might have been frightened as to what the defence had found out about his wartime activities.

In any event, when Campbell called Rudolf Oebsger-Roeder, for the second time, he did so knowing that the witness was safely in custody and would be brought to the witness box.

Oebsger-Roeder described himself benignly as a former university assistant, a Doctor of Philosophy who had been in the SS since 1935 and had worked for the German Intelligence Services throughout the war, first for the security service and later for intelligence services relation to foreign matters. The war ended when he was thirty-five; he was a high-flying Nazi, destined for the top but the defeat of Germany had put paid to his career.

Officially Oebsger-Roeder said that he did not wish to give evidence at this trial, *"which can only result in new hatreds arising"* and he was *"willing to forget the happenings as a human being and an historian"*. I am sure that he was very willing to forget his own role in the Nazi party and in the war and the events leading up to it. The statement he made was:

"I am aged 35 years. I was employed as a University assistant in Leipzig up to 1937. I was then withdrawn from the University and posted to Konigsberg. There I met Dr Mahnke and we became friends. We remained in touch with each other throughout the war. I joined the SS in 1935. By virtue of the technical nature of my work my connection with them was at first an honorary one but later it became an official appointment. On 28th January 1946 I was arrested by British soldiers and taken to Nienburg. I was removed from there on 25th March 1946 by Captain Langham and a Sergeant [and taken] to Bad Nenndorf. At Bad Nenndorf I was in cell 57 in the prison block. After about eight days I was removed to cell 2. About this time my first interrogation took place. This was carried out in an interrogation cell in the presence of Major Edmunds, Captain Langham and Captain Van Rije. Major Edmunds presided over the interrogation. It began at 9 o'clock in the evening and lasted about half an hour to one hour. The main theme was how far I was connected with an underground movement and what were the aims and who the members of this organisation. I was warned to speak the whole truth. I was told that I was to die in any case but that if I were to tell the truth quickly and fully, I could save myself from suffering. I was also told that my wife and little daughter had been arrested.[29] These and other menaces were made by Major Edmunds and Captain Langham.

The interrogation cell was darkened. It was only lighted by a sort of table-lamp whose light was arranged to fall upon me. I got the idea that the scene was specially arranged beforehand to impress me. I was not physically ill treated by the interrogators nor by the guards.

My first interrogation was followed by other interrogations. For a short time, I was placed in a cell with Mahnke. About the beginning of April, the furniture was taken from my cell No.2 and it was converted into a confinement cell. I remained in this cell about eight days. During this time, I was obliged to scrub the floor. There was an occasion a few days before Good Friday when I was interrogated in the interrogation cell. I was particularly badly bullied, threatened with blows, but not struck. I had to stand to attention for fourteen hours.

During this time, I was given nothing to eat and several times lost consciousness. I was restored to my senses each time by a sentry throwing cold water into my face. During this time either Major Edmunds or Captain Langham or Captain

---

[29] The Geneva Convention permitted that prisoners be told that their families would be or had been arrested and threats could be made against the families, provided that they were not carried out.

Van Rije would put in an appearance and put questions to me. On Good Friday – or it may have been the day before – I was removed from cell 2 to cell 12. I had to strip off everything so that I was standing naked in the cell. My clothes were thrown on the floor outside the cell. Inside the cell there were two soldiers besides myself. Several other soldiers stood outside the cell.

The two soldiers in the cell changed places from time to time with those standing outside. I was obliged to raise my hands and to keep on running from one end of the cell to the other. As I did so I was continually seized by two soldiers in turn and hurled from one to the other. As a result of this I scorched the skin on my hands and also grazed the skin on other parts of my body. From time to time the Sergeant-Major came into the cell.

I was very weak and collapsed several times. I received this treatment from 4 o'clock in the afternoon until 6. I was then left alone in the cell for a while. Shortly after 6 I was called outside the cell and given my evening meal of tea and bread. I received this meal in the presence of Captain Langham, who was the officer on duty. I was still completely naked. Captain Langham did not speak to me; he looked me up and down and smiled. I went back into my cell and ate my food. After that I was taken into the bathroom next door. There were several soldiers in the bathroom, but I cannot exactly say who they were. I was placed under the cold shower. My nerves were by this time in a bad state.

The water was very cold, and it seemed to me that I stood there a long time. After that, about 7 p.m., I was taken from the bathroom, driven along to corridor 3 and put into one of the larger cells there. This was cell 36, 37 or 38. There were six or eight English sentries in the cell. One of these was a Sergeant.

The prisoners always referred to this Sergeant as Robert Taylor[30]. These men placed themselves in the four corners of the room, some of them in between and compelled me while they hurled me from one to the other. I was still entirely naked. This treatment lasted several hours. I was also forced to stand against the wall on tiptoe with my hands above my head. My feet were then pulled away from beneath me so that I fell to the floor each time. As I stood with my back to the soldiers I was beaten about the body with straps in such a way that as the centre part of the strap struck my ribs and loins the ends of the strap struck me in the private parts.

---

[30] Robert Taylor was a handsome contemporary movie actor famous for romantic roles.

> *This was very painful. I collapsed repeatedly and was revived by having water thrown over me. I felt very wretched and begged the sentries to shoot me. I do distinctly remember that Captain Langham appeared and spoke to the sentries. As he did so he looked into the cell and then went away. About 11 o'clock the soldiers left the cell and left me lying in the water on the floor. Another older sentry came in. He made me stand up against the wall with my hands above my head.*
>
> *About midnight Captain Langham came along and said to me, 'Now let's hope you've had enough of this make your confession'. I was led into a nearby cell where there was a typewriter and a bed. I did write something on the machine, but I was so confused that I do not know what I wrote.*
>
> *After I had written, a sentry took the sheet of paper and let me go to bed. The whole of my body was covered with bruises. In some parts the skin was gone and there was much swelling, especially in the loins. I also had very bad pains in my heart. I have not made any official complaint of this treatment because I felt afraid of provoking further trouble for myself."*

In his evidence Oebsger-Roeder denied any knowledge of any organisation existing to create an uprising on Hitler's birthday. In the course of his evidence, he was shown Sergeant Sore, whom he knew as Blood Eye, and Company Sergeant Major Mathers, whom he also identified, and Thomas – Robert Taylor.

Curtis-Bennett asked a few questions about Oebsger-Roeder's Nazi credentials, establishing that he had joined the Nazi Party in 1931, not as he first claimed in 1935. The difference in dates is significant. Hitler came to power in 1933 and Oebsger-Roeder wanted to give the false impression that he had only joined the SS after Hitler was in legal power of Germany. At the end of the third day of the hearing, Curtis-Bennett had persuaded the court to view the cells at Bad Nenndorf on the following morning so it was not until 14:15 on Friday 5 March the court martial resumed, with Oebsger-Roeder facing the cross-examination of Curtis-Bennett.

Every successful advocate must have a powerful voice, not necessarily a loud voice, but one that commands attention and makes it appear that a witness's answers are almost being dragged out by the advocate if the witness is being cross-examined or sympathetic to the witness, if the witness is one the advocate wants the court to believe. It must be a charismatic voice. Intonation is important, so that the advocate can express surprise, simplicity, disbelief, or agreement simply by the tone he uses. This usually has an effect upon a witness, who feels from the advocate's voice that his evidence is incredulous or in some way unsatisfactory.

These are the games that lawyers play. Curtis-Bennett was a master of these devices but in Oebsger-Roeder he faced a highly intelligent witness skilled in questioning and cross-examination, and in some other techniques that no member of the English bar would approve.

Oebsger-Roeder told Curtis-Bennett that he assumed Frank was the leader of those who were physically violent to him, but not during the interrogations. He said that after he was beaten, he was kept in solitary confinement for four weeks and not allowed to speak to anyone and therefore could not make a complaint. Oebsger-Roeder admitted that a duty officer came round at various times – at least three times a day – and that Oebsger-Roeder did not complain to any duty officer. Oebsger-Roeder then said that some days he never saw the duty officer, and therefore that he thought it would be futile to complain to the duty officer. He did see a German doctor on Easter Sunday, shortly after he was beaten up, but got the impression that the doctor was timid, or a prisoner, and he did not mention to the doctor that he had been beaten up.

Clearly whether Oebsger-Roeder could have complained about his beatings was important to the case, and Curtis-Bennett was able to establish, with the reluctant agreement of Oebsger-Roeder, that between Easter Sunday on 21April 1946 and 4 December 1946 Oebsger-Roeder did complain, but only about rheumatism, toothache, and constipation.

Curtis-Bennett then turned to Oebsger-Roeder's knowledge of the English language. Oebsger-Roeder said that he understood about half the questions in English but not all of them. Curtis-Bennett established from Oebsger-Roeder that although he was physically exhausted after he was beaten up his mind was working at more than normal tempo – super fast. That was when Oebsger-Roeder typed out his statement. He then turned to the statement, prepared, and read to the court when Oebsger-Roeder had escaped. He asked the interpreter to read out one passage:

> "I was brought into a neighbouring cell where there was a typewriter and a bed as well. I wrote something on the typewriter, but I was so confused that I cannot say any longer what I wrote."

The Advocate General checked the translation, *"I do not know any longer what I wrote"*.

Curtis-Bennett had pulled a master stroke of cross-examination by showing a serious inconsistency between what Oebsger-Roeder had just said in cross-examination and what he wrote at the time. The Advocate General appeared to attempt to dilute the force of the inconsistency and reduce its impact on the court. Curtis-Bennett was arguing that Oebsger-Roeder could not have typed such a logical well-typed document if he was as exhausted as he says. If Oebsger-Roeder was as badly ill-treated as he claimed, surely, he could not have typed out such a logical statement, Curtis-Bennett asked Oebsger-Roeder who replied, *"theoretically I cannot answer very well"*, claiming that he did not swear that this was his document he had typed. Curtis-Bennett pointed out two scratching outs on the document and Oebsger-Roeder said he could not identify the document from that as his. Curtis-Bennett asked Oebsger-Roeder that the document could not be a copy, because no one would copy those scratching outs, and when the President said that he understood the point Curtis-Bennett rattled back, *"Yes, I know you understand it, but I am trying to get an admission out of him and if we sit here six weeks, I shall go on trying."*

It is not usually good tactics to get angry or feign anger with the Court, and Curtis-Bennett then diffused his shortness by asking permission for the document to be shown to Frank who was waiting outside, whereupon the court decided not to make any decision about whether Oebsger-Roeder had typed the document before it. The fourth day of the trial ended.

Friday night is never an easy night for a barrister who is set to resume cross-examination. He must spoil his weekend in preparing the cross-examination in the light of what he has already learned about the witness. In this case it was even more difficult than normal on Curtis-Bennett because the court would reconvene on Saturday morning at 10 a.m. It was a sleepless night, and with the chain smoking Curtis-Bennett was his usual bundle of nerves when the court re-assembled.

Whereas Colonel Campbell had been polite in his questioning of Oebsger-Roeder, calling him Dr Oebsger-Roeder, Curtis-Bennett ignored his titles; his first question set the tone for the rest of the cross-examination.

"Oebsger-Roeder, did you ever say anything like your conduct had been unreasonable when you were at Bad Nenndorf?"

Oebsger-Roeder agreed that he had not. He also agreed that he had said that he had been untrustworthy. He regretted being untrustworthy and should have given the intelligence officers the names of his acquaintances but refused to do so in order to save them from the ordeal he himself had experienced. It was a mistake because his acquaintances could have cleared him. When he came into English hands Oebsger-Roeder eventually admitted that he was prepared to lie.

Oebsger-Roeder deflected the question saying it was not a low lie, and refused to answer it, but he was very keen to incriminate Langham, saying that Langham saw him naked and saw him being ill-treated *"in the full realisation of my oath"*. Curtis-Bennett asked about important details which Oebsger-Roeder had mentioned now but did not mention to the police when they investigated the case and Oebsger-Roeder replied that there were hundreds of details which he did not mention to the police. He confirmed that Frank Edmunds was the main interrogator, questioning him for nine hours altogether and that he regarded the fourteen hours in interrogation as "a pretty stern thing".

At the end of the cross-examination the court asked some questions, clarifying the type of wounds that Oebsger-Roeder received. Suddenly, the Judge Advocate asked about 'Michael' the source of the claim that there would be an uprising on Hitler's birthday. The Judge Advocate asked, *"This man Michael, was he ever at Bad Nenndorf?"* Oebsger-Roeder replied, *"Yes, he was Major Edmunds' batman. He was first a prisoner and then became a batman."* Oebsger-Roeder claimed that Michael had said he had overheard a conversation between Oebsger-Roeder and Mahnke, about a resurrection, but it was all lies. He was confronted with Michael for a few minutes, and that he noticed that Michael had shoelaces on his shoes, which were forbidden, and they were made of twine. At 11.40 the evidence of Oebsger-Roeder was complete.

The court called Lader Dubritz, a businessman, who said that he saw Mahnke on a stretcher at the Rotenberg Internment Hospital in Easter 1946, being carried by two British orderlies on a stretcher. Dubritz was assisting the doctors at the time. Mahnke was delirious, talking a lot of nonsense, his arms and legs were swollen, and teeth seemed newly missing. Mahnke arrived without a case history, without notes (which was very unusual) and had to be given a blood transfusion. Dubritz said that the doctor had told him that they had to give Mahnke a blood transfusion otherwise it would be hopeless, when Curtis-Bennett quickly objected to hearsay evidence being given.

Mr S J Mathers was the star witness for the prosecution. He was formerly Company Sergeant Major Mathers, of the Royal Inniskilling Fusiliers. Mathers was a Northern Irish soldier who joined the army in 1941, saw action and was wounded in Africa in 1942 and spent nine months in hospital rehabilitating. He was then posted to a secret camp, where they kept both military and civilians in Britain. After September 1946 Mathers transferred to the guard section of CSDIC, later DIC at Bad Nenndorf. He had to guard the prisoners and see to the cleanliness and discipline of them. Mr Mathers was now a grocer's assistant.

He explained under Colonel Campbell's patient questioning that most people who came to Bad Nenndorf went to the prison, but some went to the Diester House, or the Guest House. He explained the arrangements for guarding and looking after the prisoners, where they were interrogated, and the duties of the duty officer. Campbell in questioning Mathers did not want to get to the heart of his evidence on Saturday morning because the court would adjourn at lunchtime until Monday afternoon and some of the effect may have been lost. Having 'dealt' with some side issues the court martial adjourned until 1400 on Monday 8 March 1948 leaving star witness Mathers' most critical evidence unspoken.

CHAPTER 9

Waiting for The Star Witness

On Monday 8 March 1948 Frank returned to the United Kingdom at the suggestion of his legal team. Perhaps they worried that Frank was a distraction that they ought to remove while they considered Mathers' evidence. Perhaps they felt that Frank was not needed now, but whatever the reason Frank went back home.

I know from personal experience that a fussy client intent on examining every detail of a case against him (or in his favour) can be a very tiring experience for a lawyer. You have to concentrate as to what is being said in court, keep track of important documents, work under considerable pressure with high intensity. You then, at the close of the case when you need some peace, must speak to the client, who will, if they can, spend hours with you on matters that you already know or have already discerned. I think in those circumstances I would have been glad to find a reason to send Frank back to England.

The court started in the afternoon, and as is the way, before the resumption of evidence the barristers updated the court on what was likely to happen in the case. Curtis-Bennett explained that he had many witnesses to call in England, and that he was absolutely certain that they would have to complete the case in England.

Mathers was, as I have said, the star witness for the prosecution. He was formerly Company Sergeant Major Mathers, of the Royal Inniskilling Fusiliers. He was a Northern Irish soldier who joined the army in 1941, saw action and was wounded in Africa in 1942 and spent nine months in hospital rehabilitating. He was then posted to a secret camp, where they kept both military and civilians in Britain. After September 1946 Mathers transferred to the guard section of CSDIC, at Bad Nenndorf. He had to guard the prisoners and see to cleanliness and discipline of them. Mr Mathers was now a grocer's assistant.

He explained under Colonel Campbell's patient questioning that most people who came to Bad Nenndorf went to the prison, but some went to the Diester House, or the Guest House. He explained the arrangements for guarding and looking after the prisoners, where they were interrogated and the duties of the Duty officer. Campbell in questioning Mathers did not want to get to the heart of his evidence on Saturday morning because the court would adjourn at lunchtime until Monday afternoon and some of the effect may have been lost. Having "dealt with all the frillings" the court martial adjourned until 1400 on Monday 8 March 1948 leaving star witness Mathers' most critical evidence, as yet unspoken.

When Mathers resumed his evidence the next day, he said that he remembered Oebsger-Roeder and Mahnke at Bad Nenndorf in April 1946. He said that Mahnke was "doubled" round the cell and slapped on several occasions by Mathers and Thomas, both of whom slapped Mahnke with their hands held flat.

Curtis-Bennett intervened to ask (he already knew the answer to his question) as to whether the witness should be cautioned because he was giving evidence which might tend to incriminate him? It was a master stroke. Campbell replied that Mathers had been told categorically no proceedings would be taken against him, and that there was no competent court, Mathers having left the army more than three months previously. Curtis-Bennett had no time for this argument. *"In my submission if he is being asked to give evidence that he assaulted somebody, in Germany or Togoland, he ought to be warned that he need not give it."* Curtis-Bennett argued that some court somewhere would have the right to try Mathers, but Campbell and the Judge Advocate denied this was the case, which Curtis-Bennett described as *"a very strange position"*.

The Judge Advocate asked if Edmunds could be tried by a court, because he was taking responsibility for anything that might happen. Curtis-Bennett said that Edmunds was not taking that point – he was not saying that he would not give evidence because it incriminates him, and the point Curtis-Bennett was making was merely that Mathers should be warned, in the usual way. Curtis-Bennett asked the President for a ruling on whether Mathers should be warned and debated the point with the Judge Advocate, who took the view that Mathers need not be warned. During all this argument Mathers was in court listening to it. He heard, according to one impressive sounding lawyer, that he still might be charged for what he had done to the prisoners.

Curtis-Bennett wanted Mathers warned, even though Mathers had been assured that he would not be prosecuted and given a pardon, because he wanted to shake Mathers' confidence in those who had pardoned him; perhaps the pardon may not be watertight? The thought must have gone through Mathers' mind. He had not seen a written pardon. That was what he needed. Campbell promised to produce some law and the court, having opened at 2 p.m., adjourned at 12.30 to enable Campbell to check the law. At 4.35 p.m. the court reassembled, and Campbell told them that he needed more time. Curtis-Bennett was not in court at this time so Mr Norris, his junior barrister, agreed to Campbell's request for more time, pointing out that it was simply a question of discovering whether Mathers could be tried for the assaults to which he had confessed, anywhere, in which case he should be cautioned. The court adjourned with no decision being made on the point.

Curtis-Bennett was absent because he was going over some notes produced by David Goy, the solicitor who was anxious that the Public Security Police be criticised in the trial for their conduct. Goy wrote (as lawyers did rather formally in those days):

> "It has come to my attention that the method used by the Public Security Police for obtaining information from prospective witnesses is very much a matter for criticism, and it appears that threats were used by these officials – this fact being confirmed by evidence that Sergeant Lewis (formerly Lance Corporal in April 1946) was threatened by the officials with words such as 'if you persist in holding back information like the others, I'll knock your bloody head off' or words to that effect and a protest was actually made by Lewis to Captain Moran at the time. (Captain Moran is available as defence witness if required). Sergeant Lewis is being called by the Prosecution as a Witness. Another member of the staff, named Kheeler also protested in writing at being threatened by the Police to Major Kettler and Major Chute (both available as Witnesses if desired) and Sergeant Brant, who is also a Prosecution Witness has apparently stated on some occasion that he was told by the Police that he would be sent to prison if he did not come clean. It is believed that prosecution's principal witness CSM Mathers was coerced into coming to Germany to give evidence and that certain promises were made to him by Colonel Campbell".[31]

I think that Goy was right that these points should be made in the trial, but they were not made for reasons Curtis-Bennett must have had.

On 9 March, the Judge Advocate General queried the authority for Frank's return to the United Kingdom. He was told by Curtis-Bennett that his return to the United Kingdom was undertaken at his authority and request. The Court's question was odd, because the Court had earlier ruled that it had no power to try Frank and no military authority over him.

At 10 a.m. the court reconvened and Mathers had still not given his star evidence because of the objection by Curtis-Bennett that Mathers should be warned against incriminating himself. Colonel Campbell told the court that the law was far from straightforward but conceded that there was force in Curtis-Bennett's submission that Mathers should be formally warned. Campbell had decided, he told the court, that it was important that the prosecution lay the fullest possible evidence before the court martial and the only way to do this was to get a free pardon from the Commander in Chief at Berlin so that Mathers could give evidence free from any fear of prosecution.

---

[31] Mr Goy is in effect saying that the prosecution used similar tactics to those alleged to be used by the defendant.

Curtis-Bennett had clearly shaken Mathers who was probably refusing to give evidence without a written pardon. The prosecution had decided that the only way to get Mathers to give the evidence that they wanted him to give was to put a free pardon in his hands. Technically, the prosecution lawyers were prohibited from speaking to Mathers on this subject because he was in the middle of giving evidence, but it is hard to see how they would have come up with offering a free pardon without Mathers speaking to them.

Curtis-Bennett was scathing in his response to this suggestion, about the competence of the prosecution, and protested profoundly. The court decided to agree to the twenty-four-hour adjournment to enable Campbell to get a written pardon for Mathers.

Curtis-Bennett explained that he had taken on this case on the basis that it would take ten days; it had already taken ten days and now Curtis-Bennett would have to make arrangements to absent himself and leave the case in the hands of his junior, Mr Norris. To the echoes of Curtis-Bennett's complaints about the scandal of the delays and pardons which were prejudicing his client, the court adjourned for the day, leaving Campbell to book his journey to Berlin to get the pardon.

This was an extraordinary development in the case. The prosecution had already decided that it should not prosecute those who did the actual beatings but those who the pardoned soldiers claimed had ordered the beatings. A few months earlier at Nuremberg in Bavaria, the judges of the War Crimes Tribunal convened there (led by the presiding judge, a British lawyer) and decided that the fact that a person acted pursuant to order of his superior does not relieve him from responsibility. In other words, Mathers was still responsible even if Frank had ordered him to do the beatings, because the order was unlawful and contrary to international law, and also contrary to the law that applied to the British Army at the time. Now Mathers was to be pardoned so as to enable him to give evidence against Frank without fear of prosecution.

This was a plea bargain and plea bargains have always been somewhat of an anathema to English law, especially plea bargains which enable some accused to go free while others are prosecuted.

The case was ten days old. Not a single piece of evidence had been given to the court linking Langham to the allegations of ill treatment. The cases against Frank had been dropped on a technicality leaving Frank, the prosecution, and those baying for justice unsatisfied and Frank was the most senior officer implicated in the allegations. The Dutch Government had pressured the British Government into dropping the case against Van Rije (who was senior to

Langham in rank). Langham was the most junior commissioned officer accused. There would be no prosecution of the men who had actually carried out the mistreatment of the Nazis.

The court had heard secret evidence *in-camera* as to British methods of interrogation. Oebsger-Roeder had run away and been recaptured and Mathers, the star witness on whom the prosecution case against Langham rested had refused to give evidence until he was first given a free pardon because Mathers had apparently been one of those men who carried out the mistreatment of the Germans. I cannot think of any other case in the whole of British legal history where so long had been spent with so little effect. I cannot think of any other case outside fictional cases where so many dramatic developments had taken place as the trial progressed.

Curtis-Bennett must have been fuming. He had to now explain to Langham that the Court have given indulgence to the prosecution to get a pardon for Mathers so that Mathers would give evidence. Poor Langham. He must have thought that the Court was determined to convict him at any cost, and at this distance of time, it certainly looks that way to me. Campbell was unable to get to Berlin; fog had descended on the local airfield. He sent his Brigadier, Halse, to Berlin to get the pardon. Campbell then had to temporarily withdraw Mathers from the witness box and he then called Major Short. It seemed that Mathers would not give evidence until he had got his pardon firmly in his hands. That is quite an extraordinary state of affairs for any English court, including a court martial.[32]

Short was a major in the Intelligence Corps, which meant that some of his testimony would have to be heard behind closed doors. He was Senior Intelligence Officer at CSDIC from August 1945 until April 1947, so he was in charge the entire time that Frank was there, and after Frank left. He was under the command of Colonel Stephens. He explained that the Intelligence Bureau would arrest someone and decide if that person should be interrogated. If it were decided to interrogate, the person would be taken to DIC where Short would decide which Intelligence section should carry out the interrogation. A major would be in charge of a section and would, after interrogation of the suspect, prepare a report which Short would then approve, sign and forward to the Intelligence Bureau. If the major conducting interrogation was dissatisfied with the prisoner – perhaps because he thought he was lying, then the interrogating major could ask that the prisoner be punished by up to seventy-two hours' detention, in which case Short had to approve the punishment. Confinement meant that all furniture and bedding was removed from the cell and only at night was the bedding returned.

---

[32] American readers may find this less strange; many US prosecutors use plea bargains which have the same effect as pardons in order to secure convictions. This is quite disgracefully unjust.

When an interrogation was finished the interrogating officer would write a summary of that interrogation which was placed on the case file. Case files would remain under the control of the section major responsible for the interrogation.

Short was shown the case files of Mahnke and Oebsger-Roeder and confirmed that those cases were dealt with by C Section, which was headed by Major Edmunds, assisted by Captains Langham, Van Rije and Teare. Short said that Mahnke and Oebsger-Roeder were suspected of engineering an uprising but in the event, there was no uprising, and the plots may have only existed in the minds of Oebsger-Roeder and Mahnke.

Mahnke and Oebsger-Roeder were, Short said, *"undoubtedly mischief makers. Indeed they succeeded."*

"What do you mean, they succeeded?" asked Campbell.

"By where they are now," Short replied.

Curtis-Bennett made sure that his words were repeated, and it was brought out that Short thought that the mischief that succeeded was producing this hearing. Neither Oebsger-Roeder nor Mahnke wished to help the British authorities. He went on to describe how Mahnke was connected to a subversive organisation called 'Nursery' and even tried to recruit an American agent called Hirschfeld into it. As the court started to hear that Hirschfeld had been recruited by the Americans to spy on his own people it occurred to the President that the court should go into closed session, and so the public were removed, and the court sat *in-camera*. While *in-camera* the court discussed which documents would need to be read by the court *in-camera*. Curtis-Bennett wanted the court to understand that there were grave reasons for suspecting an uprising on Hitler's birthday.

The court martial heard Frank's plan of action for the interrogations and read the case files that Major Short produced.

There was a specific plan to interrogate Oebsger-Roeder, which was identical to the plan to interrogate Mahnke, except that the lives of Oebsger-Roeder's wife and daughter were to be threatened. Gravely, the Judge Advocate read out parts of the case files. The court heard that Mahnke and Oebsger-Roeder were threatened with their lives and the lives of their families. Even Michael, the informer, who was also undergoing interrogation, was threatened; if Michael admitted he lied about the plot for an uprising Michael would be give an attractive punishment – a thorough beating which would wipe out his crime – but if it were later found out that Michael had lied, Michael would be locked up and never let out of prison again. Michael remained 'steadfast'.

Frank's final comment was read out:

"It is the opinion of the interrogator that if Michael had really lied, he would have come clean during that interrogation. It is believed that he has spoken the truth. Conclusion: It is the opinion of the interrogator that Oebsger-Roeder has made his mind up that if he made a confession he would be shot and if he kept silent he might stand a slight chance of being spared. He seemed to be decided to take that slight chance. He does not seem concerned about the fate of his wife and child whereas clings most desperately to his own life. No useful purpose would have been served to continue the interrogation. The man was so completely finished that he would have said almost anything that we wished him to say. On account of the vital question, however, he remained steadfast."

By the time the court adjourned for lunch Major Short had hardly spoken in the witness box, most of his 'evidence' being case files read out by the Judge Advocate.

After lunch Short gave his evidence. From time to time the Judge Advocate seemed to snap at Short. I think he must have taken a dislike to the man who throughout giving evidence would always try and steer responsibility for anything that happened from himself. He did say that Langham had joined CSDIC in early 1946, and that Short would not tolerate any interrogation officer using violence to a prisoner, but mental pressure was allowed. Short would not have approved of an interrogation lasting fourteen hours, but he did not know that was happening because it happened while he was away.

The court went into closed session again so that Short could explain the three methods of getting information. The intelligence service had installed microphones secretly in the cells and the microphones were constantly monitored. The intelligence service used stool pigeons, by which Short meant Germans who had agreed to give evidence to the British by pretending to be of the same persuasion as the prisoner, and thus getting the prisoner to talk. Short conceded that the use of stool pigeons was not a success. The last method of extracting information was by interrogation.

Short explained that Michael was an informant not a stool pigeon in that he came voluntarily with information rather than agreeing to spy on prisoners beforehand, a distinction which took the Judge Advocate some time to understand.

Curtis-Bennett started his cross-examination while the court was still in closed session. He must have thought that Short was not a clever man; that was obvious from the evidence he gave, and Curtis-Bennett must have been aware that if he did not handle Short carefully, he might turn against Langham and go further than the evidence he had given, so he decided to befriend Short in the course of his cross-examination of him.

He carefully led Short into explaining that the intelligence officers were entirely separate from the administration of the prisoners. The only administration duties that had to be done by an intelligence officer was undertake three rounds of the prison a day, and that was to be undertaken by intelligence officers of the rank of Captain. Feeding and looking after the prisoners was entirely the duty of the Administration section.

The court went back into open session and Curtis-Bennett, continuing as a friend of Short, had Short agree that Langham was an exemplary character, intelligent and a thoroughly decent young man. Langham would report all irregularities he knew of and would not discuss intelligence matters with anyone like CSM Mathers, because that was against the rules.

Curtis-Bennett: the method of interrogation ... was largely left to the Intelligence Officers themselves?

Short: To the officer in charge of the section.

Curtis-Bennett: That, in this case would be Edmunds?

Short: Would be Major Edmunds.

Curtis-Bennett: Now, he was a very conscientious worker, was he not?

Short: Extremely.

Curtis-Bennett: Almost fussy to a point?

Short: Yes.

Curtis-Bennett: About being correct in procedure?

Short: He was very keen.

Curtis-Bennett: He was an intelligent officer?

Short: (misunderstanding) Yes and he had been one of them for some time.

Curtis-Bennett: And worked as hard as he could?

Short: Worked extremely hard.

Carefully Curtis-Bennett was building up a picture of Langham and a picture of Edmunds that he hoped would influence the court when they came to their verdict. It is important that every trial lawyer understands human nature and can quickly understand the client that he or she represents and can make a quick and instant understanding of a witness who gives evidence, who the trial lawyer will likely have never seen before. This exchange shows that Curtis-Bennett certainly got the measure of Frank, with whom he had spent hours, and quickly got the measure of Short, whom he had never met until Short stepped into the witness box.

Short was nevertheless still fence sitting, and Curtis-Bennett had to get him off the fence without upsetting him, so treating Short with the utmost courtesy and respect he asked about one Lieutenant Smith who thought Oebsger-Roeder was a charming man and so too was Mahnke, but Edmunds and his section thought them fanatical Nazis. Carefully, he showed Short the report that Edmunds had made, and when Short became equivocal about it he reminded him that he himself had also signed off that report. Short had no alternative but to agree. When in the course of the cross-examination the Judge Advocate asked for clarification of something that Short had said, saying *"You are puzzling the Court by your answers"*. Curtis-Bennett leapt to Short's defence, *"I am sorry, sir, he is not puzzling me"*.

Curtis-Bennett got good evidence out of Short; Dawson. Mathers did not tell Short that had beaten up the prisoners; the proper place to start an investigation as to the beatings was with Prison Control; a prisoner 'breaking' simply means a prisoner breaking down, getting him to confess, with no physical connotations; it is useless to beat up a prisoner from an intelligence point of view; it was quite usual to find a prisoner getting hysterical and writing hysterical notes. When Curtis-Bennett had finished Short was no longer sitting on the fence. The gist of his evidence was that a stern enquiry was necessary and that was what had happened.

Campbell did not wish to re-examine Short (presumably for fear of making the prosecution's case worse) but the Judge Advocate, Stirling, did. He tried to persuade Short that the grounds for suspecting an uprising were flimsy, but Short did not agree. He said that Michael was not Frank's batman, but a prisoner, and he did not know what happened to Michael. Short insisted that he had heard nothing about a beating of Oebsger-Roeder or of Mahnke.

Interestingly, when asked if there were any orders about the use of violence being prohibited in interrogation Short explained that there were none; there were standing orders, but they did not cover the point. The Judge Advocate pressed Short as to why the prisoners were moved around from cell to cell but Short could only say that he did not know about it and could not think of any reason why it should be done.

Frank, getting reports of the trial and reading them in England, could not imagine what Short said in his evidence that could cause the slightest harm or incriminate Captain Langham or himself. He could have imagined that he might deny any knowledge and thereby responsibility in respect of the 'ROME' case, its investigation and progress, the long and severe interrogations and the threats that were used during the interrogations and pass all responsibility for the intelligence investigation to the Commanding Officer, Colonel

Stephens, saying that he was away on leave. Frank also thought it possible that he might plead ignorance about the regulations concerning very long, severe, and threatening interrogations.

Frank warned the defence counsel of these possibilities and suggested that he recall Short for an appropriate cross-examination at a later stage of the proceeding, when Frank could have armed Mr Curtis-Bennett with information, which could have made things rather uncomfortable for Short.

As things turned out, it was not necessary to recall Short; his evidence did absolutely nothing at all for the prosecution and made Short look a rather ridiculous peripheral figure. Recalling him later would have simply given the prosecution a chance to 'firm up' Short's evidence and when conducting a trial if you have achieved most of what you wanted to achieve with a witness, it is usually best to stop, rather than risk undoing the good work.

In the late afternoon Short had finished giving evidence. John Timmerman, of the Control Commission for Germany, Public Safety Branch was called to give evidence. I have been unable to find a photograph of Timmerman, but I picture him as a small sharp man with a hard face. Timmerman was one of Mr Hayward's assistants and he had interviewed Langham at Bad Nenndorf. He had obtained a written statement from Langham as a result of this interview, and that statement was read out to the court by the Judge Advocate.

The statement made by Langham was not in any way incriminating. It merely recited the interrogation of Mahnke and Oebsger-Roeder including the way in which the prisoners had collapsed and were revived.

Curtis-Bennett then moved to cross-examine Timmerman. With this witness Curtis-Bennett had a different approach this time; he was going to be confrontational. He got Timmerman to admit, reluctantly, that he had heard of Mr Stokes' speech in the House of Commons. Mr Timmerman said that he was charged to investigate the allegations of beatings.

Curtis-Bennett supposed the first people Timmerman approached into allegations of beatings were those at Prison Control, but no, Timmerman first approached the prisoner. He did not approach Captain Bennett or Captain Dawson of Prison Control, but Captain Bennett was interviewed by another junior member of the Public Safety team. The team comprised seven or so people. Timmerman could not remember whether any statement was taken from Dawson or Bennett or Sergeant Brant.

CHAPTER 10
Mathers At Last

After returning from Berlin, with the pardon signed by General Sir Brian Robertson in their pockets, Colonel Campbell and the Judge Advocate General were ready to produce their witnesses, Mathers and Thomas, because those witnesses were willing to give evidence because they had their pardons. In fact, Campbell had a handful of pardons, one for every soldier who had assaulted the former SS officers and probably some for other wardens who may have been completely unconnected with the assaults.

Curtis-Bennett took the view that pardons can only be granted by the King. The legal senior member at Control Commission, Colonel S White, declared that the Military Governor's authority rested on a Four Power declaration and that, therefore, the Governor of the British Zone of Germany had full power to grant pardons for Army and Control Commission courts. The Judge Advocate General must have convinced Mathers before he went into the witness box that the promise of a pardon had been kept.

Granting pardons to witnesses to enable them to give evidence free from the fear of prosecution for their own wrong doing is a morally complex thing. In this case the prosecution would have argued that without the pardons, which were granted to the actual perpetrators, there was no possibility of convicting those who had ordered the beatings, and justice was served by granting pardons. The defence would have argued that the fact that you had to grant pardons must make the evidence of the perpetrators very suspect at least. Oebsger-Roeder had already pardoned the beatings; he was willing to let bygones be bygones. Where was the justice?

The Judge Advocate General told Mathers in open court, *"The court has decided that because of the pardon that you have been given and your position as a civilian you are in no danger as regards any of these matters."* Mathers listened intently. The former sergeant major was the only guard that the prisoners had not nicknamed. He was simply the sergeant major. In fact, I do not think that the decision of the court that Mathers was no longer in any danger would bind another court in another country. Mathers was not on trial, he was a witness. There are rules that court decisions should be binding, but only to the extent that they relate to the issues, and the issue here was whether the officers had ordered the beatings.

Mathers, with his strong Northern Irish accent, gave a brief resume of his military career saying that in May 1945 he was sent to Bad Nenndorf. There, he helped to set up the Combined Services Detailed Interrogation Camp. So far as he could remember he took up duties at this camp about four days after the General Election in the United Kingdom[33]. In

February 1946 he was appointed Company Sergeant Major in charge of Warders under the Officer in Charge of Prison Control Captain Bennett.

"Sometime before Hitler's birthday in 1946 I was given certain information and after this I remember a prisoner named Mahnke being admitted to the prison. This was in April 1946. About this time another prisoner named Oebsger-Roeder was admitted but I don't remember exactly when this happened. At the time of Mahnke's arrival he was very insolent. I remember both Mahnke and Oebsger-Roeder being interrogated by Major Edmunds, Captain Langham, and another officer for most of a night.

The following day – I cannot remember the exact day or date – I was called to Major Edmunds' office and he then gave me full details of the history of those two men. Sometime later – the same day I believe – Major Edmunds phoned me and gave me instructions to carry out any form of punishment I thought fit to induce the prisoners to give the required information relating to the uprising. He did not specifically state what that punishment should be. I have a faint recollection that Major Edmunds said on the telephone that the prisoners were very important and that the information they had was most vital to the occupation.

As a result of these instructions I gave orders to Sergeant Thomas to strip both Prisoners and to double them round their cells naked. After tea Sergeant Thomas and myself went into Mahnke's cell, stripped him and made him run round his cell. I cannot remember on what day this occurred or can I say if any other persons were present. This treatment lasted about half an hour. Mahnke did not get his clothes back.

We then went into Oebsger-Roeder's cell and the same thing happened there. Lance Corporal Lewis assisted us in Oebsger-Roeder's cell. Both prisoners were pushed about but not brutally manhandled. The prisoners were not kicked in my presence, neither were they beaten with sticks or straps.

During the punishment both prisoners were repeatedly asked to make a statement and I personally informed them that the punishment would cease as soon as they did so. I left Oebsger-Roeder's cell – as far as I can remember I was there about half an hour – and gave Sergeant Thomas instructions to report our failure to get the required information to the Duty Officer – Captain Langham, I believe – for his further instructions.

The matter was very depressing to me and I went out for the evening to the camp dance. On my return I called at the prison and looked into Oebsger-Roeder's cell and saw

---

[33] The election was held on 5 July 1945.

him fully dressed typing a statement. As a result of something I was told about Mahnke, I ordered Corporal Brant and Sergeant Thomas to bring him into the corridor and to (double) him up and down.

When I saw Mahnke, he was naked. We made him run the length of the corridor several times, naked, and he collapsed. I am certain that his collapse was not due to the treatment he had received but was, in my opinion, a fake. I examined his eyes, and I came to that conclusion. We carried him to the shower, and he was given a towel. When he had dried himself, he said something to me and in consequence I took him to his cell and gave him paper and pencil. He then wrote a statement."

The specific claim that Frank had told Mathers to punish the prisoners was the only evidence against Frank in the case. Curtis-Bennett had to deal with that in cross-examination.

His first question, so important when cross-examining an important witness, was to ask Mathers whether Mahnke was an insolent chap. Mathers agreed, and this annoyed Mathers, "*to a certain extent*". He had no love for Mahnke. He found Oebsger-Roeder insolent too. Mathers agreed that there was no question of either of these prisoners being burned with a cigarette. They were lying about that, Mathers said. He was not covered in blood and no blood was dripping from his head. They were pushed around, made to double and in one case tripped up. When Mahnke and Oebsger-Roeder were dressed, Mathers agreed, there would be nothing noticeably wrong with them. Slowly and surely Curtis-Bennett got Mathers to confirm that Langham would not have seen any damage to either of the Germans, when Langham did his rounds. He put it to Mathers that some of his recollection about the order of events was wrong, and Mathers agreed that it might be. As far as Mathers knew, Langham might well not have seen anything that happened or any of the aftermath.

Curtis-Bennett asked who would know about what was going on in the prison. Mathers said that the prison officers would know and so would the intelligence officers. Mathers knew that the two Germans were supposed to be involved in a plot for an armed uprising on Hitler's birthday; that was, Mathers said, general knowledge in the prison. He said that Major Edmunds had given him this information. Captain Langham, said Mathers, never spoke to him about this at all.

Carefully Curtis-Bennett took Mathers through some details of the evidence and then suddenly asked Mathers if he had ever mistreated prisoners of war before. Mathers said that he had never done that. Mathers admitted that he hated these two Nazis not only because they were Nazis but because they had planned to take British lives on 20 April. Curtis-Bennett

77

suggested that Mathers came back from the camp dance worse for wear and was angry. Mathers insisted that he merely had drunk a few beers. Curtis-Bennett put the statement that Oebsger-Roeder had typed and suggested that Mathers might have thought it to be a complaint against him but Mathers denied that.

Some innocent sounding questions can be highly significant and quite brilliant: Curtis-Bennett asked how Mathers had got to Germany from Ireland. It sounds like a mundane question but Curtis-Bennett must have understood Mathers' deep resentment in being called to Germany. Mathers lived in Port Stewart, County Derry. Mathers said that he travelled by boat to Scotland, then by train to London, then to Harwich by train, and then to Hook of Holland by boat and then another train. It must have been a difficult journey in 1947 and taken several days. Making Mathers describe the journey in detail seemed to bring out resentment in him. Mathers described his journey angrily and said that he made that journey voluntarily but because he believed that if he did not come, he would be brought to court. He thought the document that he received telling him to come to Hanover was enforceable by law, and if he had known that it would not be enforceable *"Hanover is the last place I would have travelled to"*. He had not, Mathers said, been threatened with prosecution if he had not made a statement but just gathered that it would be in his own interests to make a statement and in all probability that meant if he did not make a statement he would not be prosecuted. Those were the truest words that Mathers had said in court. Curtis-Bennett had finished with him.

In re-examination Campbell tried to deflect from the damage that Mathers' statement about being under the impression that if he came to Hanover he would not be prosecuted had caused. He did not succeed.

The Court asked Mathers if he had received instructions from Frank over the telephone. Mathers said that he asked Frank what he should do and Frank told Mathers to *"do anything you like"* provided that he got the necessary information. The court continued probing Mathers about the administration of the prison, the way in which Mathers was acting unofficially, and other matters. One of the members of the court asked about the information that Mathers was to get and Mathers said it was confessions, which were urgent, and related to matters at which lives were at risk, and then drew out from Mathers that Mathers thought he had obtained confessions in the form of the typed statements (Mathers did not read German), which he left on a table despite their urgency, until someone later collected them. Mathers did not think that odd, nor did he think that to double a man around a cell for a few minutes was severe. The court seemed to grasp from Mathers' account of what he had done that getting a confession from the prisoner as a result of beatings was highly unlikely. Mathers said the prisoners were slapped, but not about the head. So much for the prosecution star witness.

Mathers was followed in the witness box by ex-Sergeant Frederick William Thomas, the man who looked like Robert Taylor. Thomas served in the East Surrey Regiment from 20 July 1942 until he was demobilised on 30 Oct 1946. In August 1945 he was posted to CSDIC at Bad Nenndorf. He was then a Private. He said that he was employed on warder duties and gave evidence about the prison systems and feeding prisoners. Mathers was in charge of all of the warders.

Thomas was able to go into many more details about the ways in which the former SS men were abused. He could recall just one instance when severe physical punishment was deliberately meted out to prisoners. This was just before Hitler's birthday in 1946. These prisoners were Mahnke and Oebsger-Roeder.

As a result of certain instructions that Thomas was given (the rule against hearsay prevent Thomas saying who gave the instructions) the warders made each man strip and pushed them around their cell and slapped them with the flat of their hands. Cells 12 and 37 were used. Four or five sentries and NCOs took part. He could not remember the names of any of the sentries, but he could remember Lance Corporal Lewis and Corporal Brant taking part in the punishment. He could not remember whether Sergeant Sore was there or not. He remembered that after Mahnke had been punished in this way for some time, Mathers took Mahnke into the bathroom and put him under a cold shower. Both Mahnke and Oebsger-Roeder collapsed several times under this treatment and had to be revived. The punishment of Oebsger-Roeder carried on until very late at night.

The duty officer normally visited the prison at 6 p.m., 9 p.m., and sometime between 11 p.m. and 12.30 a.m. Thomas could not recall who was the duty officer on the night they punished Oebsger-Roeder, but the treatment was not stopped when he came, and Thomas had no doubt that the duty officer was aware of what was going on. He knew that Mahnke got water on the knee a result of it and a day or two after he went to hospital.

As the day wore on and the questions continued Curtis-Bennett observed that Thomas was getting tired. Thomas's voice got quieter with each question. The court carried on. Thomas said that the prisoners could have been slapped around for as little as five minutes or as long as fifteen minutes. At the end Oebsger-Roeder showed signs of exhaustion and could hardly stand. Thomas left him alone in the cell and subsequently returned to Mahnke's cell without Mathers with a couple of warders acting under Thomas' orders. They went into the cell, probably closed the door and slapped Oebsger-Roeder around a few more times for fifteen minutes. Mahnke did not look as bad as Oebsger-Roeder.

It was now nearly five o'clock. The court adjourned and Thomas was warned not to talk about the case with anyone.

At ten sharp the court started the tenth day of the trial. Thomas faced more questions from the prosecution, Colonel Campbell. Thomas told how he went back to Oebsger-Roeder's cell to look at him and then spoke to him, slapped him around, made him run around the cell, and made him stand up against the wall, his legs apart and his arms stretched up. He slapped him in the kidneys because "*it seemed to be the most convenient place at the time*".

Later Thomas went to see Mahnke in his cell. He made Mahnke run around the cell, slapped him, pushed him, because he was not running fast enough. Mahnke's chin was drooping so he knocked his chin back up. They kept Mahnke standing against the wall like this, spreadeagled, pushing his chin up, and Mahnke looked dishevelled, his hair in a mess, but he was not bleeding and there were no scars or marks on his body. He made Mahnke run around for another five minutes and left him there naked being watched by a warder.

While all this was happening Oebsger-Roeder was standing in another cell also naked, also spreadeagled against the wall. Thomas went to talk to him and then started to slap him around again for a few minutes, pushed him again and made him run around the cell. He seemed exhausted. Thomas left Oebsger-Roeder, attended to other duties, and then went back to see Mahnke on his own. Mahnke was standing to attention, naked. He started slapping Mahnke again, pushed him around and made him run around the cell.

About 9 p.m. the duty officer arrived, and they checked all of the prisoners one by one. They opened the door, Thomas stood in the doorway and the prisoner called out his name, and the door was shut. When they saw Oebsger–Roeder he looked dirty, and his hair was matted. The duty officer did not see any prisoners naked. Thomas did not know that the duty officer was in fact Langham.

Mr Norris standing in for Curtis-Bennett argued that Thomas giving evidence about what a duty officer saw was of little or no value when Thomas did not remember who the duty officer was. The court disagreed, saying that it attached "*considerable value*" to it. Thomas went on to say that when they opened Mahnke's cell Mahnke looked as dishevelled and dirty as Oebsger-Roeder.

Thomas explained that the prison had an internal telephone which did not connect to the main switchboard and there was only one phone in the prison connected to the outside world and that was in Thomas' room. When the duty officer finished his round and left the prison Thomas went back to see Oebsger-Roeder and treated him to more slapping, pushing and doubling for twenty minutes (during which Oebsger-Roeder had fallen down), and then went to see Mahnke where he too received the same treatment. Altogether Oebsger-Roeder had been on the end of the warders' violence on five occasions that evening and Mahnke on six occasions. Thomas then took Oebsger-Roeder a chair and a pencil and paper to write on while Oebsger-Roeder sat on an otherwise empty cell's floor.

Another guard, Thomas Lewis, was cross-examined by Norris on the eleventh day of the court martial. He said that he went in the cell with Oebsger-Roeder without instructions from Thomas, but off his own bat. He mistreated Oebsger-Roeder because he wanted to get information about an uprising from him, and the uprising was fairly common knowledge amongst the warders. The NCOs knew about it, but Lewis could not remember who told him about the likely uprising. After a second escape attempt on 17 April warders "mostly" took clothes of the prisoners except their shirts at 9 o'clock every night and put them outside the cell door until the morning. It was an exceptional thing to see a prisoner completely naked.

He was shown a pardon that had been signed by General McCreery who "*hereby condones any assault against the persons of Horst Mahnke and Rudolf Oebsger-Roeder which the witness may have committed during the month of April 1946.*"

After Norris had finished Campbell had no more questions and the Judge Advocate asked Lewis if he could not remember more "*little details ... which we might expect an honest man to remember*". He suggested that Lewis was making up some answers and Lewis appeared not to understand. He put to Lewis that he knew all about techniques for beating people up. Lewis denied it. After some more fruitless questions the Judge Advocate lost his temper when Lewis failed to understand the questions. "*Mr Lewis, you seem a very stupid witness, if I may say so.*" The more questions that the Judge Advocate threw at Lewis, the less Lewis seemed to understand and the vaguer the answers.

Finally, the President intervened to ask a question. He asked Lewis if Oebsger-Roeder was the only man he had ever beaten up.

A: To that extent, yes.

Q: So, you beat some others to a lesser extent?

A: In confinement, with water, yes.

Q: What is that?

A: Just throwing water at them.

Q: So, this confinement you are telling us about included throwing water at them?

A: To get them to scrub the floor.

Q: Yes but getting a man to scrub the floor does not mean that you throw water over him, does it?

A: That was the only way you can get them to scrub the floor. If they flatly refused to scrub, we would throw water at them.

Q: When they were naked?

A: Yes.

Reading the transcript today I get a strong impression that Mr Lewis was in his own way mocking the court. He was also trying to avoid getting himself into trouble. It is better to be thought stupid than to be prosecuted. In the course of this entertainment Mr Norris must have found it hard to keep a straight face.

Sergeant Brant was the next to give evidence but before he did so the court martial received some documents from a soldier and having read them the court went into *in-camera* so the President could explain to Brant and Sergeant Sore (who was also called into court) that they were not to mention anything about any methods of interrogation except direct interrogation and not to mention listening devices. The President also explained that the unit was to be called "DIC at Bad Nenndorf" of "74" and they must not refer to it as the Combined Services Detailed Interrogation Centre or CSDIC because that was top secret and must not be disclosed. If they had doubt about whether their answer would involve secrets they should say so. Brant and Sore said they understood, and the court re-opened to the public.

Sergeant Brant said that he was a Private when he joined CSDIC. On posting he joined the Warder Company and had been with the Warder Company ever since. He was promoted to Acting Corporal on 30 Apr 1946. He was promoted to Acting Sergeant on 24 July 1946.

He knew Major Edmunds and Mr Langham at CSDIC. They were the interrogation officers. He remembered Mahnke who had been in bed sick and Oebsger-Roeder. He remembered an occasion when he was in his office, when Mathers and Thomas went to cell 12 whilst Oebsger-Roeder was still there. Brant went with them. They all went into the cell and made Oebsger-Roeder take off all his clothing. They then took him outside the cell and made him run up and down the corridor for about twenty minutes. They made him run by shouting at him. Two of them were at one end of the corridor and one was at the other. At the end of this period of twenty minutes they took Oebsger-Roeder back to the cell and made him run round the cell.

Altogether he was running for about half an hour. In the cell Oebsger-Roeder twice slipped down. He leant against the side of the wall and slipped down. He seemed very exhausted. At the end of this period Mathers left. Sergeant Thomas also left but before he did so, he told Brant to carry on. As a result of this he went on pushing Oebsger-Roeder around for five or ten minutes. Oebsger-Roeder slid down to the floor again. When he did this Brant decided to leave him there. He walked out of the cell leaving him naked. All this happened sometime during the afternoon. He looked in the cell on several occasions after he had pushed him about.

On these occasions Oebsger-Roeder was dressed in his clothes and seemed to be alright. The next day, Oebsger-Roeder was shifted to another part of the prison. Brant never saw him ill-treated again.

At no stage did Brant say that any of the interrogation officers involved knew or sanctioned the mistreatment of the prisoners. Norris concentrated his cross-examination on details of what Brant said and established that the telephone that existed in this part of the prison was just a field telephone, unconnected to the exchange and only communicated between the two offices in the cell part of the prison, so you could only speak to the Administration section over that telephone and not to the Intelligence section. It would have been impossible for anyone using the telephone in the prison to speak on it to the intelligence officers.

When the Court asked Brant if he had heard about an uprising fixed for 20 April Brant said that he had not; those things did not interest him, and he gathered that somebody wanted to get statements out of Mahnke and Oebsger-Roeder.

Brant's evidence had not damaged the defence at all.

The court then adjourned until Monday 15 March 1948, and the President told the court that it would sit until Friday and then continue the hearing in London.

Sergeant Sore was then called on Monday, a regular soldier who joined up in 1934. He told of the ill-treatment he saw meted out to Oebsger-Roeder. He too was shown a pardon that had been signed by General McCreery.

Sore proved a confused witness. He did not remember events accurately and sought to lessen his role in them. At one stage during his evidence the Chief Judge Advocate pointed out that his pardon did not extend to perjury. Norris objected saying that it was for the prosecution, not the Judge Advocate, to take that line and started to cross-examine Sore. He did not need to ask him much because Sore's evidence was very confused, and confusion usually is helpful to the defence. The Court then tried to un-muddle Sore's evidence, cajoling him, pointing out that on some things he had a good memory and on other things he had a bad memory.

There was evidence about the guard book which was supposed to log the comings and goings at the prison. All that evidence showed was that the guard book was an unreliable record.

The prosecution then recalled Major Short to ask about the telephones in the prison. Short said that there was a central switchboard, that linked the buildings to the rest of the world and that switchboard was only manned until 6 p.m. or 7 p.m. every day. There was a line from the central switchboard to the room occupied by the sergeant in charge of the cells in the prison. An officer could not communicate with the prison by telephone after the switchboard had closed down. An NCO in charge of the prison could not communicate with anyone by telephone at night.

That closed the case for the prosecution.

CHAPTER 11
Back in Blighty

Frank could not understand why the prosecution picked some of their witnesses, because some of them might almost have been called by the defence. All of those who were on duty at the time the violence was committed agreed and confirmed that Oebsger-Roeder and Mahnke were beaten up and that they took part. However, not one of them could incriminate any interrogation officer. Frank had not been in the United Kingdom for more than a few hours when Mr Fullerton, Frank's solicitor, telephoned to tell Frank about the questions asked by Mr Skeffington-Lodge M.P. in the House of Commons[34].

RELEASED ARMY OFFICER, GERMANY (RECALL)

HC Deb 08 March 1948 vol 448 cc798-800799

75. *Mr. Skeffington-Lodge*

asked the Secretary of State for War on what grounds Frank E. Edmunds, until recently a serving Army officer under military government jurisdiction in Germany, was allowed to travel to that country.

The Under-Secretary of State for War (Mr. Michael Stewart)

Captain Frank E. Edmunds was recalled to military duty from release in order to stand trial in Germany, together with another officer on charges arising from allegations of the ill-treatment of persons held in the Detailed Interrogation Centre, Bad Nenndorf. After his recall and return to Germany, he was allowed to return to this country on compassionate leave, to attend to the business he had set up between the time he was released from military duty and his recall. This leave was due to expire on 28 February, and his trial in Germany had been fixed for 2 March. In view of a recent High Court decision concerning the jurisdiction of courts-martial in relation to officers released from military duty, the case against him was dropped. His solicitors were at once informed, but it was too late to stop him from returning to Germany in the normal way as an officer at the end of his compassionate leave.

Mr. Skeffington-Lodge

Can my hon. Friend say whether this man, who has endeavoured to whitewash himself for the offences he is alleged to have committed in Germany, will be brought to book, and will at any rate be made to develop some sense of responsibility? In my view, he has behaved disgracefully.[35]

---

[34] Thomas Cecil Skeffington-Lodge was elected Labour MP for Bedford in 1945.

Mr. Blackburn

> On a point of order. Is it in order, Mr. Speaker, when a man has not been charged, for an inference to be made against him that he is guilty of a charge?

Mr. Speaker

> The hon. Member for Bedford (Mr. Skeffington-Lodge) is entitled to say so if he thinks the officer was wrong. A Member is not forbidden to criticise actions, and the hon. Member was criticising this officer through the Minister.

Mr. Stewart

> I was about to say that I could not agree with my hon. Friend, and that I could not express any opinion on this matter, since the officer has not been brought to trial.

Mr. Bellenger

> Can no action whatever be taken against officers and other ranks—against whom a prima facie case has been made out—so that they can be tried somewhere or other?

Mr. Stewart

> That is another question; the full implications of the High Court judgment are now being studied.

This question, with its implication of Frank's guilt raised in Parliament, was an act of gross cowardice by Skeffington-Lodge, who had been elected as Labour MP for Bedford by a very slim majority and believed in a Fabian style of patrician socialism. He knew that he could say virtually what he liked about Frank, under the protection of Parliamentary immunity, without facing any legal consequences. Mr Fullerton advised Frank that matters should not be allowed to rest and that the ill-founded statements by Mr Skeffington-Lodge should be followed up. Fullerton sent a letter to Mr Skeffington-Lodge and simultaneously a personal letter to his friend, Sir Patrick Hannon M.P.

Fullerton also proposed in both these letters that David Goy (who had been made a junior partner during his absence in Hanover) should follow up matters with a personal interview with both gentlemen following his return to the United Kingdom. Fullerton's letters had no effect.

Mr Skeffington Lodge would not let this go, because he raised, more obliquely, the matter again in the House of Commons on 24 March.

Mr Wilson Harris

---

[35] Mr Skeffington-Lodge has in his own mind decided the outcome of a trial in progress.

asked the Secretary of State for Foreign Affairs whether he will issue instructions prohibiting British intelligence officers in Germany from threatening prisoners with the death of their wives in order to extract information from them.

Mr Mayhew

No, Sir. I am informed that no instructions authorising such practices have ever been issued by any Government department.

Mr Harris

In view of the statements made in the court last week by a British colonel that it is perfectly proper to threaten German prisoners with the death of their families in order to get information from them, will the Minister say whether that method is approved, and whether it will be adopted in this country also?

Mr Mayhew

The method is certainly not approved; but I would not like to comment upon the statement in question, because the case is sub judice.

Mr Skeffington-Lodge

Is not my hon. Friend aware that the public are rather disturbed by a series of incidents in which British Service personnel have been involved in allegations of behaving badly towards Germans in Germany? In such cases, would he use his influence to bring the personnel concerned back to this country, where they can do no further harm in that direction?

Mr Mayhew

That is another general allegation without supporting evidence, which I am very sorry that my hon. Friend has mentioned.[36]

---

[36] http://hansard.millbanksystems.com/commons/1948/mar/15/prisoners-examination#S5CV0448P0_19480315_HOC_81
It is quite extraordinary that a Member of Parliament made these comments in the middle of a trial that was being heavily publicised at the time, but I suppose the publicity was useful to the MP.

CHAPTER 12

The Defence Opens and Richard Langham Gives Evidence

When the prosecution closed their case, it meant that they had no further witnesses to call. English law and procedure look askance on the prosecution introducing new evidence after their case has closed so the defence team knew what they had to face and what evidence they had to try to rebut. With Curtis-Bennett away on other cases it fell to Langham's junior counsel Mr Norris to make an opening address on behalf of the defence.

Norris argued that there has been virtually no evidence that Oliver Langham caused anyone to be subjected to brutal treatment. He did not argue that there was no case to answer because he conceded there was at most some possible evidence that Langham may have aided the brutal treatment of Mahnke and Oebsger-Roeder.

He pointed out the unfairness of the prosecution, its notoriety. He said that the first word spoken by the prosecution was unfair – that *"on the 15 January 1921 Richard Oliver Langham was born at Munich"*. He described that statement as *"a nice bit of prejudice to start with. The dog that leaves the pack bites hardest; someone who was a German dealing with Nazis at the time that he saw them."*

I deduce from Mr Langham being born in Munich and coming to Britain in 1934 that Langham was a Jew who fled Nazi persecution. He probably spoke English with a slight German accent.

Norris reminded the court that Mahnke and Oebsger-Roeder were said by the prosecution not to be men of good character. They would have been shot on sight three years ago. He pointed out that Mahnke and Oebsger-Roeder were not people who thought it dishonourable to lie. He pointed out the discrepancy in the dates when the treatment was alleged to have occurred; it could only have been on the night of the 17 April, which was when all the NCOs were on duty.

The next day Norris analysed the gaps and errors in the prosecution's case in their witnesses. The Judge Advocate interrupted Norris to point out that his address was in the nature of a closing argument, because an opening address is usually meant to outline the case for the defence and criticism of the prosecution case is usually reserved for closing speeches.

Norris thanked the Judge Advocate for his intervention and proceeded, in a time-honoured way among good advocates, to ignore it. He was, he said, clearing the ground and then would proceed to outline the defence. Norris continued to 'clear the ground' with more pointing out of inconsistencies in the prosecution case. Even when he got round to outlining the defence and explaining what witnesses he would call and what they would say, Norris did not hesitate from taking every opportunity to criticise the prosecution's case.

He concluded by saying that the prosecution's case was only based on the evidence of the two SS men, and a rather flimsy corroboration of a rather bad type of NCO who has a good reason for lying. He took the unusual step of pointing out that although he was not making a "no case to answer" submission, the court could at any time stop the case and acquit Langham. It was a peculiar and novel invitation, one that the Judge Advocate had never previously encountered, but great cases have peculiar and novel features which is what makes them great cases. There had already been plenty of novel and peculiar features in this case and there would be more to come. Norris had harangued and annoyed the court for long enough and his speech ended. He called his first witness for the defence and Richard Oliver Langham entered the witness box. Having listened to evidence against him for the past twelve days it was his turn to state his case and defend himself.

Dick Langham simply and quietly denied, in answer to straightforward questions from Norris, that he had anything to do with force or violence in any interrogations of prisoners including the two SS officers and that the use of violence was contrary to his training and instruction as an intelligence officer. Langham joined the army in 1940, was commissioned in the Royal Armoured Corps in November 1994, served in reconnaissance duties in North West Europe and was asked to join the intelligence corps in 1945 due to his knowledge of the German language. He arrived at Bad Nenndorf on 21 January 1946 and was interviewed by Colonel Stephens and Colonel Short. He was told that the use of force of any sort or physical violence was strictly forbidden.

He saw Michael, who had made the claim about an uprising to coincide with Hitler's birthday. Michael picked out Oebsger-Roeder from an identification parade as one of the conspirators of the planned uprising, and that was separately and independently confirmed by American intelligence sources. Those sources also pointed to Mahnke being involved. Major Edmunds and Langham went to the American Zone, met the FBI case officer, and arranged for them to send Mahnke to the British Zone to be interrogated. While the intelligence officers did not expect an uprising in the sense of barricades being thrown up, they visualised attacks upon troops and military buildings and ambushes and things "something like what is going on in Palestine[37]" to coincide with Hitler's birthday.

---

[37] At the time the British Army was being attacked in Palestine. Less than three weeks before Langham spoke on 1 March 1948 twenty British soldiers were killed and thirty injured when the Bevingrad Officers Club was bombed by Jewish forces and on the same day twenty-eight Britons were killed when a train was bombed. Remember, Langham was Jewish.

Langham said that Major Edmunds decided that the suspects should be given a severe and lengthy interrogation in an attempt to break them and on this point Langham was clear: 'break them' meant getting the story out if them. In the course of the interrogation Langham found the prisoners responses long-winded and thought that Oebsger-Roeder was feigning tiredness, because he suddenly became lively and after a while leant against the wall and slid down it. Langham was not convinced of the genuineness of those collapses. *"In a flash he sort of changed from that to a completely live and excited man in full possession of his mental and physical faculties."*

Langham described in detail the procedure for checking the prisoners.

By 16 April Major Edmunds reached the view that no useful purpose would be served in continuing the interrogations; they had obtained some names of friends of the suspects which should be transmitted to the Intelligence Bureau to take what action they saw fit.

The only punishment that Langham knew of was to put a prisoner in a punishment cell, which was completely empty, and remove his boots. That would be done by Prison Control, not intelligence officers.

He never saw any prisoner naked, or any prisoner harmed in any way. He quite often saw prisoners who were depressed and got rather hysterical statements from them. Langham was taken through some administrative procedures.

Suddenly, the court went into secret session because there were some matters that Langham felt he could not talk about in an open court. When the court was cleared of spectators Langham dropped a bombshell which underlined the political sensitivity of the case.

"I have been told by one of the officers" (he meant witnesses) *"for the defence whom I saw, Captain Van Rije, that a person who had been detained at Bad Nenndorf and had signed a confession to the effect that she was a Russian Agent attempted to get into the court this morning".*

As is usual with these bombshells, the words were repeated by the President who asked if she was a lady with a blue scarf. The suspense was a little relieved when one of the members of the court martial said that the lady with the blue scarf was his wife. A Russian agent had been stopped from entering the court by a policeman; certainly, a female Russian agent had tried to enter court but had failed to do so.

There was a second matter that Langham did not want to mention in open court. He and Captain Van Rije had arranged for a secret microphone to record certain sessions that he and Van Rije had with Mahnke and Oebsger-Roeder. Secret microphones were advanced technology at that time. The microphones picked up the interrogation, and Langham could listen to it, but when Mahnke spoke to Oebsger-Roeder they whispered and the microphones, which Langham though to be the finest in the world far in advance of anything the Germans or Americans had, could not pick up the whispers. One whisper the microphone did pick up was from Oebsger-Roeder to Mahnke: *"They cannot have any proof because there is nothing. You can safely tell them about that silly agent, and you can tell them about your personal history."*

Langham then told of the confrontation he had arranged between Michael the informant and Oebsger-Roeder, before which Oebsger-Roeder appeared worn out and tired but when he saw Michael, he changed into a fit active man shouting at Michael denying the allegations most vehemently.

It was, Langham told, perfectly proper to make threats against prisoners and their families provided that the threats were not carried out. He also explained the way in which special prisoners were separated from ordinary prisoners at the daily meal collection times. The trial then resumed in open court.

Norris asked Langham about Timmerman's questioning of Langham at a time before Langham knew he was a suspect or going to be charged. He said Timmerman told him, *"Of course I want to make it quite clear to you that we have got all the evidence we want. All we want to do now is to pin it on somebody, and I personally do not care who it is."*

Curtis-Bennett had missed a trick. The statement by Timmerman shows a prejudiced investigation, but Timmerman was not asked about that statement when he was cross-examined. No advocate has ever conducted a trial perfectly, but it strikes me at a distance of nearly three quarters of a century that Curtis-Bennett should have put this to Timmerman.

Major Edmunds, said Langham, was a very hard working and extremely conscientious officer and was extremely fussy in obeying regulations. *"He was much too fussy really on security. It was in some cases ridiculous the way he insisted on security. He would not even allow us to discuss cases with 'I' officers of another section sort of off duty, and I am sure he was the fussiest officer on security in that section."*

He spoke about Mathers, and how he was feared by the prisoners. They were certainly scared of Mathers, but Langham had no reason to suspect that Mathers had used physical violence. When he heard Mathers brag about how he was going to beat up a prisoner after his demob party, when Mathers was worse for wear, Langham took Mathers on one side and told him that he would overlook the matter because it was his demob party, but if he found

Mathers still in the prison, demob party or no demob party, Langham would put Mathers under close arrest.

Norris sat down. Langham had said what Norris had expected him to say; he had come up to his proof of evidence, as the lawyers say. Now Colonel Campbell rose to his feet to cross-examine Langham.

Cross-examination elicited that the Mahnke and Oebsger-Roeder interrogations were unusual. Most interrogations were carried out by a single intelligence officer, but these cases had three intelligence officers working on them. The intelligence officers were in constant communication with each other about the interrogations.

Langham was asked about typing; he could not type but Edmunds and Van Rije could and did type. Campbell asked about a document typed by Oebsger-Roeder which had bloodstains on it. Langham made it clear that he had not seen that document and any document with blood splatters would be bound to raise enquiries as it would have to go through a number of hands, and someone would have asked what those dark stains were on the document. It was put to him that he might have seen blood spatters, retyped the document and destroyed the original. Langham replied, *"the only trouble is I cannot type."*[38]

All intelligence officers took turns at being prison duty officer, every two weeks or so. Langham was the duty officer on 17 April, and he signed the duty book three times in all – each time that he inspected the prison.

He explained that when a prisoner was punished, he was taken into a cell which had all the furniture removed; punishment consisted of being in a cell without furniture. Some cells were kept without furniture as it saved carrying the furniture in and out; it was simpler to move the prisoner from one cell to another. Punishment was not just used when a prisoner ceased to be of interrogation interest, but also for disciplinary offences within the prison. Langham did not know of any disciplinary offence which would have confined Mahnke and Oebsger-Roeder into a punishment cell.

When Langham did his rounds as duty officer, he would simply see that the prisoner was in his cell and tick his name off the list. Langham had no idea that any prisoner had been beaten up.

---

[38] Today, typing is second nature to most people because we hammer down on computer keyboards. The typewriters of 1946 were very different from keyboards of today. A certain degree of force was needed, and a far greater degree of accuracy than most people who are amateur typists can reach. At the end of every line you had to return the carriage, and that meant that you had to have the art of knowing where the keys were, because typists looked at the paper while they typed and not at the keyboard. Typing was a real skill then and quite hard to teach yourself.

Campbell specifically asked whether Langham said to Mahnke, *"You aren't dead yet. Do you want to confess?"* Langham denied that he said this to Mahnke. He might have asked Mahnke if he wanted to say anything. Campbell asked why should Langham ask that? Surely Mahnke had ceased to be of interrogation interest. Langham replied that a prisoner never ceased to be of interrogation interest because one is never certain that one has got all the information from the man. Langham thought that they could get no further information from Mahnke, but they were by no means certain that they had got all the information – the man might still be hiding something. He thought there was a possibility that further information might be had, but the intelligence officers had done their job and passed their report to the Intelligence Bureau, who would decide if more questions should be asked.

Langham believed that Mahnke was not in possession of information the army wanted. He called him a "little man", meaning of little consequence. Oebsger-Roeder might possibly have some important information yet to be disclosed, but not Mahnke. Oebsger-Roeder was the stronger character of the two.

When Langham did his rounds, he had not noticed any marks on either prisoner. That was, Langham said, likely to be because the prisoners were in bed covered in blankets and when he looked into their cells they only needed to move for the duty officer to tick them off the list.

Campbell homed in on the fact that Mahnke was seriously ill when he went to the hospital on the morning of 18 April and Langham had not noticed anything wrong with Mahnke during his rounds the night before. Campbell scornfully put Mahnke's written statement to Langham. *"Do you really ask this Court to believe that you attributed the contents of that statement solely to hysteria."* Firmly and quietly Langham replied, *"I most certainly do."* Word by word and phrase by phrase Campbell read the statement to Langham claiming that the words suggested something far more serious had happened to him than the conditions of his confinement and intensive interrogation. Langham refused to change his evidence. The words were consistent with hysteria and despite numerous suggestions by Campbell that the words were evidence, that Mahnke was beaten up and Langham should have known it or did know it, Langham stood fast to his account.

Ruthlessly, Campbell probed Langham; every question suggested that Langham knew about the beatings and had been involved in sanctioning them. He put to Langham that there was a plan to beat these two prisoners. Langham steadfastly maintained his position in the face of rapid questions, every question pouring scorn upon Langham's truthfulness.

The last question of the day is an important one for an advocate. It leaves the court with an impression. Campbell chose his last question to be about the written statement that Mahnke had made, saying that Langham knew perfectly well that Mahnke had been beaten up when he read *"those dreadful remarks about please leave me alone"*. Langham turned the question back to Campbell and made his strongest point.

"I want to say that I most certainly did not [know about the beatings] *and I would like to add that I think the best evidence that neither I, nor Major Edmunds, nor Captain Van Rije knew anything about it is that this statement, this 'frightful' document, had gone into the report, a report which went out to all sorts of agencies including very senior intelligence officers."*

On that strong point for the defence, to Campbell's chagrin, the day's cross-examination ended to be continued on the following day.

Langham would not have been allowed to talk to any of his legal team: when a witness gives evidence, the lawyers are not allowed to talk to the witness until after the conclusion of the evidence. Langham spent a lonely night because he would face further cross-examination and might face re-examination on the morrow.

Whatever Langham might have feared, Campbell asked a few more cursory questions and sat down. Campbell could not think of any new line of questioning to put to Langham.

Mr Norris asked a few questions on re-examination, bringing out the fact that the prisoners may have been in fear of their lives, by the threats made to them during their intensive interrogations. Those threats could easily account for Langham's understanding of their hysteria, without knowing anything about the beatings.

Langham told the court that the kind of hysterical statements that Mahnke made were not remarkable, and as far as Langham was concerned the typed statement was an example of a hysterical statement written wholly as a result of Mahnke being under severe interrogation during which he had a fear of death as a result of the threats made during interrogation.

The Judge Advocate then asked Langham some questions on behalf of the court. Langham was asked about the evidence from the NCOs who had incriminated themselves before there was any question of a pardon being given to them. He said that as far as he was concerned the NCOs made every attempt to hide the beatings from him, and if Prison Control had heard about the beatings there would have been an inquiry there and then. He admitted that the intelligence officers had shrewd and skilful minds who were seeking information of great importance to the state, yet none of these interrogation officers, himself, Major Edmunds or Captain Van Rije had any idea of what was going on.

It was vital, Langham agreed, that a man should not be asked questions except by intelligence officers or interfered with while that man was under interrogation, that warders were never allowed to talk to the prisoners about their cases.

The Judge Advocate seemed very concerned that Mahnke had received a 'real hammering' and that Langham did not notice this just a few hours later. Langham was asked why these prisoners would have been shot on sight three years ago.

"They were definitely SS and SD officers, both of them, and Oebsger-Roeder certainly if a certain one of the Allies had got hold of him, he would have been shot on sight. ... he was responsible for running the whole organisation, political and intelligence, against Russia."

When asked by the Court that Oebsger-Roeder would surely have to be tried first, Langham replied, *"I am afraid that is a question I would not like to answer. I am not referring to the British authorities."*

He was, of course, referring to the Soviet Union's position. The Soviet Union was not party to the Geneva Convention and so both the Russians and the Germans treated prisoners of war from the other side without pity or formality. The Soviets would have shot both prisoners out of hand, if they had captured them.

The court probed some details of the way in which the prison was run, but nothing of any value was said and at 11.20 Richard Langham's evidence had finished.

Frank made the following notes about this phase of the case:

From evidence of some of the Prosecution Witnesses and information obtained by David Goy that threats were used to obtain statements from some members of the Prison Staff, it seems likely that it was in this way that CSM Mathers was induced to make the allegations he has made against me. It is also significant that certain expressions were used by some of the witnesses in their statements which give the flavour of having been put into their mouths by the police.

For example, that of Sergeant Thomas who stated that both Mahnke and Oebsger-Roeder collapsed several times "and had to be revived" which were the identical expressions used by me in my – as you thought unwisely – worded Summary of Interrogation and there is no doubt that these words were then well in the minds of the police investigators, who had specifically noted these expressions on the original summaries on the case file. There can be no doubt that to some extent the allegations of violence and irregularities made by Mahnke and Oebsger-Roeder, following the self-incriminating evidence by CSM Mathers and other NCO's highly exaggerated, must have been enacted by members of the Administration ("A") side of the centre although it is – to my mind – quite impossible and virtually out of the question that they should have been authorised by the Commanding Officer.

It would, therefore, seem evident to me that they were carried out on the initiative of Prison Control or by CSM Mathers without his superior officers' knowledge.

Had a complaint been made at the time of the irregularities by anyone of the persons concerned, i.e. anyone of the Warders involved – or NCO's the CSM – Prison Control Officers – one of five Duty Officers – both prisoners – the German doctor – the British Medical Officer of a German hospital official, the case could have been cleared up and disposed of with the greatest of ease and as a result the person or persons responsible for the actions could have been dealt with summarily – and this could have happened nearly two years ago. Oebsger-Roeder said that he refrained from complaining as he did not wish to provoke further trouble for himself. This does not seem unreasonable but will fall to the ground under cross-examination.

He had had an opportunity to complain to at least ten different officers. Later on Oebsger-Roeder was made a privilege prisoner, so I understand (this was after I had left the unit). He had then plenty of opportunity to complain to an officer about the treatment he alleges to have received on 17 /18 April 1946. Mahnke said, "There were no officers to whom he could have complained". This is untrue. He could have complained to the following between the date of the alleged incidents, i.e. the 17 April 1946 and the 23 April 1946, the day of his arrival at the Nazi Hospital at Rothenberg:-

(a) The Prison Control Officer (Capt. Dawson), who inspected the prison daily (Bennett – although the prosecution do not seem to be aware of this – on leave at the time).

(b) The Duty Officer on the 18 April, who inspected the prison on that day at 1800 hrs, 2100 hrs and midnight.

(c) The Duty Officer on the 19 April as in para (b) above.

(d) The Duty Officer on the 20 April as in para (b) above.

(e) The Duty Officer on the 21 April as in para (b) above.

(f) The Duty Officer on the 22 April as in para (b) above.

(g) The German Doctor who saw him, I believe on the 18 April at 1440 hrs.

(h) The British Medical Officer who saw him on 19 April in the morning.

(g) Mahnke could have complained to the Camp Commandant in writing. I understand that there was a notice hanging up in all prison cells, telling prisoners how to complain.

(i) He could have complained to one of his Nazi friends at the Rothenberg Hospital.

(j) He could have complained to the protecting power, the Swiss Red Cross.

If the investigators had acted impartially and fairly, instead of attempting to build up a case for the prosecution and finding scapegoats (they acted for the Commander in Chief and his intentions have become known quite officially through his mouthpiece Brigadier Maynell) the evidence compiled by the defence would have been obtained by the so called investigators, which would have made it clear to them that there was no case for the prosecution.

The investigators appear not to have been willing to carry out further investigations after they had seen one or two NCO's, whose word they had accepted without so much as checking it (which would have been a very simple matter, since their Superior Officer was available).

When I was interviewed by Mr. Hayward, the information which I gave him appeared to be of no consequence at all, since joint charges against Captains Van Rije, Langham and myself had already been formulated!

From the point of view of the "I" side and interrogations, it is clear that no irregularities were committed. Allegations in this respect can all be disproved. A few examples: Oebsger-Roeder alleges that there were two table lamps in the interrogation room and no light in the ceiling. This is untrue for the simple reason that – as you know – it was not possible to interfere with the ceiling light and it was equally as impossible to have one or more table lights, because there were no plugs in the rooms. Corporal Kennels, Royal Signals could be called to confirm this.

Oebsger-Roeder said that during the long interrogation people came floating in and out. This is quite untrue. Interrogations were carried out in relay, as is shown in the Summaries of Interrogation. Both Oebsger-Roeder and Mahnke allege that they 'collapsed and were revived'.

Warder witness Scholes should be called who can state that he was called into the interrogation room to give the prisoners drink of water and that subsequently they, (the prisoners) were perfectly alright. The prisoners were not standing all the time during the hours' long interrogations.

Alleged instructions by me or any of my interrogation officers to any person of the Administration side to punish a prisoner or beat him up were quite unfeasible. Whilst to an "outsider" such instructions would not seem at all impossible, looking at it from the point of view of security and conditions at CSDIC, such an accusation of any intelligence officer would appear simply monstrous and outrageous. In giving such an unlawful order to an NCO, the officer giving the order would seriously expose himself, as the NCO would certainly never act on such an order but immediately report it to his superior officer – Bennett or Dawson, who would undoubtedly have referred it to SIO or CO.

A further point arising from the allegations is that matters of a top-secret nature would never have been mentioned at all by anyone on the telephone which was an open line (no internal phones were available), leave alone to an NCO who was not even on the Interrogation side of CSDIC.

My instructions to my staff in this connection were readily available on the Internal Memoranda file of my Section.

Telephone operators were not usually working on Sundays and Public Holidays and some of the alleged telephone instructions did coincide with one of the Easter days. Oebsger-Roeder was trying to pass all the blame onto Captain Langham. Either Oebsger-Roeder saw the German newspapers or heard it from Mahnke or some other person that charges against Captain Van Rije and myself had been dropped and Oebsger-Roeder as an ex-Nazi Intelligence Officer was quick enough and clever enough to change his statements.

As I have done from the outset, during my discussions with Mr. Hayward, in my written statement and subsequently, I will take full responsibility for the "I" investigation and will continue to take full responsibility for the "I" investigation and the methods interrogation adopted. If the Court might think – whilst being cross-examined – that I am doing so because charges against me have been dropped, Mr. Hayward, could be called to give evidence which confirms my statements have been consistent.

The interrogations were not unlawful, despite the Nazi's allegations. Ultimately even the Prosecution Witness Lieutenant Colonel Short had to confirm it. The prisoners were not touched. Food was not withheld and would not have been withheld, even if interrogation officers had overlooked the times for the feeding arrangements. The Plan of Action, which Col Campbell called a "savage treatment", had nothing to do with "treatment". It was a proposed plan – by necessity for very intensive and severe interrogations, as duly published in the Final Report, which was supplied to higher Authority and the War Office.

There is an important point about Duty Officers in Lt Colonel Short's evidence. Lt Colonel Short said that Duty Officers were only allowed inside the prison at the times of 1800 hours, 2100 hours and midnight whilst making their rounds. They were not allowed inside the prison at any other times.

In view of Oebsger-Roeder's statement that Captain Langham visited him frequently between these hours, Colonel Short's evidence assisted my case.

At my request strong representations were made by Defence Counsel about Intelligence Officers' real names having been divulged in Germany and in open Court and published in the Press without the slightest consideration about the Officers' safety and security. Throughout my career as an interrogation officer, it was the most elementary rule that real names of interrogation officers must never be publicly divulged, and this rule was observed by even the latest recruits on the warder staff. The purpose of the rule is obvious; interrogation officers could be at risk from reprisals from those they interrogated. It seems obvious that the Police Investigators and Hayward and Company are responsible for this grave breach of security.

Of course, when you are intimately involved in a case you think of every possible argument that you think supports your side of the case. I am giving you Frank's thoughts which will inevitably colour your view of the case to some extent. I am unable to offer the views of the prosecution.

Frank made some important points and Frank's note is important for these but perhaps it is more important in that it shows the kind of man Frank was, the principles and ethos by which he lived and the meticulous, fussy nature of his character. He sent his notes to his defence team.

I think that it is clear from what we have learned so far that the two Germans were beaten up by British soldiers, although the beatings were probably moderate. There is some evidence from Mathers that Frank either ordered the beatings or knowingly condoned them. There is plenty of evidence that Frank and his team had messed around with the minds of the prisoners and that caused the prisoners much distress and no doubt affected their mental wellbeing, but the team had not been charged with causing mental distress; as far as the law was concerned causing mental distress of the nature caused was not going to be considered as disgraceful conduct of a cruel kind in 1948. Three quarters of a century later in most

European countries it would have been considered to be such conduct, but probably not in the USA or many of the countries in the world where physical and mental torture is considered perfectly acceptable.

CHAPTER 13
Defence Witnesses

Norris then called Major Boothroyd, an officer in charge of Production and Registry at Bad Nenndorf, who collated, edited and revised all reports that CSDIC issued. All CSDIC Bad Nenndorf reports went through his hands. He explained that there was a marked separation between the Intelligence section and the Administration. At Bad Nenndorf the commandant, Colonel Stephens, was additionally the camp commandant and also chief intelligence officer. The Senior Intelligence Officer could give orders to the Officer in Charge of the prison, but only on intelligence matters. The interrogation officers would not go into the prison, but had to interrogate prisoners in interrogation rooms, and should not have entered the prison unless they were a duty officer or if there was an emergency. The prisoner would be taken to an interrogation room by a warder. It was forbidden by standing orders for an interrogation officer to give orders to a warder. He explained that punishments were to be approved by the Commanding Officer, and that men were never, to his knowledge, stripped naked as part of punishment, although their boots were removed. Intelligence officers had nothing to do with punishments.

He said that Langham quickly became a first-class interrogator. He had served with Frank Edmunds in England and was very popular in his section. Frank was so hard working that he undermined his health and when he was demobilised in July 1946 he had to go to hospital before returning to England. He had been trained in England in what was regarded as the best unit of its kind.

Boothroyd was asked about the allegation from Mathers that Frank Edmunds told him to use force, if necessary, to get statements from the prisoners. He regarded it as extremely unlikely on two grounds. Edmunds was very much averse to discussing top secret matters with people who were not entitled to hear them, and Boothroyd doubted whether he would have discussed these matters with anyone from the administration side. He doubted that he would have discussed such matters over the telephone as there were constant reminders in the unit about the danger of speaking over telephones, even internal telephones.

Boothroyd remembered reading that *"the prisoners had now reached the stage where they will make false statements implicated themselves in the hope that they will escape further interrogation."* He also remembered Mahnke's written statement, *"I must make these statements despite the fact that they are not the truth because I am desperate and do not know what to do. Please shoot me."* He took it to mean that Mahnke had been subjected to a very lengthy interrogation. He knew nothing of any violence until the Court of Inquiry made its findings. The statement by Mahnke did not arouse any suspicions in Boothroyd.

The court then sat *in-camera* – in secret session with the public having withdrawn, because Norris wanted Boothroyd to give evidence about the work of Frank Edmunds' interrogation section. Boothroyd said that this section was regarded as the 'star' section in anti-Russian counterintelligence work. It was investigating matters so secret that few knew of the work they did. The section had the highest security. The section was given the case of ROME because it was so highly regarded; normally the case would have been given to M section which specialised in subversive cases.

He explained that threats of shooting the prisoner were quite normal, especially in the field, but when the prisoners reached CSDIC, they knew that they were relatively safe. The interrogators were entitled to use threats, provided that the threats were not carried out. In a grave emergency Boothroyd would have no hesitation in using threats. There was no time limit for interrogating prisoners. Boothroyd agreed that a fourteen-hour interrogation would be exceptional. There was no system for grading prisoners who were suspected of being likely to commit suicide, no arrangement to take special precautions in respect of a hysterical prisoner and no prisoner was ever sent to CSDIC that Boothroyd was aware of who had been identified as a potential suicide risk. If any case an occurrence of a nature which indicated that a prisoner might try to commit suicide, then special measures would be taken but Boothroyd knew of none. It seemed clear that the British authorities were unconcerned about potential suicides among the prisoners, possibly because none of their prisoners had ever committed suicide.

Personally, Boothroyd would not have approved of the threat, outlined in Frank's plan of action, to tell the prisoners that failing a complete confession *"he will have to suffer the extreme penalty"*, but that was a matter for the interrogation officers. Boothroyd, who had only interrogated prisoners on the field and not in DIC, thought that prisoners would not believe that these threats would be implemented. *"I think most of the Germans' idea of the English is that we do not do that sort of thing"*.

The secret session ended and at 12.50 the court resumed its open hearing with Colonel Campbell rising to cross-examine Boothroyd. He did not ask many questions, getting into a muddle when asking Boothroyd to explain the procedures for drafting reports, editing them, and then finalising them. When the court asked questions, it was interested to see whether an intelligence officer would report if prison discipline became lax. Firmly, Boothroyd said that was not the job of an intelligence officer, except when he was acting as a duty officer, going round to check the prison.

Captain KI Van Rije of the Dutch Army would have been on trial along with Langham had the Dutch Government not objected to one of their officers being court martialled by a British Military Court. Now instead of being tried he was called to give evidence for the defence. He gave evidence in the English language in which he was fluent, and Mr Norris drew out his evidence. Van Rije went to Bad Nenndorf in October 1945 as an intelligence officer and worked under Edmunds in C Section. He was there when Langham arrived. He said that he was part of the intelligence side, quite separate from the administration side at Bad Nenndorf. He only dealt with the administration side when he was carrying out the role of duty officer. Physical violence against any prisoner was never allowed in any circumstances.

When he arrived the Commanding Officer, Colonel Stephens, saw him (and all other new soldiers) and made the rule against the use of violence clear. There were also standing orders to that effect. The use of threats was allowed, but if they were threats of violence carrying out the violence was not allowed. Punishment for recalcitrant prisoners was confinement; the prisoner would not be allowed to work or converse with other prisoners, although he would be allowed out of his confinement cell to use the lavatory. A man in confinement was not deprived of all his clothes. Punishment was the province of Prison Control, who were the administration, and intelligence officers had no power to order punishment. The usual punishment was confinement for three days. Occasionally that was extended to a week but only with the approval of the Senior Intelligence Officer, Colonel Short. Interrogation would continue while a prisoner was in confinement.

Campbell did not get very far with Van Rije in cross-examination. Van Rije answered the questions carefully and supported Langham's case, as you would expect. He was asked about 'punishment cells' and said that any cell could be converted into a punishment cell, merely by taking out the furniture. He was asked if his note which said that Mahnke and Oebsger Roeder were placed in punishment cells meant that he ordered them to be punished. No, said Van Rije, it must have been authorised by Colonel Stephens. He could not throw any light on the fact that according to the official documents and the guard records Mahnke was said to occupy one cell, but in fact he occupied a different punishment cell. He had no explanation for that. He did not think that these prisoners were put into punishment cells on the orders of Major Edmunds.

Van Rije did not think that he saw Mahnke on the morning of 18 April. He was distracted from work because he was going off to be married, but because he was interested in the case, he stopped off at the prison to help Langham translate the statement. He seemed reluctant to commit himself on this, suspecting that the cross-examination was trying to trap him, despite assurances to the contrary from Campbell and the Judge Advocate. He was asked about discipline in the prison and said that he found it lax; there was bad turn out on the part of the warders, much was left to the NCOs and there seemed to be little supervision on the part of Prison Control.

He knew, he said, that Mathers became aggressive when "in his cups" and that the prisoners seemed more afraid of Mathers than they were of the officers:

Q: And yet when you heard in the mess it mentioned in passing that he (Mathers) had beaten up a prisoner, you were not surprised?
A: No, I did not say that I heard he was beaten up. Mathers was mentioned in connection with it.
Q: I am sorry. I made a mistake. You said you were surprised?
A: Yes.
Q: Well, do you not agree that those two things are apparently contradictory?
A: There is a difference between being aggressive and actual manhandling.

The Court then cleared the public and asked Van Rije to explain about putting Mahnke and Oebsger-Roeder in the same cell, with a secret microphone placed to pick up what they said to each other. Many questions were asked about moving the prisoners from one cell to another, and who had to give authority for such moves. Van Rije's answers showed that Prison Control did not keep accurate records and discipline was not strong. The court then opened its doors to the public and Norris asked a few more questions which established that Van Rije did not know about or control which prisoner went into which cell.

Corporal French was then called as another witness for the defence. He was then a fusilier in the warder company responsible for the prisoners at Bad Nenndorf. His duty was to attend to any reasonable requests or complaints of the prisoners and escort them to the lavatory and back. He supported what the court had been told about the duty officer's evening rounds. He had never seen a prisoner naked when he got his evening meal. He had never heard intelligence officers discussing top secret matters at Bad Nenndorf. Intelligence officers would never discuss these matters with NCOs –"*they did not do that kind of thing because they would have been in the cart right away.*"

He served with Frank Edmunds in England and had never known him or other intelligence officers to divulge any intelligence matters.

French's memory was such that he remembered some things but not other things. Colonel Campbell told French that he found that "a bit odd". At the time of the beatings French could not see anything, but he heard shouting, and recognised Sergeant Thomas' voice. He thought that somebody had done something wrong and that had upset Thomas. French's memory continued to be sporadic, perhaps some might say that he remembered what was convenient for him to remember. French was sure about one thing: during his time at Bad Nenndorf he never saw any sign of any prisoners getting beaten up. He never heard rumours that a sergeant had carried out the beating. He first heard about the beatings a long time ago, when he was at the prison but still did not know and never heard that Oebsger-Roeder, and later Mahnke, was beaten up on 17 April in the afternoon:

Q: You still do not know that?

A: No

Q: Not been told by a soul?

A: No

Q: And what I am telling you now is absolute news to you?

A: Yes.

President: I understood him to say that he heard about it some time afterwards.

Campbell: I thought so.

French: Yes, some time afterwards.

President: What did you hear?

A: Just a man had been put in confinement. I never heard of any beating up or anything like that. I never did see any beating up.

Q: Do you mean to say some time afterwards you would hear that a man had been put in confinement?

A: As soon as he is put in cell 12 it is confinement automatically. That is the confinement cell.

Q: You knew that there was a man in confinement in cell 12 on this day?

A: Yes.

Q: Well, why should you hear alter that there was a man in confinement? Why should someone tell you what you knew?

A: I do not know. Perhaps it just slipped his memory.

Q: Slipped whose memory?

A: I do not know; whoever was speaking at the time.

Judge Advocate: Mr Prosecutor is this worthwhile?

Colonel Campbell: No. I feel weak.

It is much harder to cross-examine a stupid person than a person who is clever but not intent on telling the truth.

Sergeant Jones was next called, and he gave evidence about Mathers. *"To me, CSM Mathers was of the bullying pig-headed type. He liked to show off and let everyone know he was the big 'I am' he was a true Irishman and had got a true Irish temper."*

When Norris suggested that this was perhaps a little unkind to the Irish the Judge Advocate hastily directed that the Irish members of the court were to take no notice. Jones went on to say that Captain Bennett was rather lax on discipline and that he called Mathers "Paddy". He said that there were strict orders that no violence of any kind was to be used against detainees.

Norris had no other witness to call in Germany and the prosecution took the opportunity to recall Mahnke who had to give evidence without an interpreter, but Mahnke spoke enough English to be able to do this.

Mahnke agreed that he wore false teeth in April 1946, and these were not damaged by the assault.

Norris put to Mahnke that when he came to court, he used a stick and walked with a limp but when he walked out of court, he put the stick under his arm and walked normally. Mahnke had difficulty understanding this question, or more likely difficulty in answering it. After some abortive attempts Norris suggested that Langham be used as an interpreter. This in itself is unusual, possible unique that the accused interpreted part of the cross-examination of the victim, but this case is full of unusual and unique features and by now all those following it must have come to expect the unexpected.

Mahnke made some excuses about walking short distances without a stick but needing it for long distances. When it was put to him that walking from the corridor outside into court was a short distance but Mahnke had used his stick, he said that he found using the stick more comfortable.

Thursday 18 March 1948 was the last day of the hearing in Germany. The Court adjourned to England; there was no more evidence to find in Germany.

CHAPTER 14

The Court Martial Moves to London

The proceedings, after fifteen days at Hanover, continued at first *in-camera* in London at the Duke of York's barracks in Chelsea on 22 March 1948. The barracks had been used to try German spies in the Second World War. The court martial of Theodore Schurch was held there in March 1945. Schurch was found guilty of treachery and was hanged. He was the last person in Britain to get capital punishment for an offence other than murder.

The first witness to be called was ex-Lance Corporal Hunt, whom Frank knew as a conscientious and reliable warder. He was a warder at CSDIC in March 1944 as a Private until about September 1945. He remained at Bad Nenndorf until he was demobilised in October 1946. He was promoted to Lance Corporal in February 1946. Like all witnesses, Hunt was warned about disclosing secrets in his evidence without first telling the court that an answer might involve revealing confidential information.

Hunt said that he was struck by the difference in atmosphere between the UK and CSDIC. At CSDIC the handling of prisoners was distinctly tougher, if not rough. He disliked the fellows from the Commanding Officer's crowd because of their attitude towards prisoners.

He remembered CSM Mathers, who, in his opinion was a smart NCO, but disliked his attitude towards prisoners, at whom he shouted, doubled up and down the corridor and generally treated them in a rough manner. Hunt would call him a hot-headed Irishman. Mathers was on very friendly terms with Sergeant Thomas who was, like Mathers, a boisterous and rough type.

Captain Bennett was an officer who Hunt thought was too friendly with the NCOs and men, whom he treated like old pals rather than the way an officer should treat his subordinates. Captain Bennett was on particularly friendly terms with Mathers – whom he called Paddy – and also Sergeant Thomas. The friendliness was mutual. He thought Corporal Sore was potty and a most unsuitable NCO. He did not deserve even one stripe and Hunt was amazed to hear that this man was now a Sergeant. Sore was always hanging about the prison or in the CSM's office to gain favour with his seniors, but when it suited him, he would try and swap duties with a colleague.

Hunt confirmed that the 'I' side (Intelligence) was kept distinct and apart from the 'A' side (Administration). Apart from the Commanding Officer, the medical officer and his orderly – Prison Control officer and CSM Mathers as in-charge warders – and the duty officers, who visited the prison at 1800 hrs, 2100 hrs and midnight, nobody was allowed inside the prison. Duty officers were 'I' officers below the rank of Major. Hunt never saw Major Edmunds inside the prison.

He remembered Major Edmunds as an 'I' officer. He had nothing to do with the administration of the prison. From his knowledge of Major Edmunds, he considered it quite impossible that he would have told an NCO or even an officer of the 'A' side matters relating to intelligence and as far as the alleged order to beat a prisoner up was concerned, he thought Major Edmunds as likely to have given that order as King Kong. It was forbidden to ill-treat a prisoner. Any specific treatment of a prisoner – punishment cell, privilege block, movement of a prisoner from one cell to another, had to be authorised from upstairs (Prison Control). When on one occasion he was told to take part in the pushing around of a prisoner named Mahnke, he took it for granted that the order had been given by the officer in charge of Prison Control.

The incident was not reported in the guard book. Hunt was surprised at this because everything out of the ordinary routine, it did not matter how inconsequential, had to be written down in the guard report. It surprised him to hear that Sergeant Medcraft, who took over from Sergeant Thomas (the sergeant who was on duty on the day the incident took place), was not told anything about it. It was customary for the NCO going off duty to tell the relieving NCO everything that had happened during his turn of duty of an unusual nature. This is quite apart from the written report. He assumed, therefore, that Sergeant Thomas must have known that what he did was not authorised and he feared that it might be reported if he mentioned it to another senior NCO.

Hunt's evidence was thus:

"One day in April 1946 – according to photostats of guard reports shown to me, this must have been on the 17 April, when I was on duty, I remember the following incidents taking place.

> *(a) Sergeant Thomas was the NCO in charge. I was his second in command. Corporal Brant was on duty in Block 1 - 2. Lance Corporal Lewis was his second in command. I do not think that any of these NCO's was relieved by another NCO during the 24 hours duty, although this could have been possible. I have a faint recollection that Corporal Sore was in the Prison that evening, and he might have taken over from Corporal Brant, from after tea.*
> *(b) I remember the two prisoners Oebsger-Roeder and Mahnke.*
> *(c) I was told – I believe by Lance Corporal Lewis – that they were members of an underground movement which would rise against the British Occupation*

troops on Hitler's birthday on 20 April 1946. I think this information must have been obtained by CSM Mathers from the Prison Control office or through one of the Picket Guards on the main door who might have heard it during an interrogation of one of the prisoners. This information appeared to have been common knowledge amongst the staff. I should say 75% of the NCO's and men on duty knew about it. I have no idea where the information came from, but I thought at the time that it must have come from upstairs (P.C.), as otherwise the pushing round of the prisoners would never have been carried out.

(d) I had never touched a prisoner until that day and only in view of what I had heard did I gladly assist in pushing Mahnke around.

(e) I did not see Oebsger-Roeder being punished, although I believe I was told that he was pushed around similarly to Mahnke.

(f) I remember Mahnke in cell 37 on that day. The cell was completely bare of furniture.

(g) Sometime after the prisoners had had their tea, 1800 hours I I remember this distinctly because it was after dark and after the Duty Officer had made his rounds, I was told by Sergeant Thomas to assist in pushing Mahnke round his cell. I believe I received a telephone message for Sergeant Thomas and this is why I went down to the cell. Mahnke was in his cell, naked, and we – as far as I remember CSM Mathers, Sergeant Thomas and myself – pushed him around. I am sure that neither Corporal Brant nor Sore were there. Mahnke was not badly ill-treated. He was made to walk and run round his cell and I remember that Sergeant Thomas hit him once or twice with his open hand and I dare say we all hit him in the process of pushing him around. I believe that someone – I believe it was Sergeant Thomas – said that we should go easy with Mahnke – but possibly the reference was to the other prisoner in cell 12 – as he was suffering from a weak heart.

(h) I do not remember how long this treatment lasted. I left Mahnke's cell well before 2100 hrs for my office and I was joined there by Sergeant Thomas.

(i) I am absolutely certain that the treatment stopped during the Duty Officer's round at 2100 hrs. I do not know whether Mahnke was given back his clothes, but I think this must have been so as otherwise the Duty Officer would have noticed something unusual and would have reported it. I do not remember that

> the matter was mentioned in any way either before or after the above incident by any of the Prison Staff. Mahnke was move to Cell 12 after the Duty Officer had done his round at 9 p.m., probably on CSM Mather's instructions to Thomas. He (Mathers) probably told Thomas to move the prisoner whilst he (Mathers) was at the camp dance.
>
> (k) I went to sleep soon after the Duty Officer had left the prison. It appears from the Guard Book that I rested until about 0315 hours.
>
> (l) I heard in the morning that CSM Mathers had come in again during the night and that Mahnke was then again put through the same thing. I know nothing about this, however. I did not know that Mahnke suffered injuries as a result of the treatment. Whilst I was there and took part in pushing him around he seemed alright except that he was very exhausted."

Hunt had given his evidence under caution, issued by the Court, to the effect that he need not answer questions which Hunt thought may incriminate him. Hunt's evidence was impressive, and he delivered it in a straightforward manner. He was closely questioned on his evidence that he thought that there had been an order to do the beatings; he said that was his assumption, because it came from Company Sergeant Major Mathers.

When Hunt's evidence had finished, Norris raised the question of Oliver Langham's security. Langham felt that he was a marked man as a result of the trial and was concerned that photographs were being taken of him. He had operated in the field of Russian counterespionage, and at Bad Nenndorf operated using aliases. He was fearful that photos might be taken and that he might well become a target. The Court did two things: it banned the taking of photographs in all parts of the barracks and arranged for Langham's temporary accommodation within the barracks for the length of the trial; Langham was most grateful for this.

Intelligence officers serve the public and in doing so take risks with their personal safety. In this case Langham did not want to be scooped up by the Russians or have a German whom he had previously interrogated exact revenge upon him.

The defence next called Mr Medcraft, who was a warder sergeant at Bad Nenndorf. Medcraft reiterated that the use of violence was forbidden and that he knew about a slight rumour about an uprising but only knew after Hitler's birthday. He told of his round the day after the beatings when the prisoners seemed normal to him. Campbell, cross-examining, sought to pick holes in Medcraft's evidence and succeeded in showing that in some matters of detail Medcraft's recollection was wrong or his evidence was unreliable. Medcraft changed his testimony but not in any way that cast doubt on the defence's case; for Medcraft the prisoners showed no signs of having the most appalling beating the night before. He did not know if beatings had taken place. Campbell suggested that Medcraft was misleading the court, and must have known, if only from the later press, about the beatings.

Norris called Mr Teare next. He was now a civil servant but had been a trained intelligence officer with MI19. He had heard of the long interrogations of the two Germans from Frank and Langham. He worked at Bad Nenndorf next door to Frank and there was a communicated door between the offices. He never saw Mathers visit Frank or communicate with Frank. This would have been a remarkable occurrence. He never heard or saw Frank discussing intelligence matters with an administrative warrant officer or an NCO. The whole Intelligence section was very strict about communicating top-secret matters. They would never do so over the telephone. When Norris asked him about the use of physical violence Teare said, *"that was absolutely taboo. The C O had the strictest views on the subject and he actual believed that no officer could possibly morally or in any other way, justify physical violence on interrogations."*

Norris then took Teare through the procedure for dealing with statements that prisoners made. He then got Teare to explain how the punishment for a prisoner not co-operating with the interrogation had to be approved by the Senior Intelligence Officer and was confined to keeping the prisoner in solitary confinement for twenty-four hours, but the SIO's approval had to be first obtained. Teare explained about statements that prisoners made, and how they used to get many internees with bad consciences and how they used to write long moral justifications about what they did, and that they ought to be released and that they were innocent.

Norris got Teare to read Mahnke's statement in which Mahnke wrote that he could not stand it any longer. Teare drily commented that the sentiments Mahnke expressed had been expressed by other prisoners on other occasions and those prisoners had been interrogated for far shorter periods than Mahnke experienced. Teare said that having got such a note he would have concluded that he had reached the limits of useful interrogation with that man. *"An answer to please is absolutely useless"*. The statement made by Mahnke did not lead Teare to suspect that any violence had been used. In fact, Teare ran across many similar statements made by "paratrooper types" who had been subjected to prolonged and intensified cross-examination.

The court then went into *in-camera* to enable Mr Teare to give secret evidence. Although the *Guardian* newspaper at the time published an article that most of the Langham trial was held *in-camera* this is untrue. As you will have seen from this account the court martial held very little of its proceedings in a closed court and then only when top-secret matters had to be given in evidence. Most of the proceedings *in-camera* revealed evidence that was helpful to the defence and showed the difficulty and sensitivity of the work carried out by intelligence officers.

In this case the evidence that Teare gave *in-camera* was about the reasons to shift a prisoner from one cell to another and the officer in charge of the prison would need to know from the intelligence officers not to put two men together because of the nature of their associations, and other intelligence reasons. After no more than five minutes *in-camera*, the court martial resumed in open session.

Teare had given his evidence well, in a lucid easy manner. The fact that he described himself as a civil servant made me wonder about his precise occupation; perhaps he was still working in intelligence. In cross-examination the prosecution elected the helpful evidence from Mr Teare that Frank was very conscientious about not talking to unauthorised people about intelligence matters and it was out of the question in his mind that Frank would talk about these matters to the warder staff.

Teare was pressed on whether he had read Mahnke's written statement. He could not remember; they dealt with sixty cases at a time and would get between ten and twelve such statements. By "I can stand this no longer" Teare said he thought that Mahnke meant that the interrogator had got under Mahnke's skin, psychologically with the interrogation. Teare was cross-examined on almost every word in that statement. Barristers do this and it is surprising how many different interpretations can be read into a simple form of words and how many inferences, true and false, can be drawn from a few lines. Teare remained steadfast in his evidence – the statement made by Mahnke simple showed that further interrogation was useless, no more and no less.

Teare explained the art of the interrogator in this case like this:

"The man will have in his mind a very very high state of tension and anxiety, the result of a fairly successful interrogation. He will be in a highly nervous state, mentally. At this stage we were satisfied, I think we were satisfied, that there was nothing in this plot and the man himself felt in all conscience that he was, he knowing the inside facts that he was not involved, that he was not a suspect, still had no assurance that we would not start again on him in the same long interrogation if we were not satisfied, and I imagine the case officer would not have said to him 'all right, now you are finished'. That is cooking their own goose. They leave him in a state of anxiety until we are absolutely satisfied that a long interrogation

will not be necessary." In fact, the object of a long interrogation is to set up what Teare called an anxiety complex in a man's mind.

Norris, on re-examining just sought to remind the court that the intelligence about the uprising came from an incoming signal.

When the court cross-examined the prosecution they put it to Teare that Mahnke writing "*I am making a confession but at the same time what I am telling you is untrue*" was very unusual. Teare assured the court that it was not at all unusual. He did not agree that the statement should be attributed to some form of violence.

Mr Norris then called George Wigglesworth, a former Royal Air Force Squadron Leader who served in intelligence duties. He knew of the interrogation of the two Germans and that it was urgent. He sent out the signal, a provisional warning, about the potential uprising and required the interrogators at Bad Nenndorf to see what information could be obtained. He considered that Mahnke and Oebsger-Roeder might have information of vital importance. He thought there was substance in the information they got about a potential uprising from Michael. The interrogation of these two Germans, Wigglesworth reiterated, was of vital importance and he felt that the results were inconclusive. He still felt that the Germans might have been concerned with an uprising on 20 April 1946.

Mr Dawson, a former lieutenant at Bad Nenndorf, was called next. He was Captain Bennett's assistant at Prison Control. He found Bennett an awkward man to work with, a disorganised excitable mind. He said that it was an invariable rule that if a prisoner made a statement which was given to Prison Control their warders were to give the statement to the Senior Intelligence Officer immediately and not send the statement to the Interrogation Division. Moving a prisoner from one cell to another, not for intelligence reasons but other reasons, was done by Prison Control, having first checked with the Intelligence Division that there was no objection to the proposed move. The only form of punishment permitted was confinement to a cell which had no furniture. The man confined kept his blanket, his clothes and his boots. He knew from their names that the two Germans were prisoners. He did not know them individually. Mathers told him that after a hectic party he had found Mahnke fainted and in order to revive him had splashed his face with water, using a floor mop. Mathers also told him that he had placed his hand against Mahnke and hit Mahnke's hand, but not so as to harm him or mark him or injure him. Mathers had committed a breach of discipline because violence was not permitted.

Dawson thought that Mathers was under the influence of alcohol; he presumed that Mahnke must have been truculent when brought out of faint and Mathers had just committed a lapse. If Dawson had reported the matter very severe disciplinary action would have been taken against Mathers, but as Dawson considered the incident very slight it would have been a gross miscarriage of justice if Mathers had suffered for such a slight lapse on his part against a person known to be a virulent Nazi.

The questioning went like this:

Q. *What sort of punishment of prisoners was known to you?*

A. *The only form of punishment to a prisoner was to be confined in a punishment cell – cell 12, I think was the usual cell used. It was not a very large cell and it had no furniture in it.*

Q. *Was there any question that you know of, of a man being deprived of his clothes to that he was naked?*

A. *No I do not remember that.*

Q. *Do you remember during April 1946 an occasion when CSM Mathers said something to you, which was unusual either about Mahnke or Oebsger-Roeder?*

A. *Yes, there was one such occasion. I cannot remember the exact date. It was sometime during the middle of the morning. I cannot specifically remember about the time.*

Q. *And where?*

A. *In the Prison Control Office.*

Q. *Do you remember if at that time Captain Bennett was there or was away?*

A. *I do not think that Captain Bennett was there. I remember he had a leave during April, and I think this must have been during his leave.*

Q. *At any rate were you alone in the room with the CSM at the time he spoke to you as far as you can remember?*

A. *Yes, as far as I can remember. He was talking to me in general conversation.*

Q. *What did he say?*

A. *He said that on the previous night.*

Judge Advocate General: *Wait a minute. I want to get this verbatim.*

MN (Malcolm Norris): *If you are answering without his exact words you will say so, of course.*

A. *Yes.*

Q. *On the previous night...*

A. He said that on the previous night he had returned to the prison after a party, I believe he said a hectic party, but I cannot be certain and had found that the prisoner Mahnke had fainted. He said that Mahnke was taken to the ablutions.

Q. Did he say by whom or if anyone was with him?

A. By himself and I believe he said Sergeant Thomas, but I cannot be certain. And there, in order to revive him, water was splashed on the prisoner and for this purpose they had used a floor mop. CSM Mathers also said that he placed his hand against the prisoner and hit his hand. He said he had not marked or harmed or injured the prisoner in any way.

Q. Do not answer this if you cannot, but did you get the impression?

Judge Advocate General: Is that the end of it?

A. That is the end of what CSM Mathers told me.

The President: Just a moment. (The Court confers).

MN. I think it was put in almost those terms to Mathers.

JAG. The great trouble I am having as legal Adviser to this Court is that naturally the members keep on saying : "Why do we hear one thing and why do we not hear another" and the President was merely asking me now why we have this as it seemed to be within the realm of hearsay. But I am prepared to advise the Court that owing to the course that has been taken it is quite proper that you should put this.

MM. It is, of course in fact in rebuttal of Mather's denial.

JAG. I think it is alright Sir. It is certainly for the benefit of Mr Langham.

Colonel Campbell: I am not objecting, Sir. I agree with Mr Norris about it.

MM. Thank you. What I was going to say was: Did you get the impression that Mathers was telling you everything that happened?

A. Yes, I did.

Q. It appeared from what was said, although he did not speak of any great violence against Mahnke that he had used some violence against the prisoner?

A. Yes.

Q. Was any violence allowed to be used against prisoners?

A. Certainly not.

Q. What did you say to him and what happened after that, after he had told you that?

A. As he had told me that he returned to the prison after a party, I presumed it to mean that he had committed this act under the influence of alcohol.

Q. Yes?

A. As it is one of the primary duties of every officer to look after the welfare and protection of the men serving under his command, I gave the CSM a severe dressing down and told him that he had been wrong in his action.

JAG. This is the CSM, is it, of the prison?

A. Yes.

MM. Did you consider that that was sufficient action to take?

A. Believing that he had committed this act under the influence of alcohol and knowing that the prisoner against whom the act had been committed was a member of the SS and most probably a virulent Nazi against whom feeling was running very high – much higher than it is now, two years later – and knowing that CSM Mathers was a disciplinarian, I presumed that he had been drunk when he returned to the prison and that the prisoner must have been perhaps truculent after being brought round from the faint and I presumed that it was just a lapse on the part of the CSM.

Q. I asked you, did you consider you had taken sufficient disciplinary action?

A. I did in view of the circumstances.

Q. Whether you were right or wrong at the time in view of the circumstances you have enumerated, you thought that that was enough?

A. I knew that if I had reported the matter, very severe disciplinary action would have been taken against the CSM and I considered the incident very slight and that it would have been a gross miscarriage of justice had the CSM suffered severe disciplinary action for such a slight lapse on his part against a man who was known to be a virulent Nazi.

Q. Did he say at any time either then or at any time round about then that he had done anything to Mahnke or anybody else on the orders of an Officer?

A. No, he did not say that.

Q. Or in particular on the orders of Major Edmunds?

A. No, he did not say that.

Q. Or Captain Langham?

A. No.

Q. Did he tell you if the Duty Officer or Captain Langham knew anything about what had happened when he returned from the party?

A. No, he did not mention the name of any officer or the name or appointment of any officer.

Q. I had very nearly finished the examination in chief, Mr. Dawson, but will you just look again at Exhibit 11, which is the Guard Book for Blocks 3 and 4. Turning again to 17 April 1946 and taking your mind back to the morning of 18th April 1946 when Sergeant Thomas must have brought that book to you – do you agree with that?
A. Yes.
Q. Did he say anything to you about any unusual occurrence during his tour of duty in the prison?
A. I do not remember Sergeant Thomas making any such remark.
Q. Would you have remembered had he said anything about any prisoner being subjected to violent treatment?
A. Oh yes, I would have remembered that.
Q. Would you have had to take action of some sort had he told you any such thing?
A. Yes, normally I would have taken some action had any such thing been told.
Q. Then are you in a position to tell the Court that he did not tell you that any prisoner had been subjected to violent treatment during his tour of duty?
A. Yes.
Q. Did he say anything in particular to you about any of the moves which are mentioned in the remarks column?
A. No, I do not remember any move being mentioned to me particularly.
Q. If he said anything about any move being connected with the administration of violence to any prisoner, would you have remembered?
A. O yes, because violence was not allowed.
Q. You are quite sure of that, are you that he did not say anything about any violent treatment being meted out to any prisoner?
A. The only knowledge I have of any violence is what CSM Mathers told me. Dawson knew about the suspected uprising and that Mahnke and Oebsger-Roeder were connected with it in some way. He might have mentioned it to Mathers. Dawson said that Mathers did not say that violence was used against the Germans on the orders of Frank or Oliver Langham or any duty officer. They were not mentioned at all. The court adjourned for lunch.

After lunch, Derek Curtis Bennett, fresh from his other trial, took his place in the court. His first act was to object to a question put to Dawson in cross-examination about whether the Sergeant of the Guard would know a move had taken place. The Judge Advocate pointed out that Curtis-Bennett had not been in court in the morning and had not heard the previous evidence. Curtis-Bennett said that he had been in court long enough to object to the question, because Dawson could not possibly know the answer. Curtis-Bennett prevailed. Campbell put to Dawson that his father – confessor role with Mathers was so extraordinary that no reasonable person could believe it. Dawson responded, "I claim to be a reasonable person and I am stating under oath."

He said that he felt he had no duty to investigate why Mahnke had fainted, and that he never heard a rumour to the effect that beatings had taken place.

It can be hard for an advocate to step into a case which he has left for several days. Mr Norris had done excellent work so far, but Curtis-Bennett was happy to take over and started the re-examination of Dawson, even though Norris had examined Dawson. He was quick and to the point; Dawson said again that no knowledge of the beatings had come to his attention nor had any wounds from beatings. There were plenty of medical facilities should the prisoners need them.

> *Q. (Colonel Campbell): Do not you think it likely that such a serious matter as the beating up of prisoners, it was common knowledge amongst the warders, would have reached your ears?*
>
> *A. Apparently it did not.*
>
> *Q. I know. That is not an answer to my question. I said do not you think it likely that it would?*
>
> *A. No.*
>
> *Q. You do not, why not?*
>
> *A. It appears that the Sergeant Major did this off his own bat whilst he was drunk, and the warders would not be likely to tell the officer of something the CSM had done illegally.*
>
> *Curtis-Bennett: Very well. You remember Colonel Campbell asking you just now – he was somewhat surprised as to why you did not hear. Can you tell the Court why you did not hear about this beating-up? You started off "Mathers off his own bat". Just go on from there.*
>
> *A. What I said was in reply to Colonel Campbell's question whether I should not have heard if the warders were talking about it, I said that it would be unlikely that any of the warders would tell me that the CSM had done something which he should not have done.*

The Judge Advocate asked Dawson about the quality of the warders. Dawson said when men were demobilised they had very poor-quality replacements. Mathers was a very smart soldier, a disciplinarian, and could command discipline by his voice and his penetrating eyes. The prisoners were scared of his tone of voice and eyes. *"The sergeant-major had authority over the prisoners by virtue of the respect they had for him, or call it fear, if you like, but I think it is respect."*

While the President of the Court was asking Dawson questions, he put the court *in camera* for a short while, while he sought information from Dawson about the movement of prisoners. The evidence given *in camera* was not enlightening in any way but in fact was confusing.

Curtis-Bennett called Scholes, a private and a warder at Bad Nenndorf. Scholes said that Mahnke and Oebsger-Roeder were two of the worst type of Germans. They were insolent and Mathers shouted at them a lot. Scholes knew that these two had planned an uprising on Hitler's birthday. He heard it while standing guard outside the interrogation cell, the door being left opened on Frank's orders, and heard it when Frank conducted the part of the interrogation in English and in German: Scholes had picked up some German while at Bad Nenndorf. Other warders knew. Private Pawsey knew. Scholes told Corporal Sore about it. There was also a story going round the prison, Scholes said, that Mahnke and Oebsger-Roeder were planning an armed escape, by taking a revolver from a sentry and using it. The rumour was spread by Thomas. He also heard about the beatings and that Mathers instigated them. It did not surprise him in the least, because these prisoners were very insolent. Scholes had never heard that any officer had given orders for the beatings. Scholes agreed that Frank made the soldiers work very hard.

In cross-examination Scholes admitted that it was unusual for doors to be kept open during interrogations. Frank, said Scholes, must have known that a warder was outside the cell during interrogations; this was the custom for the protection of the interrogator.

Another hard day's evidence ended.

We move to the eighteenth day of the trial with Curtis-Bennett firmly back in the saddle and into the flow of the trial.

Scholes was pressed about a discrepancy in his evidence about time, which differed from the guard book records and whether Mahnke was given food or not. It was put to Scholes that his evidence was wrong, which Scholes answered thus:

"May I make one point quite clear to the court? I have no liking for Major Edmunds. I never had any time for Major Edmunds. I have had to spend a lot of time doing quite unnecessary work for him. I came to this court for only one reason, this was to see a little bit of justice done. If I am confused with my times, I am sorry. It was two years

ago, and I cannot quite remember the times, but I am sure that I was on interrogation duty between seven and nine. If I have made a mistake and there was a man who was resting, then it was my mistake. But I have not wasted my time to come to this court to tell a lot of unnecessary lies, because as I have said I have no liking for Major Edmunds."

It was a heartfelt statement from Scholes and certainly had the ring of truth. Curtis-Bennett must have kept the pleasure from his expression when he heard Scholes say this. The President told Scholes "*do not get excited about it*" which perhaps revealed where the President's sympathies lay. Scholes went on to say that he thought that Mahnke was the ringleader of the uprising and came to this conclusion when he heard Frank tell Mahnke that Frank would not tolerate the lives of British soldiers being endangered. That was said in English, not German.

Scholes was questioned on how such a strict officer such as Major Edmunds would allow a warder to overhear interrogation. Scholes could only reply that when warders did overhear interrogation, they were honour bound not to repeat it. He remembered that at times Major Edmunds allowed him to sit on the floor. When he took over duty from Private Lucia, he noticed with disapproval that Lucia had used his own mug to give Mahnke a drink of water. Scholes would have used a mess tin for this purpose.

Scholes finished his evidence in the morning of 24 March 1948, and at that stage all the witnesses, bar Frank, had given evidence. Just before this on 23 March solicitor David Goy took stock of the state of the case. The solicitor set out his stock, taking in a note to the barristers:

> *The case for the Prosecution seems to be collapsing fast with the bombshell exploded during Prison Control Captain Dawson's evidence and Cross-Examination. Had the Police and JAG done their investigation properly, they would have checked Mather's self-incriminating statements, interviewed his superior Officer Captain Dawson, found out what we did over two months ago and not brought a case at all against any of the intelligence officers.*
>
> *The most extraordinary part of the Court Martial is that although proceedings was this: following the withdrawal of charges against Major Edmunds are exclusively directed against Captain Langham, the Junior Officer, the prosecution case against Captain Langham rested almost entirely on the alleged accusations by CSM Mathers against Captain Langham's superior officer, Major Edmunds.*

Whilst Mathers' statement that he had acted on information and instructions from Major Edmunds did not directly incriminate Captain Langham in any way, it might be anticipated that prosecution will construe that Captain Langham was in the confidence of his superior officer and was fully conversant with and gave approval to the actions of Mathers and his co-operators.

The Prosecution have completely bungled the issue concerning the date when these beatings are alleged to have taken place. Even their charges give the dates wrongly, as 18 and 19 April 1946, at which dates absolutely nothing happened, and they have continued during the proceedings to stick to these dates, whereas it is blatantly clear from evidence, however contradictory in parts that in fact the fateful date was the 17 April 1946, the day Captain Langham was Duty Officer and made his rounds of the Prison at 1800, 2100 hours and midnight. This was the main if not only point which could incriminate Captain Langham, since he could possibly have seen evidence of the ill treatment at the time of his tours of duty of the prison. Evidence, however, given by witnesses for the defence tends to show that at the times when the Duty Officer would appear at the prison, namely at 6 p.m., 9 p.m. and midnight, both prisoners were dressed and in such a condition that no indication would be given as to the treatment to which they had been or were being subjected to. Furthermore, it is more than coincidence that certain things were done, for example. the changing round of the two prisoners in their cells at times when the Duty Officer would be known to be not likely to return.

Several witnesses who were called by prosecution, including Sergeant Brant, Sergeant Sore and others are also giving evidence in Colonel Stephens Court Martial case, which evidence will divulge information of other irregularities committed in the Prison by NCO's without instructions from or permission by any "A" and/or "I" officer. Also several German Detainees at CSDIC, other than Oebsger-Roeder and Mahnke gave evidence at Colonel Stephens Court of Inquiry that they were subjected to violence by a number of NCO's and warders. (Dieter Albrecht, Lueneburg, Menzel Hamburg, Graf Buttlar-Brandenfels, alias Herrmann), which shows that such violence was not exclusively meted out to Oebsger-Roeder and Mahnke.

If you consider it desirable to show once more the quasi impossibility of Major Edmunds' disclosing Top-Secret information and giving orders for brutalities to be carried out as is alleged by CSM Mathers, we have in reserve two of Major Edmunds' ex colleagues, Majors Boothroyd and Cochrane, who have said in their sworn statements – which I have available – that Major Edmunds is a man of intense energy, integrity and activity and that he was fussy regarding the strict compliance with regulations and that it was anything from most unlikely to impossible that Major Edmunds should have disclosed Top Secret information or given orders for brutalities to be carried out. They have also given some inside information of the atmosphere inside this camp regarding interrogation procedure to show that this allegation, so far as Major Edmunds and Captain Langham are concerned, is completely unbelievable from the point of view of an experienced Intelligence Officer.

Captain Langham was a Military Officer who was transferred to intelligence duties only shortly before April 1946 and prior to the matters complained of in the charges. His experience of interrogation work was certainly limited but certain of the witnesses who have known him have given evidence that he was conscientious and devoted to his duty. It is perhaps more important to note, however, that as a Junior Officer, he stood in great awe of Colonel Stephens from whom he had received express instructions regarding matters of security and treatment of prisoners, and it is hardly credible that he would have acted in direct defiance of his Commanding Officer.

I think that David Goy was a little over optimistic in his view that the prosecution case was collapsing. Certainly, its case was not the same case that it had opened, but there was enough evidence to convict Langham, if the court was so minded. Every person takes a different view of evidence; the standard that the court had to adopt was whether Langham was guilty beyond reasonable doubt, not whether Langham was guilty beyond any doubt.

CHAPTER 15

Frank Gives Evidence

Curtis-Bennett K.C. had decided to call Frank last to give evidence for the defence of Captain Langham. It was not an easy decision, because it was evident that Frank would be fiercely attacked by the prosecutor, Colonel Campbell. Frank spent over five hours in the witness box. The master interrogator would be interrogated.

Curtis-Bennett took Frank gently into his evidence. He gave Frank the opportunity to state how much Frank would wish to defend these charges but was denied the opportunity of doing so and asked Frank about his military career. Frank said that he would never talk to Mathers about intelligence matters over the telephone and would never talk to Mathers about intelligence matters at the office. Violence was never to be used; that was perfectly clear from first to last. All his officers knew that. He denied that he had ever given Mathers instructions to use violence. Violence was never to be used. By 17 April 1946, the case was, from an intelligence point of view, closed. It was necessary to have information three or four days before the expected uprising (on 20 April) to get field security into place. As far as Frank was concerned the case ended with the last interrogation of Oebsger-Roeder at five in the morning on 16 April 1946.

"I sent him back to his cell with the understanding that if anything happened on 20 April he would be in serious trouble."

By 15 April, Frank told the court martial, Mahnke was of no further intelligence use, and Frank closed the interrogation because the prisoners might have given wrong information and false information. There was no point in going on with the interrogation. He said that when Langham came to him, Frank found Langham a conscientious officer, who had made excellent progress and he recommended him for promotion to captain. He had never known Langham to be party to any physical cruelty and Frank was certain that he would not be a party to any violence.

Frank then detailed the long and arduous interrogations of Mahnke and Oebsger-Roeder – which he said were intended to be harsh. He explained that they had two independent sources with information about their involvement in a planned uprising and the two sources did not know each other. Also, he had quite a bit of supporting evidence. Frank had gained secret information about this from an American general.

Frank said that he had interrogated several thousand prisoners during the war and was particularly busy before and during the invasion of Germany.

At this stage, at Curtis-Bennett's request, the court went into *in camera* and members of the public left it.

Frank said that he had interrogated privates, SS men, Field Marshalls, N.C.O.s, junior officers, and generals including Field Marshal von Runstedt. He also interrogated a number of SS men who guarded Hitler's Chancellery and one private at Auschwitz whose duty it was to cremate hundreds of bodies daily, bodies of those who had been gassed, men women and children at Auschwitz concentration camp. He talked about interrogating the operational people responsible for the V1 and V2 rockets and he discovered information about Operation Sea Lion, the German plan for the invasion of Britain. He also found intelligence about German Tanks. *"I produced for Major General Briggs personally a photograph of the Josef Stalin Tank which was so-called non-existent and which Mr Churchill had been asked to obtain information from Stalin at the Yalta conference"*. From Bad Nenndorf Frank had got one piece of information which was top top-secret – at this stage the President of the Court who was becoming very nervous about this evidence even though it was given *in camera*, and said that the court would accept that the information was of the utmost importance and that there was no need for Frank to recount it.

Frank then was asked about the guests at the Dieterhaus. There were many low-grade people, but there were also people who turned out to be spies, chiefly German, but also Poles and Belgian and Russian, who were spying (or trying to spy) on what went on in the Dieterhaus[39]. Frank was greatly involved in discovering 'the Russian Angel'[40]. Finally, Frank explained that he was one of the few people who had studied both a specific interrogation course at Oxford and an interrogation and the order of battle course at Cambridge.

Curtis-Bennett was satisfied that enough secrets had been exposed *in camera* and asked the court to resume an open session.

Frank also explained that Prison Control A was quite separate from the Intelligence section. Frank as an 'I' officer could not command an 'A' soldier, except by making recommendations to the senior intelligence officer. Frank had no contact at all with Mathers.

His interest in the prisoners was only intelligence: *"we might have dealt with murderers. We were not interested in that part. Our interest was intelligence and intelligence only"*.[41] Frank said he had no idea about whether Oebsger-Roeder and Mahnke were

---

[39] The spies, I think it safe to assume, were spying for the Soviet Union, no matter what their nationality might have been.
[40] I have been unable to uncover what this was about.
[41] Clearly Frank and his team had interrogated many murderers.

concerned in conspiracy against British troops. *"I was not satisfied at the time and I am not satisfied in my mind today"*.

Curtis-Bennett took Frank through the report that Frank had prepared of the interrogations. It would be circulated to about sixty different agencies. The statements made by the prisoners after interrogation, including the dramatic statements made in this case, were explained as was the telephone system and other reasons why Frank would not put himself into Mathers' hands, even if he had wanted the prisoners to be beaten up. However, Frank's instructions were to obey the Hague and Geneva Conventions and he did this. Further, Frank gave extensive written instructions to the effect that the prisoners' food was not to be interfered with. Curtis-Bennett then asked a question about the informer 'Michael' who was one of the sources of information about the uprising.

Michael, said Frank, was an informer on Russian Intelligence matters. Frank was satisfied that his case was genuine and arranged for Michael to act as an assistant to batmen working in the garden. He was interrogated about fifteen times and stuck to his story about the uprising. He was a co-operative prisoner who came voluntarily.

The court went back into open session.

From the information received Frank thought that the plot was real, and Oebsger-Roeder was the leader of it. He was the far stronger character of the two had had done important work for the Nazis. Mahnke was the weaker of the two. *"The fact that a prisoner collapsed during interrogation could not deflect me from my purpose, nor was I convinced that the collapse was genuine. I rather felt it was simulated in order to get over a rather embarrassing series of questions. The few hours at my disposal were running out and I would not let the prisoners get away with the idea that they could enforce a termination of the interrogation by the simple expedient of simulating a collapse."* Without hesitation, Frank took full responsibility for the cases of Oebsger Roeder and Mahnke. With an affirmation in the innocence of Langham, Frank's examination-in-chief ended and after a ten-minute break Colonel Campbell rose to cross-examine Frank.

Frank had answered Curtis-Bennett's questions carefully and sensibly. He had given the appearance of a witness who was trying to be painstakingly truthful and was obviously an intelligent intelligence officer who had by his work shortened the war and saved lives. This presented Campbell with a problem in cross-examining Frank.

Campbell first tried to question Frank about the filing of statements in Frank's section, but all this cross-examination brought out was that Frank was snowed under with work and that it was not possible to file every statement made; the section had insufficient personnel to do this. Some statements were translated, but not all. Campbell tried to make a point that Oebsger-Roeder's statement was translated and asked why this should be. Frank calmly replied that there was no particular reason and no value in the statement, but perhaps it was translated because it was short and would only have taken a few minutes. Such translations were left to the discretion of the case officer. Campbell asked Frank about filing and dealing with documents.

Campbell was clearly flustered; he asked general questions based on premises which the Court pointed out were inaccurate but moved on eventually to the specifics of the case. Whatever he had hoped to prove by his questions about filing, Campbell had simply reinforced in the mind of the court that Frank was a methodical, fussy, and careful intelligence officer who followed the rules.

Frank established that he prepared the interrogation plan without the assistance of Langham and Van Rije but showed it to them after he had prepared it. Frank was asked about the threats made to Oebsger-Roeder.

Q: *Was he in fact frightened by that particular interrogation?*
A: *He presumably was.*
Q: *What was your impression; you interrogated him, did you not?*
A: *Yes.*
Q: *Was he frightened? Did he seem to take your threats seriously?*
A: *That was the idea of the interrogation.*
Q: *You are not answering my question. You saw him, you saw the way he looked to what was said to him.*
A: *Yes.*
Q: *Did he give the impression that he took what you said seriously?*
A: *I think so.*

Campbell pointed out the various threats made by Frank in the course of interrogation. In some cases, Frank had threatened a thorough beating, which Frank agreed was not the same as threatening a prisoner with death. Campbell put to Frank, *"whereas you might not be prepared to take a man's life you might be prepared to give him a thorough beating"*. Frank answered calmly:

> *"I think I have said before, threats were never carried out. I have interrogated for years, interrogated thousands of prisoners and I have never touched or made any person under my command touch a prisoner or a prisoner of war."*

Frank remained steadfast when being cross-examined about the treatment of Mahnke. Reading the transcript, I get the impression that Campbell had somewhat lost his way in the cross-examination and that the court did not see the point of much of it. This sometimes happens when an advocate tries to prove something by documents, which the documents do not necessarily prove but simply admit the possibility of what the advocate is trying to prove. From Frank's point of view, however, being cross-examined was an ordeal, however well or badly Campbell was doing it and the arduous ordeal ended, temporarily, at 5 p.m. when the court adjourned, only to be resumed the following morning on Thursday 25 March 1948, which was the nineteenth day of the trial.

As I have explained, a witness, in the middle of testimony, is kept away from his lawyers under the English system. The lawyer cannot speak to the witness without special permission of the court so Frank spent a lonely night away from Curtis-Bennett, Norris and Goy who were probably relieved to be away from Frank for that night. Frank probably never felt more alone. He would not have known how the court would be regarding his evidence. He only knew that he had done his best to tell the truth, but he also knew that on many occasions doing your best is not enough.

Campbell, however, had time to think about the cross-examination and started at ten o'clock the next day. Campbell tried a new tack. He asked about Frank's habit of keeping the cell door open during interrogations; these interrogations were top secret and could not the warder, in this case Scholes, hear what was said in English? Frank agreed Scholes could have heard but said that the little that was said in English would not have provided Scholes with any top-secret information. Frank said that he did not say anything in English from which Scholes could have gathered that Frank was investigating the possibility of an uprising.

> *"You see what I am leading up to is this. We have had a number of witnesses before this court during the course of this trial all of whom have told us it was common knowledge among the warders in this prison around about 17 April that Mahnke and Oebsger-Roeder were there because they were suspected of engineering a subservice uprising for Hitler's birthday on 20 April."*

This was the strongest point that Campbell had made; how did the warders find out about the suspected uprising? He asked Frank how they found out and Frank said he did not know.

> *"To my knowledge these warders had no knowledge of German and most of the interrogation was conducted in German and I did not think for a minute that the warders would understand what was going on."*

Campbell pressed the point. Frank was unable to comment on it and unwilling to comment on it, although it seemed fairly obvious to him that the warders might have concluded that the interrogations were unsuccessful.

Campbell asked about the differences in handwriting on Mahnke's statements, which Frank attributed to hysteria. Campbell said that the differences in handwriting could only be explained by Mahnke being beating up, and Frank agreed, but pointed out that in 1946, when he attributed the handwriting differences to hysteria, Frank did not know about the beatings. Campbell, as with all good advocates, tried to end the cross-examination strongly, but Frank firmly and carefully, sometimes fussily, answered his questions. He re-affirmed that violence in interrogation is completely useless, because the results obtained are completely unreliable. When asked *"would you agree that the Gestapo often got very useful information from direct violence"* Frank answered, *"not from British personnel"* and *"my considered opinion is that violence used in interrogation provides completely valueless results"*.

The purpose of re-examination is to enable a lawyer to clear up any apparent discrepancies that may have arisen in cross-examination. The questions asked are usually easily answered and so it was in this case. Curtis-Bennett established that the court would not regard the keeping of the prisoners standing to attention for long periods of time as physical violence, and Frank then left the witness box. The case for the defence had closed.

The court adjourned over the weekend, which permitted Mr Curtis-Bennett to study matters and prepare his final speech, which he was to commence on Tuesday 30 March 1948, nearly two years after the events in question.

CHAPTER 16

Curtis-Bennett's Closing Speech

30 March 1948 was the twentieth day of the trial. It fell to Mr Curtis-Bennett to make the first closing speech to the court martial. He had been chain smoking ever since he woke up but from the moment he walked into court he could not smoke. He was his usual bundle of nerves, but appeared calm and collected, as good advocates must. It would be a long speech and one that would command the attention of the jury from the start. I will offer my own analysis of parts of it, as we go along, but remember this was delivered in one long session and in truth Curtis-Bennett had to keep the jury entertained, like every excellent raconteur. This is what he said.

May it please you, Sir.

A lot of water has flowed under London Bridge since we started this case, which looks like lasting exactly one month. Therefore, I shall be pardoned (though I do not ask any apology or offer any apology) if I take some time in addressing you this morning, on behalf of my client, Captain Langham, for whom I appear with my learned friend, Mr. Norris. I should like to start by saying that all of us for the defence have been very sensible and very grateful to you and all of you, for your courtesy throughout this case, and I personally am very grateful to my learned friend and to those instructing me, for the help they have given me, particularly with regard to the time that I was not able to be in Germany with you. Having said that, I am afraid I have a good many uncompromising things to say about this case.

It is a lovely expression, that a lot of water has flowed under London Bridge. He could have said "a lot of water has flowed under the bridge," or even " a lot has happened," but the expression he used reminded the jury that they were in London, not Germany, and that they would be deciding a complicated case about which he would have to be frank and uncompromising.

I say them in the exercise of my duties towards my client, having had, through your courtesy, ample time to think things over, over the week-end. Nobody who appears for the defence in a serious case – which after all, this is, because Captain Oliver Langham is a young man of good reputation and repute, whose whole career and future is at stake, and you will not therefore, expect me to spare words, providing they are proper words, describing this case or the attitude taken up by various people in it.

If you do not agree with what I say, well, that is a matter for you to decide later on but I ask you to bear with me as you have borne with me, patiently, all the way through this long case – because this is one of the most important cases ever to come before a court of

British law, in my submissions, and I am saying quite quietly and deliberately, that I hope by the end of my address, you will agree with what I now submit, quite firmly that this case is one which should never have been brought against Captain Langham – never should have been brought.

He explains his duty to defend Langham while saying that the prosecution should never have been brought.

It is one which has caused him to suffer agony in preparing and waiting and listening to this case, and giving evidence in it, one which he started, you remember – I am bound to go back to the beginning, and it would be madness to start at the end; I am bound to remind you that he came over to Hanover at the beginning of March or the end of February last year, to face his trial along with Major Edmunds. Not the least extraordinary thing about this extraordinary and quite astonishing case, is that originally, he faced his trial, together with Major Edmunds, upon the same charges, Major Edmunds having been seen in September (I think September 1st) the first time Hayward saw him – October, November, December, January, February.

He counted the months on the fingers of his hands, six months, emphasising the delay in bringing the prosecution.

The Judge Advocate General, not Colonel Campbell, who, if I may say so, has also behaved and conducted this case, certainly in a manner of charm which becomes him so well – not until two or three days before we were to meet at Hanover did the Judge Advocate General (and now I am speaking of the high official) know what the law was, and found out that he had illegally arrested Edmunds, illegally caused him to be brought, or be told to go to Hanover. Yet, when he finds out what the law is, not one piece of paper countermanding these orders, but a telephone message to Mr Goy, my instructing Solicitor, which, for all we know, might have been from the office boy at Spring Gardens.[42]

So he goes out there at our suggestion and our advice because the orders had not been countermanded officially, and you know, and I am not going to dwell upon it, the protest I made, one of many protests. I am not going to repeat it to-day; (it is not becoming because he is not before you) – one of many protests which I shall have to repeat to you to-day. I am not going to repeat every one. Time will tell and, in the proper place, proper proceedings will be taken in due course.

---

[42] I have no idea what this was. It seems Curtis-Bennett must be referring to a telephone call to David Goy of which Frank was unaware, as it does not appear in his notes.

So you have the curious position now that of the three people in C Section which was devoted to this case of Mahnke and Oebsger-Roeder, the only one before you is the junior officer, one who had only joined it in January 1946. Major Edmunds is free. And let me just pause to say this because I am his counsel. If anyone here or outside should happen to think that Major Edmunds thinks himself lucky not to have been charged here, let me disillusion them. There is nothing he would have liked more than to come here, or he did come here, to come here and entirely free himself from the charges.

I dare say you have seen him another place somebody has said, my learned friend Mr Attorney General, has said that he will look into the matter to see whether he may be prosecuted somewhere else. Major Edmunds would further that and hopes that the Attorney General may find the place where he can be tried, so that he can be not only tried, but acquitted. Let no one think that Major Edmunds considers himself fortunate.

He wants to weave the fortunes of Langham into those of Frank.

You have to deal with the junior officer, of first class character, the man who had least to do with it. A summary taken against Captain Van Rije, no case brought against him; Major Edmunds prosecuted, no charge against him. This man left for you to deal with. Sir, upon what charge or charges? "When on active service..." Of course, he is still on active service and therefore the learned Judge Advocate General does not need to know much more law about that, but he is right for once), –"caused"– that is the charge, nothing else, not anything else "caused" – I say there is no evidence at all that my client caused Mahnke and Oebsger-Roeder to be subjected to brutal treatment.

We started this case you know, with my learned friend Colonel Campbell, opening this case to you at Hanover and I do not know (he had long enough) but thinking back, and looking at the very valuable note which I have here, which is not mine, but which I have been using, do you remember the first words almost that fell (I am sure by mistake – it must have been by mistake) from Colonel Campbell? I am not using his actual words, because quite frankly, I am so astonished by them that I had not taken them down.

Curtis-Bennett was so surprised by something so amazing that Campbell said that Curtis-Bennett did not write it down. Believe that if you will! It kept the jury's attention.

He said on 15th January 1921, Richard Oliver Langham was born at Munich in Germany. It is true that it is in the statement that Langham made, as were lots of other things which were irrelevant and were cut out. But what had that got to do with it? What does the Judge Advocate General mean by instructing his officers to open the case in that way? Of a man who is a British Subject, who has been used by his country in time of war against the enemy, the Germans.

There could not be any other purpose than to put in your minds; here is a German born man. There could not be. Some of us know that some Germans are brutal people. We all of us have had good evidence of that in the last nine years. It does not matter whether Langham was born in Timbuktu or Tooting, and if he had been born in Timbuktu or Tooting, you would not have heard that matter from my learned friend. "Born in Munich!"

Now I have sufficient confidence and have good reason to have, in this court, and in you officers, you gentlemen, to know that that is the sort of thing that is going to be wiped right out of your minds, but I must deal with it because that is the way this case started. Those were the first words practically said, and then we had all that business you knew, about what day it was that the beating up of those two men took place. Colonel Campbell told you that Oebsger-Roeder and Mahnke were working indirectly through a string of people under that pleasant gentlemen Himmler, which must surely have recommended Oebsger-Roeder and Mahnke as a couple of nice people.

Racism was not a term used in 1948; what Curtis-Bennett accused the prosecution of was racism, carefully distancing Campbell from the decision to talk about where Langham was born.

But this brutality took place on—he said, I think you will find, it must have been on the 18, and there was I, and perhaps you will remember, perhaps rather painfully, trying in vain to draw your attention to the fact and saying—because it is in a sense against my client, but we are here to do our duties as advocates and we are not here to mislead you, although people not in the law very often think barristers exist for that purpose.

You know from your own experience on courts martial that they do not, but they exist to help. But you wave this thing about and nobody will look at it seeing it is the 17; nobody will look at it; nobody would pay the slightest attention to me. But now it is correct that it was the 17. Bear in mind that I was pointing it out. The 17 showed that Langham was Duty Officer.

Be that as it may, it was against my client, and I should have loved to agree with Colonel Campbell that it was the 18, as he said with six months study of the case, because on the 18th Langham was not Duty officer at all. Is that the proper way to present things of this gravity to you?

Curtis-Bennett established his truthfulness and his own accuracy, unlike that of Campbell.

It is the 17 and we now know, having heard the Judge Advocate agree, we will now agree, thanks to my having pointed it out to start with. We all know it now to be the 17. I know, and I want it to be understood before I start almost, that it does not matter if the Nazis killed six million, was it, people in Europe, it does not matter. We cannot touch a hair of their heads now. That is the law here and we stand by it, and we are proud of it, of course and we are not descending to that level.

They can kill six million people in Europe or sixty million, but still you are not allowed to touch a hair of their heads and I am not suggesting anything to the contrary. It is not my case that because these two men were parties to killing six million people in Europe, we can beat them up. If that were my case, then this would be a plea of guilty. It is not. It is that that young man there played no part at all in any brutality on the 17 April 1945 whether he was Duty Officer or not.

The evidence in the case, to start off the evidence, is take evidence of those two charmers, Mahnke and Oebsger-Roeder those two trained liars, those two deceivers, those two Nazis.

Charmers, trained liars, and deceivers. Curtis-Bennett referred to them rather politely, knowing the jury would have stronger views.

Once you have said that, you have really said all that can be said against them. I have had the privilege of appearing on more than one case before your present Judge Advocate where German witnesses are concerned and I think I am right in saying (he will correct me when he sums up on it and I shall be delighted if I am wrong) that there has yet to be a court of law which has accepted by itself, the evidence of Nazis against British Officers or men by itself.

But they were called and Colonel Campbell, although he told you they were not very nice men and he did not think they were people of very good character (I think that is something we would have gathered without being told perhaps) spent his time afterwards reading to you bits out of Lieutenant Smith's report, which said that Mahnke thought it was dishonourable to lie.

I do not think I need dwell a great deal upon them. Their evidence took an awful lot of time, was bound to, but there is one aspect that I can say – of course, their stories are hopelessly exaggerated, in my submission to you – hopelessly. You see, one gave evidence on the summary, and one did not, because one had run away and escaped.

You remember Oebsger-Roeder had run away and Mahnke gave evidence. They talk, both of them, curiously enough, perhaps having got their heads together at some time, about being burned with cigarette ends and hit with brushes and brooms and bleeding, particularly, Oebsger-Roeder – blood was pouring from his head, dropping down, according to him.

Yet Mahnke, who went to hospital – and we heard a gruesome description of his condition when he got there – not a word about burns. You noticed that, and one of your number for which I am grateful, asked whether there were any marks on certain parts of his body where he said there were burns, like on an ear. You remember he said he put his hand over his ear and an attack had been deliberately made on it.

No mark on his ear or hand; no mark where anybody could see it outside his clothing. A hopelessly exaggerated and lying story by two men who were confirmed and trained liars the whole of their lives of course, what evidence it was. One always regrets having evidence in camera as I think the learned Judge Advocate told you, the less camera we have, the better, in this court. We stand for open, free trials in this country, but there were certain matters which had to be held in camera, and one of the matters was the useful work the section had done.

I am not going to repeat it to you, because it was held in camera, but it is only right that I should say in public that a volume of evidence was given showing that this section of this unit did very valuable work in the national interests during the war. Anyone who thinks that just because someone gets up in the House of Commons and questions something, that this camp spent their life beating up prisoners of war, is quite wrong.

They did some very valuable work and Major Edmunds told you on Thursday (Wednesday or Thursday), some of these valuable things which were done, without which, many of us, at least civilians sitting here, might not have been here to-day.

Here Curtis Bennett was not only playing to the jury but also to the press that had not been present when evidence was given *in camera*.

So it is a unit which is worthy of some respect and therefore the members of it are worthy of some respect. Not easy work. If you hear, you know, from two sources, that the Germans are going to cause an uprising in the British Zone, on the anniversary of Hitler's birthday, on 20 April, and you are a member of this particular sort of unit, you are not going to take that lightly. Supposing there had been an uprising, and Edmunds had not done what he did. Do you imagine he would have been let off lightly? "You had in your charge the ringleader Oebsger-Roeder. Why did you not do all you could do, not to touch him, no, no, you must not touch him, not a hair of his head, why did not you do all you could do, short of violence, to break him down".

That expression, which is a perfectly innocent expression, means to make him tell the truth.

At the beginning of this case and entirely because of what Colonel Campbell said to you, it seemed to me (I may be wrong; if I am so be it), it seemed to me that the Court was taking the view that there never was any sort of conspiracy or any justification for thinking there was any conspiracy for the 20 April. Of course, that is all gone now, because you know it was common knowledge in the prison that there was a conspiracy or thought to be a conspiracy, to have an uprising in the British Zone of Germany on the 20 April and Mahnke and Oebsger-Roeder were two people in it.

Major Edmunds gave you seven reasons for thinking that was genuine, one of which was the information from Michael, one of which was the information from the other source which I wrote down, the American source; the third of which was something which we heard in camera, the fourth of which was their own view as Intelligence men—and I am sure you will agree with me (I did not hear Captain Langham in the box but I will deal with that in a moment), I am sure you will agree with me, whatever else I say, that Major Edmunds is a very intelligent, thoughtful, careful officer.

That cannot be neglected. British lives were at stake. So these two men were put through a sort of interrogation, including one of nine hours in the case of Mahnke and one of fourteen hours in the case of Oebsger-Roeder, at which certain things happened. With regard to the interrogation, I am going to submit to you, that nothing that happened at it, nothing that happened during it, can be taken or ought to be taken in any way against either of my clients.

It is not enough to say: "Oh, there are no charges on those days". Of course there are not, but I am not content in the least with that. I am submitting that nothing that happened at these interrogations ought to be taken into account against them. Why do I say that? I say that because of the Judge Advocate General's letter of 22 January, which is exhibit 18 in this case. You know it is signed by Colonel Campbell, but it is a letter of Sir Henry MacGreagh the Judge Advocate General, he is responsible for it and a very proper letter in my submission it is; I am not criticising it at all. It was brought to your knowledge quite early in this case by another protest of mine which I suggest (it is for you to say), was absolutely justified.

Having said this was a severe interrogation in his opening, Colonel Campbell brought the matter of the interrogation right up to the forefront by saying (and I suggest with respect to him, without the slightest justification) that Mahnke and Oebsger-Roeder were innocent men, innocent of this conspiracy. But of course, once he has said they were innocent men, having said they were not men of good character, it seems rather a queer joint statement to make, in a way.

You are brought up against what happened to them at this interrogation and then when he called Mahnke first, instead of saying "In view of this letter"—which I am going to read to you in a moment, instead of saying that, he took Mahnke through his evidence:

"Well, Mahnke, you were taken in and you went through a very hard and severe interrogation?"

"Yes."

"Well, I am not going to deal with that because it is not part of my case" and passing on.

You know, he is not the only person in this case who has done some prosecuting in his time, and in view of this letter, I think that was the only way to examine these men. He goes into almost every conceivable detail of the interrogation. I protested and I said really, this is a breach of faith, and you said (rather you ruled and I am bound by it and I will bow to it now as I did then) that that is part of the background and Colonel Campbell is entitled to bring it out. All right, I bow to that ruling as I am bound to, but I am most disturbed about this part of the case.

I confess to it being a thing which has disturbed me more than anything else over the weekend, because, you see, you may not have it both ways. The Judge Advocate General says he does not propose to make any allegation of improper conduct during the long interrogation of either of these two men. He will not allege that there was any improper conduct on the part of your client when interrogating the above mentioned personnel; does not allege cruelty at or during the interrogation above referred to, is concerned only with the case of Mahnke and Oebsger-Roeder.

Some parts of this speech when read in print lose the magic, the resonance of Curtis-Bennett's voice and the outrage that details of the interrogations were given as background, when they were irrelevant and were only led to prejudice the jury against Langham.

A very proper letter, because of course, in the emergency which Major Edmunds and the rest find themselves, a severe interrogation short of violence was the only thing. Otherwise you might just as well let our soldiers be killed on the 20 April without any trouble at all. But why am I worried about it? I had thought and I had hoped that by now this Court would have not only realised that there were no charges with regard to the 15 or the 13 (that we know already) but that this Court was not going to take either or anything of these interrogations into account against them.

But I found after Thursday last, Major Edmunds being asked whether when a man slips to the ground three or four times and that is caused by interrogation that is, in part, a part of physical cruelty; you will recollect that I said something about it and I was told "Oh, we are not suggesting there is a charge or anything like a charge on that interrogation, but I am just asking Major Edmunds to see whether he is telling the truth when he says he does not believe in violence."

I hope I am carefully paraphrasing what was said. I conceive it to be my duty to try and point out (maybe that view is changed already) to try to point out that, in my submission it would be very, very wrong for any member of the Court to take anything of that interrogation into account against this man, when the Judge Advocate General says it is not part of his Case.

It is not part of the Court's duty to invent a case of its own. I do not say invent, but to put a case of its own. They are the people who ought to have known their case, having had six months to prepare it, and those who write these sort of letters are no fools at all (you know Colonel Campbell better than I do) and you know Judge Advocate General cannot be forced into writing letters. They wrote this letter in January and I saw it in January and I ask you to imagine the position.

Do not think I am complaining of being handicapped by it, because if I had, I should have asked for an adjournment. But cannot you imagine that earnest, anxious, worried, and rather fussy officer Major Edmunds, coming to see me and saying: "In view of this letter, have we got to go into the question of the interrogations. I am perfectly prepared to, but it means, of course, witnesses being collected from all sorts of places". Can you imagine me looking at that letter? I expect (I am not going to tell you what I said, because I cannot say – I cannot give evidence) but you will say to yourselves that probably I said something about: we can act on that: we need not worry about the interrogations now; we will concern ourselves with the violence of the 17 which we spotted after six weeks on the case, not six months, they did not spot it, yet when we got to Hanover, on the very first day we realised as we went back from that Court on that first night, that we had to get down and plough our way through the whole of these interrogations.

If I had felt we could not do it in the time, or were not prepared to do it, I should have said so and asked for an adjournment and I know you would have granted it. I am not making any complaint – we had plenty of time out there to turn our minds (it was not an easy task, I might add), to turn our minds on to this other picture, which we thought was eliminated.

With this Curtis-Bennett was accusing the prosecution of incompetence; be look, he goes further.

I hate to use the words bad faith but I would say this that there is something very wrong in the Judge Advocate General's office, if they are writing a letter like that and then go to Hanover and producing the very evidence—which I am not suggesting is improper – there can be no purpose in that.

You see, it reacts upon you. I am not complaining about your attitude about it. It is what Colonel Campbell said, without the authority of the Judge Advocate General, that took weeks to rub out, for a poor, humble, civilian advocate like myself. It has been playing through some of your minds all the time, and I am not surprised, not a bit, but I hope that the time has now come, on the twentieth day of this case, when you will agree silently to yourselves, that you cannot, and ought not, to regard any of that interrogation as wrong.

We started off with the learned Judge Advocate, he will pardon me reminding him of it, asking questions about food in the interrogations – quite proper questions; but after this letter, it shook us to the core, those questions, and we had to turn our minds to something entirely different, and it was only through the grace of heaven, that one has been in this case very properly instructed and very fully instructed, that one was able, by getting down to it in the evenings, to plead the case in order from that point of view.

But that does not the position that, having come out to meet one case, we found we had to meet two. Having come out to Hanover, to make a defence upon what Colonel Campbell calls the 18, and when everyone ought to know from one look at the book[43], was the 17 we had to meet allegations and questions and answers about these interrogations. Of course, they were severe, and you know Colonel Short (against whom a Summary of Evidence was taken and there have been no proceedings, quite properly), told you that. He discussed a plan – he did not discuss the actual plan of action, because he was away, but he discussed the matter of Mahnke and Oebsger-Roeder with Edmunds and that he would approve of the plan of action, except, he said, if he had been there, the interrogation would not have lasted quite so long, but he did not now criticise it. You will remember I asked him: "What are you to do if it was true", as it rather looked as if it might be to start with, that there was no real belief in this uprising, that is one thing, but as precautions were taken by Rhine Army, as they had

---

[43] The guard book.

seven reasons for thinking it was going to take place, as it quite obviously might have taken place; what alternative was there but a severe and long interrogation, such as would not be tolerated in civil life here. Nine hours, 14 hours, 24 hours – I suggest any length of time you like would be justified, and it is not their job to find out guilt or innocence.

They are interrogators – they are intelligence officers; if they do not succeed, then they drop the case and away it goes. Yet you are told that these two men were innocent men. Well, Edmunds has told you that even now, he does not know they are innocent men – it is inconclusive. And what is to be said about these interrogations except that they were severe. People were asked to stand to attention – and why not?

I was not aware that Mahnke (and I have looked at the evidence over the week-end) ever said that he had not had any food during the interrogations. Oebsger-Roeder plainly did, but as I shall plainly show you in a few minutes, this memory of him sticks, because during food times, Langham was not interrogating either, so do not hold against this man what ought to be held against somebody else.

I am going to read out the details in a moment. There was no time at which Langham was interrogating these men when they ought to have received food. Well, perhaps people do collapse. You know one has often seen people collapse in the witness box, being cross-examined in open court. No one suggests brutality. Sometimes it is because they do not like the question being asked.

Sometimes it is because they are lying and find it very difficult to persist in these lies and Mahnke and Oebsger-Roeder are trained liars. In my respectful submission (and I say it and pass from it) the fact that these men may or may not have collapsed, or simulated collapse, is a matter which it would be wrong to take against whom?

Against Edmunds? He is not in the dock – against him (pointing to the accused), when you are trying him for causing brutal treatment? And you know – I hope you will have this right too – that although you are not trying Edmunds, in your minds you have got to decide whether Edmunds is guilty or not, if you were trying him in your minds yet have got to decide that, in my submission, because the case against Langham does not start, being the third most junior officer, does not get on its feet, does not get off the ground, until you have found that it was Edmunds who caused this brutality of the 17.

So, if you think that Edmunds cleared himself, or if you think he may be innocent, reasonably, of causing this brutality – and Edmunds after all is a very, very experienced officer in intelligence work, fussy to a degree who reduces everything to writing, and puts notes on the file, a very upright, honourable gentleman, doing his job brilliantly, so hard-

working that he was ill after it all, a man who had been trained at places which we mentioned in camera, and had been taught over and over again no violence, no violence, no violence. Is that the man who is going to constantly break all his learning and training and be brutal?

In my suggestion, it is ridiculous nonsense.

Sometimes it is good to descend from beautifully composed rhetoric into the vernacular of "ridiculous nonsense".

I say if this investigation had been made by the police, in the proper quarter, you would not have Mr Langham sitting in the dock because if the police had investigated this case properly (which, in my submission, they have not), the person you would have had in the dock would be Mathers and Co., not because they are other ranks, or non-commissioned officers, or company sergeant-majors, but because they would (the police) have taken a proper statement from Captain Dawson and Captain Dawson told you that Mathers confessed to some sort of ill treatment or touching of prisoners of war. For some reason which I am not going to guess at, for some reason which is hidden in the breasts of these investigating officers, or perhaps of those instructing them, a dead set seems to have been made at the intelligence officers.

This was as close to accusing the trial as being politically inspired as Curtis-Bennett was to get.

Let us see whether that can be justified, because I am not in the habit, I hope, of making statements that cannot be justified. Who has the summary of evidence been taken against in this case? Colonel Stephens is awaiting trial; the Medical Officer is awaiting trial; Colonel Short – no proceedings; Major Edmunds "illegal" Captain Van Rije – no charge; Captain Langham – arrested. No summary of evidence or any proceedings whatever one can take against the other ranks, against Mathers, who Johnson says told him he had come back from a hectic party, and, assuming he had rather been under the influence of drink when he did it, Dawson gave him a "ticking off".

If that is true, if Dawson's evidence can be true, on my submission, there is an end to this case, because this shows quite plainly that this was a beating up done off their own bats, for their own reasons by the non-commissioned officers. Do not misunderstand me. You know it is quite true that Dawson does not say he told him he had been beating up these two people, since two o'clock or four o'clock in the afternoon. You see how Mathers works.

He told Dawson enough so that if it leaked out that there had been a touching of prisoners, well, he had had his trouble, he had told Dawson and had been rebuked and rebuffed and "ticked off". It was a very clever move on Mather's part. You cannot expect

Mather's to tell Dawson the whole thing, because then he would have had to put him on a charge at once (and that is why I started by saying so this morning) could not have been made or ought not to have been made against Oliver Langham at all.

You see, it has always been our case that this must have happened by these men off their own bats, always has been our case – not to throw the blame on company sergeant-majors or other ranks but because it is the truth. You see, Langham could only be brought into this case if you say to yourselves "Well, he must have seen naked Mahnke at six o'clock, naked Oebsger-Roeder at six o'clock naked Mahnke at 9.15 or nine o'clock and naked Oebsger-Roeder at nine o'clock: and if he saw these things – he must have known they were beating up these two men and he acquiesced in it". So I say you must find Edmunds guilty in your minds, first because Langham cannot have acquiesced - not with his training and character and the sort of appointment he has, unless he was acting on the orders of a superior.

And you know I got from Mathers, that gentleman whose presence in Hanover was procured by a most unfortunate means, which I hope will never be called again in any Court Martial – that man who would not have given evidence if he had not been pardoned (and if the pardon is legal, I am not going into that, because it is not a question I can raise again here); we had the spectacle of Mathers a civilian, and he get to a certain stage in his evidence and I interposed, you will remember – so long ago.

But before we get there, how did Mathers get to Hanover? By train, I suppose, and boat, but as the result of a letter which those that wrote it knew quite well was a deceitful letter:

Curtis Bennett would have raised his voice at this for emphasis.

"Your presence in Hanover is required at a Court Martial" – words like "is required" – reaching Mathers, who has not got the time or money it takes perhaps, to go to a lawyer, believed he was required and if he did not come he would be prosecuted.

He told you that if he had known that that letter was a piece of rubbish, not worth the paper it is printed on (and the paper was pretty poor, too), he would not have been there. And you remember, not in answer to anything I asked him, Mathers, how he turned upon Colonel Campbell, who took it like the man he is, straight on the chin – didn't mind (of course, he is not a member of the Bar, who is subsequently brought before his benchers) and said "don't you remember Colonel, you said to me that you (Colonel Campbell) did not want to turn nasty". What do you think there would have happened to a wretched civilian barrister like myself, whether one of His Majesty's Counsels or not, who dared to say to a witness: "If you do not go to Hanover or Hampstead, I will turn nasty." Marched straight to the Benchers, or, if a Solicitor, straight to the Law Society and struck off the Rolls, for improper conduct. That is what it is and we have to face that fact.

Of course, Colonel Campbell can say now, as we have come to England "I could have subpoenaed him here and he could have been brought; but at that time, I think the Court were hoping to complete the case up in Hanover. I had not realised or I had just realised that we had to deal with the interrogations and all these witnesses had to come to us and so forth. And the wretched Thomas, his presence was procured by, I use the word quite quietly but deliberately, by deceit by a public department, Well, if that is the right way to conduct a prosecution, then I have got to re-learn 22 years all over again. Maybe I am wrong – what do you think of it? Well, let us pass from it, because there they were, anyway, by deceit or not, and we have, to deal with their evidence.

It is unusual to attack the prosecution, as opposed to the prosecution's case, but Curtis-Bennett deliberately did so.

Mathers, the man whom I suggest is the cause and origin of this case, who knows of the violent feelings we held about Nazis, particularly in 1946, in April—and one can forgive Mathers a good deal, you know, I am not casting too many aspersions upon him, because it was known in the prison generally as it was, and you have heard the evidence.

Some people seem to have heard, and others do not seem to have heard, they were there, Mahnke and Oebsger-Roeder, because of some alleged plot, and, knowing, by that mysterious bush telegraph which goes round prisons, and all other places where there is no communication really supposed to go, that the interrogations had not been successful and set about it themselves.

No prospects of their being discovered by officers – it was done between four and six and then between six and nine and then after nine o'clock and after midnight, all at times when Langham was carefully out of the way. Do you remember, Mathers said: "If Mahnke and Oebsger-Roeder were dressed at six, there was nothing you could see about their condition which would affect anybody but me." He said, furthermore: "If Mahnke and Oebsger-Roeder were dressed at nine, there is nothing Captain Langham could have seen which would have upset him at all."

*Now can you believe **that** man would tolerate seeing a naked prisoner bleeding or blood pouring from the head of one of them, without reporting it? You see, Mathers and Thomas having been pardoned by Sir Brian Robertson, they could say what they liked (unless the pardon is illegal, which it may well turn out to be) if it is a good pardon, but they had a* statement taken from them, no doubt both, by the police, before any question of pardon arose. That is the time you have got to take; that is the time they told their story.

Of course, they blame somebody, and they put the blame, Mathers does, squarely upon the shoulders of Edmunds. He has got to you may think. I would not say got to, but, being a human being, he does. "I did this because Edmunds rang me up, had a conversation on the telephone, and then I saw him in his office, and he told me to do what I liked with them provided I got a statement out of these people". Of course he says that. [44]

What of course may (and I am not here to prove my client's innocence I am suggesting that we have done that actually, but I am not necessary to prove my client's innocence, as you know) but that that is possible, that these men acted upon their own, must be quite obvious to all of you gentlemen.

You know it is easy to be wise after the event; people are awfully fond of being wise after the event. Think back to April 1946, think of the feeling that then existed against these monsters, who had been causing all of us so much trouble and unpleasantness for years; think of the prison, where it is known that two men are there, planning an uprising against British troops. It was going to make more widows more orphans by Brutish soldiers being killed.

Do you blame (you have to at a Court Martial – if you were trying Mathers you would have to) but as men, do you blame Mathers and Co. for what happened that day? Because you know, let me hope, that you will accept this that their account of what happened is vastly different from Mahnke and Oebsger-Roeder and probably the truth lies between the two, do not you think about the beating up?

According to the other ranks, N.C.Os., they were only run round the cells and slapped and made to put their hands against the wall and so forth, and on one occasion, Mathers shoved a chair in front of one of them, Mahnke or Oebsger-Roeder, and he fell over it, Mahnke. A vastly different and minor account of time, you know – five or ten minutes – than Oebsger-Roeder and Mahnke. Probably not true, you know, as you probably think yourselves. Not true because they are trying to minimise what they did. Might I not be right in thinking that? I think you will agree with me that the truth probably lies somewhere between the two – the lies of Mahnke and Oebsger-Roeder and the inaccuracies of the N.C.Os somewhere half-way between the two.

---

[44] The equivalent of Mandy Rice-Davies saying "He would say that, wouldn't he?" giving witness in the Profumo affair fifteen years later .

The men Thomas and Mathers, who had to throw the blame somewhere, and who are not supported by the other ranks that have been called in the detail of what happened at all, either as to clothing, when it was returned and so forth; and Mathers of course admits, not being in the dock, merely in answer to Colonel Campbell who quite properly asked him, having received certain instructions from Thomas: Did you do so-and-so beatings? That is the part of the case I came to meet, not the interrogations. That was the part of the case I cannot agree more with every question that Colonel Campbell asked was right and proper.

Yet when it gets to a stage where Mathers is obviously incriminating himself, or about to (I think he actually had done) being goaded to my feet by my learned junior and those instructing me (and not needing much goading at that), I said that it was about time that Mathers was cautioned. I suggested that it was about time the Court should take the view that Mathers should be cautioned that he need not give evidence, because it is a very important thing that he should know, having been deceived by the Judge Advocate General's letter, that he should at least know what his right position was, that he need not give evidence at all. Colonel Campbell in that charming way said oh, very well ~ give me five minutes.

You adjourned and had a cup of tea. Five minutes elapsed and two hours elapsed and Colonel Campbell asked to adjourn overnight. It seemed to me when he said that, that he might be thinking that possibly there was something in what I had said, that perhaps for once in my lifetime I had been right on a point of law. We all went early that day and my learned friend had his experts in Hertford or somewhere wherever they live these days when all the experts are out of England and in Germany) and the next morning we assembled, Colonel Campbell had to say (and he did it with the utmost charm) "my learned friend is quite right – the witness ought to be cautioned". You will remember I said so the night before.

All I can say is, if a British man can do bodily harm in Germany and not be liable to some Court, I am astounded. But away we went to Berlin.

COLONEL CAMPBELL: I did not go.

MR CURTIS-BENNETT: Then somebody else must have gone instead but away they go to Berlin and this affair is gone through. What Sir Brian Robertson and General McCreary would say now, if they heard the case now, heaven knows; how they could pardon Mathers and Thomas now we know what we know?

Curtis-Bennett takes Campbell's rude interruption in his stride after having been self-deprecatory about not knowing much law and then saying he had been right on the law.

It is pretty doubtful, should not you think whether they ever would have been pardoned at all if they knew what you and I know now. But in some way (it is not my duty to inquire into it) that great gentleman, Sir Brian Robertson was persuaded to sign a pardon and General McCreary, (an officer of the greatest experience as we all know) was in some way persuaded to sign a pardon for the military witnesses. We had a day off, you remember.

All because the Judge Advocate General cannot even think out procedure of the simplest kind which, as I said then and I say now, if it was a civilian counsel the case would be stopped, and he would have been rebuked and nobody would have sent him a brief again. Off he went, or somebody else did, and then these documents were put in and sighs of relief: Mathers proceeded to give evidence in the witness chair although it was quite clear by then that the proper place for it was the dock – and it still may be if perhaps I am right for the second time in my life that this pardon is just as valueless as Colonel Campbell's letter, because, as I suggested (and I pass from it) the only person who can give a pardon is His Majesty The King on the advice of his Cabinet.

Released from peril – you may think quite wrongly, because they ought to be sitting where Oliver Langham is sitting now, Mathers gives his story which involves, as I had to bring it out as you will agree (because if I had not brought it out Colonel Campbell would have and it was far better that I should bring it out first) that he had got his instructions from Edmunds. Now, do you believe it? Do you believe that that officer with all his training and all his care for procedure, who would not even speak to the police without getting leave of the Deputy Director of Military Intelligence about top secret matters, who hardly talked to me now about security matters and who certainly would not talk to you on Wednesday and Thursday unless he was forced by a pitchfork even when in camera which only shows what a good security officer, intelligence officer, he is.

You saw the reluctant way in which he answered questions I quite deliberately asked him in camera when he could say anything he liked (the walls here have not got ears). No, he hardly said a thing. And when the police (and you may think that is a most astonishing part about Edmunds' evidence) when a police officer comes and wants help about some investigation that has arisen because someone in the House of Commons has talked up, spoken up a bit more than usual, says "No; I cannot talk to you. I must get release from the Deputy Director of Military Intelligence" – a perfectly proper thing to do. Is that the officer who is going to order a man to be beaten up? Just think of it as intelligent men, as you are. This is a man who says to you, at the end of this interrogation, these two men were useless from an interrogation point of view. "They were ready to lie to please". You will remember that expression. He knows perfectly well that if you get a person into a state where he lies to please he is finished from an intelligence point of view. What on earth is the good of adding to that by having a beating up? Quite pointless.

One of the Judge Advocate's questions was to ask Major Edmunds whether he did not know that the Gestapo got wonderful results by physical cruelty. But as far as I remember about the Nazis and the Gestapo, it was not altogether sure that they did get very good results: their brutality was extreme and horrible torture. And of course if a man knows where a particular body of troops are and he is branded with red hot irons, possibly he will either faint or say where they are, I do not know; but this is not brutality of that order, running him up and down corridors, slapping their faces and so forth.

And, as Major Edmunds said, he is not at all of that view, that there is any point in violence. You see, violence is no good on top of an interrogation which has shattered people mentally. Therefore how could he have done - how could he, that man who will not speak up even in court about security matters, ring up on the telephone Company Sergeant-Major Mathers of the "A" Branch (you know "I" and "A" are separate) and quietly tell him over the telephone – it is not even secret; on top secret matters send for him to his office and tell him the whole story and say, "do what you like provided you get statements."

Somebody who is not an intelligence officer, maybe, but that man whom you have seen—and I called him because I thought you ought to see and hear him, in the interests of Captain Langham's defence which we are only concerned with. Does it ring true? You have got to judge these things broadly I mean. I am going to take up some time this morning but I am not going to go through the evidence A, B, C, D: if so, we should be here forever. Because I think what you want from me is a broad view of the case from the defence point of view, dealing of course with the case against me, not ignoring it at all, but dealing with it in a broad way. How does it strike you, that man ordering violence after all his training and experience in "I" matters, with an "A" man?

If you do not think that that happened or if you think that may be untrue, there is a finish to this case, coupled with Dawson's evidence, coupled with Langham's own evidence. Are you to disregard those three witnesses, Langham, Dawson and Edmunds? And van Rije for that matter, whom you heard, whose wing Langham was under after coming into the section, van Rije. Are they all to be disbelieved because they are defence – they are defendant or defence witnesses?

And is Mathers and Thomas – are Mathers and Thomas to be believed and Oebsger-Roeder and Mahnke to be believed in preference to and to the exclusion of these people? It is not a matter of balancing one up against the other and seeing which weighs the heavier. You *have got to disbelieve Langham before you can convict him in my submission: you have got to disbelieve Edmunds; you have got to disbelieve Dawson; you have got to disbelieve Van Rije; and you have got to think that Colonel Short has a pretty wrong view of his officers. You will remember the praise that Colonel Short in answer to questions by myself, had for this young man – and he is entitled, you know, to use his character and the sort of work he does and the way he has done his work, in asking you to say not that he is innocent because he has got a good character but he ought to be believed, ought not to be disbelieved at least.*

When this case has wound its tortuous way across Germany and England, and the end will come to-morrow, Captain Langham will hear whether or not his brother officers have convicted him or acquitted him of about as grave a crime as can be alleged against any officer.

Thomas, you know – both of them; I noticed that both of them (you I am sure noticed) they could not face the ultimate lie. Thomas talked a lot about the duty officer being there who if it was the 17 was Captain Langham; Mathers, not much. Neither of them would name Captain Langham: they could not face that ultimate lie.

Powerful words "that ultimate lie".

You will remember that Thomas (that is the man who is known as Robert Taylor – you will remember them – was known by the prisoners as "Robert Taylor"), he was asked and he threw his head back and paused: No, he could not remember. Well, of course, he remembers perfectly well if it ever happened because this was the only beating-up we have heard about that took place at the hands of Mathers and Thomas and others and every detail of it must be quite plain in their minds, particularly who the officer was who so far forgot his duty that he failed to report what he saw.

They could not face the ultimate lie, in my submission, that is they would not name Langham: they talked about the duty officer, leaving it for the documents to say who the duty officer was and for us indeed to point out to you these documents in the early stages of the case.

You can look through that evidence. I have done over the weekend from start to finish. You will not find these two men mentioning Langham by name because they dare not face the lie; they dare not perjure themselves to that extent, pardon or no pardon. Of course, gentlemen, Sir Brian Robertson and General MacCreagh cannot pardon people for perjury in that witness box, and if they were to say things which were material to this case, as that statement would have been, it may be that they would realise that they are in danger or might be in danger of another prosecution for perjury. They dare not face it. They know quite well they have thrown the blame successfully by reason of the inadequate and quite hopeless investigations into this case, on to the officers. You know, they just bunked that issue and let the Court assume, whoever the duty officer was—it is not our fault, look at the book: it happens to be Captain Langham, we know.

Now, gentlemen, I was dealing with Robert Taylor who dare not face mentioning Langham either except talking about the duty officer and saying what the duty officer may have said. I do not know how Thomas impressed you as a witness. I heard him in chief. You heard him being cross-examined; you heard his evidence. I do not know quite how that evidence impressed you or he as a man impressed you.

He was the man, if I am right, who wrote the remarks on the guard report of 17 April – and a great deal has been asked about that – and Thomas fell into the most hopeless pitfall of his own making, did he not, when he said that it was after nine o'clock, after the round of the duty officer when he had been rung up and told to move these two men around (and of course Colonel Short was rung afterwards). And I think it is plain to everybody now (it certainly is in reading the note of the evidence that once Captain Langham had gone away from the prison after five o'clock when the Minden exchange was shut, he could not have got through on the telephone at all unless he walked back to the prison and spoke on the internal line when he could. have just gone and spoken to the man himself.

So Robert Taylor just having to find some excuse for moving these men, having to find something on the spur of the moment in the witness box, tells a lie; says he was rung up on the telephone I think he said, by the duty officer or something like that after the duty officer's round.

He writes down this switch over of these two men; knew these moves were illegal moves, they would not have been made without the proper authority and the proper authority was not obtained. They were made, the moves, and no doubt they had to be recorded in case somebody found out 'where these two prisoners were, and so they were recorded. What is to be noticed about these moves is the time – nine fifteen, a quarter of an hour after Langham was out of the way, a quarter of an hour after he had left. Of course, we know these signatures' of Captain Langham's were appended at the end of his prison tour, not at the beginning.

A quarter of an hour after he left for some reason Thomas writes down that Mahnke and Oebsger-Roeder are switched over from one cell to another. Why? Had it got something to do with the fact that in Block 3 (I think it was) there was a cell which was kept for warders who were off duty to sleep and the noise of any beating up might be heard, and so Mahnke's move to cell 12 – or not, I do not know. They were moved about, and then about the simplest things which must have been quite apparent to them on the day all these N.C.Os differ.

The defence had insisted that the court view the prison. This information would have been from that viewing.

You may remember the evidence of Oebsger-Roeder that he had a typewriter – to put his clothes on and typewrite a document. And I think it was Thomas who said he provided Oebsger-Roeder with a pencil. Well, there is no pencil document by Oebsger-Roeder.

Why is it that all these differences arise, and they are not small differences? I mean, if you see me writing with a pencil it is quite different to seeing me banging with two fingers as you would with a typewriter, on a typewriter. And, you see, all they had to do, these people, Mathers &Co was to dress Mahnke and Oebsger-Roeder at six and Langham would have noticed nothing; all they had to do at nine was to dress Mahnke and Oebsger-Roeder and Langham would have noticed nothing – that is common ground.

We were told by Mahnke and Oebsger-Roeder that they walked out of their cell and got their food. The English N.C.Os, were not sure whether or not – Thomas told you he was not sure – whether or not the food was brought into their cell. There is no certainty in it; and I suggest that if either of us or any of you were sitting there instead of Langham you would not believe a court of your brother officers would convict you on that sort of evidence. And then of course there is the final move, which is scratched out, of Oebsger-Roeder at 0020 hours just after Langham has finished his duty tour again. It is scratched out we know, but if that move was ever made it was after he had gone round, and from such things like that, as I was trying so hard to draw your attention on the first day of this case, there is much material for thought.

These moves were being done just after the time when Langham would be paying his visit to the prison. Why? Now, if you expect me to prove a case against somebody else, I am afraid you have made a mistake. As you know, I am not here to do that. But, why, ask yourselves? Does it fit in with his knowing about it, does it fit in with Edmunds authorising it? It fits in with nothing except the view that this was a beating up done by angry men who thought these people were going to rise up on 20 April; angry N.C.Os acting on their own behalf, subsequently blaming officers who are not responsible, Mathers having already told one officer that he had done something off his own bat himself on that very day. That is the most vital piece of evidence we have yet reached.

Now, if we may turn from the actual beating up to another subject at this stage – the statements.

Sir, before I turn to Exhibits 2, 3 and 5 which I was just going to turn to, I have been reminded of two of the rather more I suggest, crushing lies told by Thomas which may help you to judge him: one of which I was coming to which is that he told us or told you rather that he told Medcraft all that had been going on when he (Medcraft) took over. Medcraft came and said, "No that is quite untrue". And, you know Thomas, did go to bed at an unwonted hour, three-fifteen, and if you look at this guard-book you will not find Sergeant Thomas going to bed as late as that on any other night. This was obviously, from Thomas's point of view, a gala night of some sort: he had been beating-up or taking part in the beating up of these men.

The other thing which I was reminded of and have not made (and I am grateful for the reminder) was that (I was not here when he said that, I think) Thomas said that the duty officer came on that round, the last round at 1110 hours, and when he looked at the book he could see it was 0010 hours. One can pick out people's evidence and find discrepancies in most people's evidence, and I am not trying to be the pernickety lawyer trying to do that, because I hope that by now you will think that even if one is rational one is human as well. The importance is that he is trying to make the duty officer know what was going on after twelve o'clock. That sort of lie (for it is not a mistake), that sort of lie is not told – one does not tell a lie for fun. He has got a purpose in fixing the blame on the people – that is to say to fix the blame before he was pardoned.

Now, to turn to Exhibits 2 and 3, there is a great danger. These ill-written documents, described by yourself somewhat picturesquely, certainly so far as one of them was concerned, as being painfully and slowly written. I agree with the description but it is a very dangerous thing to describe documents like that now that we are so wise after the event. You see, you and I now know that they were written by a man sitting on the floor who had been beaten up – quite plainly.

Curtis-Bennett was attacking the guard book records. They were confusing and the points he makes were fairly made from the evidence.

Supposing you were not trying this case but were an intelligence officer and out for intelligence information and not caring – well, not caring about anything else, and you saw two documents like these, the translation of which you have got on page 13 of the summary; they do not mean a thing from an intelligence point of view and you have heard evidence I think from Captain Teare and other people that hysterical documents were not unusual to come from prisoners of war, at this camp, hysterical documents meaning nothing. I am not going to read it all to you, but of course the allegation is made – and it is a perfectly proper way of putting the case and I am not going to say anything else about it, except that it is obviously part of Colonel Campbell's case and a proper part, that these documents were written up after a beating up at the instructions of Edmunds with the acquiescence of Langham. It cannot be more than acquiescence of Langham because Langham never caused more than a fly to be hurt.

Yet he is charged here with causing it all. But you will pay some attention to them, I know, these documents which could (and I agree, could) bear the meaning which is attributed to them. But there never was a more dangerous thing with regard to documents or letters than to try and put a meaning to them. Look how often it has been done in breach of promise and divorce cases, letters looked upon after the event, seeming to mean all sorts of things when in fact they were quite innocent and done for some quite different reason. What was it that was said? "Do write and fear no man: don't write and fear no woman." Here it is, "Don't write or you will fear the Judge Advocate General and his department or the police" who will say that not only is this written after a beating up (naturally they are right) but that is part of the case against Captain Langham who knew all about it and wanted the statement – that was the very purpose for which the beatings up took place.

Look at them. I am not going to read them, but I will read the bits that are against him, just to content oneself with that because one never does the case any good to ignore the case against one. I am happy to take it up and beat it down by logical argument until there is absolutely nothing left and so that Colonel Campbell can talk until next Easter without ever being able to put it on its feet at all.

Look at that: "I can stand this no more. I tell for the last time the truth that I belong to no opposition movement, know nothing similar of Roeder. If I am treated again like this I shall incriminate myself and Roeder with untruths because I can no longer stand this. As God is my witness I cannot do otherwise". And then again: "I cannot stand it." Then again, "I am forced to write more. Thus I must continue to write untruths. For this may God forgive me".

You know, that was no use, if that was all that happened after a beating up on Edmunds' instructions, as the case for the Crown is. It was a pretty poor result: in fact, it was not a result at all. None of these documents contain any "I" information of any sort or description.

And yet, why is it you have these documents before you at all? The answer is because they were on the file, which Major Edmunds likes keeping on a file – personally I hate them but he likes them and it is his job and not mine. They are there on the file. I do not know what you think about that, but if it is so obvious they were written painfully and slowly, if it is so *plainly (being wise after the event like we are all trying to be now) written by a man sitting on the floor suffering agonies of the damned. Why did not Major Edmunds tear them up and throw them away? No use to man or beast from an intelligence point of view. If he caused these men to be beaten up and this was the result, why on earth are they in existence? You would have thought that the first thing he would have said would be "Where are the two documents painfully written after a beating up? I shall tear them up and they won't go on the file". If he is wicked enough to order a beating up, surely he is going to protect himself and destroy these documents. Yet they are in this report, part of one of them is in the report on the Mahnke Case.*

An advocate is used to making speeches and King's Counsel were very used to making long speeches. Here, Curtis-Bennett had to go through all the evidence, putting the defence's interpretation of it, keeping the interest of the jury of officers. He would pause now and then (a pause is a very powerful thing) and modulate his voice so as to keep the jury entertained. He has to try to get them hanging on very word, and every nuance. He has to talk to the jury in a friendly style, as though he was talking to them as friends, revealing bits of his own philosophy of life, letting them enter his thought. He continued.

You know, one can almost criticise almost anything in this world. People write documents and they say either too much or too little; they never saw the whole thing. I do not know what is going to be said. Colonel Campbell has the advantage of being able to answer me back for once and I have no doubt he will take advantage of it and I have to guess what he will say. I do not know, but probably he will not say it now, but he may have said "Oh, well, if you look at Appendix C, second page or third page of Appendix C you will not find anything about the first statement in it". That is quite true, but what is remarkable is not what is not in it: what is remarkable is what is in it.

A translation more or less of that second document, a translation of it, a translation of the statement is given to show prisoner B's state of mind. Well, you could take one or the other; certainly, you could take the other and put it in and say the same about it but he took the second one but the amazing thing is that it is there at all if he is guilty of causing cruelty, because this document, circulates to some sixty different sources – not the whole file but SIR 29.

You notice the note on the bottom: "In a subsequent interrogation the prisoner B is admitted that the statements made above are a complete fabrication", which is eloquent testimony that Edmunds was telling the truth when he has told you that he sent Langham down to find out what it was about. And Langham has told you he went down and Mahnke said it was all lies and said he was tired of being in the place, something like that. If they were party to this they would never have been there, these two letters would never have been there.

It is quite all right for you to look at the real writing and say, "it is very different". I see that, but why should this man who has twenty-five live cases on his hands at the same time, is pressed and rushed for work—is he supposed to be a detective finding out exactly what is going on in the prison? He does not know.

You may think that is prison control part of the case. I suggest to you that that is a very important point: they would not have been there. Appendix C page 3 would not have been there if Edmunds or Langham were guilty of this offence.

And do not forget, all the time I am talking and saying to you that you should find Edmunds guilty in your minds first before you can proceed to Langham; and even then you have still got to find it positively proved, as your learned Judge Advocate will tell you, proved beyond reasonable doubt that he is guilty. And I do not know, I have searched long and far, and you will have to ask yourselves: upon what? Upon what are you going to base a finding of guilty in this case, on the junior officer in this case, upon what evidence?

Upon the Nazis? You cannot do that, surely: they must be corroborated. Upon the British personnel? They are accomplices so they must be corroborated. Who were they corroborated by? The Nazis. Well, you go round and round in circles like that and the only thing that remains is the thing which we brought to your attention, the fact that Langham was duty officer on this day in question.

On Appendix C comment is made – and Major Edmunds welcomes criticism. I am not saying questions ought not to have been asked or that certain lines ought not to have been taken. You are here, I quite appreciate, to discover the truth. We are trying to do that, and one of the ways is to make suggestions to people and see how they react to them. At the beginning of Appendix C "Below are given statements made by the two prisoners after they appeared to have broken completely as the result of prolonged and very severe interrogation." Then "Prisoner A was plausible though. It may not necessarily have been the whole truth. Prisoner B lost his head completely and made a number of false statements implicating himself in the hope that he would escape interrogation. Interrogation was suspended at this point as prisoners gave impression that they had reached the stage when they would make untrue statements implicating themselves, even at the risk of a trial by a military court rather than face any further interrogation". "Interrogation was suspended at this point" – and it was put by Colonel Campbell in one of those phrases and suggestions which were quite proper, that that looks as if it meant that the statements had been obtained by interrogation and the interrogation had stopped there. It is quite proper that that should be put but I think Major Edmunds said that was a mistake. You see how it has arisen. It is quite clear what was meant and you are not going to convict a man because a word here or a word there does not read as completely as it should. The prisoners have been broken completely as the result of prolonged and severe interrogation. "Interrogation was suspended at this point". That is really how it should read. Then it should go, "I append two statements" or "statements made by the prisoners, one of whom has made a number of false statements".

That is how it ought to read. He has put it in the wrong order. "Two prisoners have been broken completely as the result of prolonged and very severe interrogation. Interrogation was suspended at this point. Prisoner B appears to have lost his head and to have made a number of false statements". Then, turning over to the third page, a translation of the statement was given to show prisoner B's state of mind. I suggest it is as plain as a pikestaff, and I do not retire a bit from the line I took to start with, that he is not saying that the statements were obtained by interrogation at all; he is not saying that having got these statements he ceased to interrogate them, but it may not be well worded.

People who write as many reports as Major Edmunds does must not complain if, looking back on it and being frightfully wise as we are now, criticisms may be met. That always happens, because after all even Lord Chancellors make invalid wills sometimes. So it is really a bit hard for Edmunds, who you are not trying, that he is criticised because he used a phrase which on one view says these statements were made as the result of the interrogation; when the obvious sense of the whole thing is that here there are two men who are finished, they are washed out so far as interrogation is concerned. And Appendix C: "I append statement to show the state of B's mind", you can see he could not have included and left the original on the file if he is guilty of brutality. He would have seen at once, if he had been guilty of brutality, that it was re-written – and painfully and slowly written; but not being guilty of brutality he does not do so. All he looks for is intelligence information and there was none, and on the file it goes. If he had been guilty it would have gone into the wastepaper basket.

SIR 29 is a whole document signed by Colonel Short, published apparently on 2 May 1946 but got ready as far as part of it is concerned on 17 April, but of course Appendix C cannot have any existence then. Part of it later is a very revealing document: it puts out the whole of this uprising on the 20 and what happened and the Michael version and the other information, the Oebsger-Roeder history, Mahnke history; makes no secret of the fact that the interrogation was rather prolonged and uses the words "collapse" and "revive" and all those sorts of things. No secret about them: quite plain that that man considered he was doing his duty properly, is not it, from that document?

You see the expression used there at the bottom of the first page Oebsger-Roeder has proved himself to be an unscrupulous and apparently convincing liar. He managed to pass himself off as a harmless high-minded intellectual. He was so successful in this pretence that he was assessed in an interrogation report as likely to be was useful tool for the political education of the German nation. (I am leaving out the top secret matters in that sentence).

There was one stage I think when Colonel Campbell read that out, having said that Oebsger-Roeder was a man of not good character – he was "a useful tool for the political education of the German nation". It sounds to me like suggesting he was a good character, but still: there is the end of that paragraph – page 2 – "Prisoner claims he was disillusioned about National Socialism during the war. This is, however, a well-worn tale and it is considered that he remained a good Nazi until the very end."

Then Mahnke, halfway down the first paragraph: "It has been proved that Prisoner B is far from 'the man who feels dishonourable to lie' as stated in an interrogation report. On the contrary a few whispered words from Oebsger-Roeder in the truck that took them to camp so and so, to the effect that they should withhold certain information, were enough to launch Prisoner B" (that is Mahnke) "into a flood of lies".

Again, there was a time in this case when Colonel Campbell, I think, read to a witness, if not to the Court ~ that Mahnke considered it dishonourable to lie. Well, is their Nazi line that it is dishonourable to lie? What nonsense. He puts them up first as people of bad character, then as people of good character. Where are you? That report with its clear statements and its Appendix C, could not have existed if Edmunds was guilty of this brutality.

Now, that is documents 2, 3 and 4. And if the learned junior, who has been so very helpful to me in this case, said all this in his opening speech, I cannot help it; I must conclude Captain Langham's case properly. You will not grudge the time I spend, I know.

Exhibit 5, is it not, is the Oebsger-Roeder statement?

THE JUDGE ADVOCATE: The statement of Oebsger-Roeder of 17 April is Exhibit 5.

MR CURTIS-BENNETT: What a business we had about Exhibit 5, did not we, at Hanover. Your learned Judge Advocate seemed to think at first it was impossible it should be an original and there were a whole lot of questions fell (quite properly) on to the witnesses about it. Now we have ended the case or nearly. You see if Oebsger-Roeder in the first place

– if that is a copy it does not matter a great deal because if it is a copy then it is a copy of something Oebsger-Roeder typed. It is a sensible (you can read it) logical, ordinary thought-out document. The point I make about it is that it is not the document of a man who is practically finished by brutality.

But of course, I go much further than that now that Major Edmunds has told you it is the original. It comes from a file. I do not suppose a prisoner was given both a typewriter and a pencil; he might have been given either. It is true Thomas says he had a pencil and other people say he had a typewriter, but no one says he had both at this time. They had no German girl typist there to copy it out. As Edmunds told you, they never copied a statement in that form; put it into a report, yes, but they never copy a statement.

And so (if I may have it a moment) I suggest it is the original document (document handed to Curtis-Bennett). He has even written it in pencil the word "Berliner", has Oebsger-Roeder, in his little printed handwriting, which Edmunds told you about. He has written – or somebody has (I remember seeing it in Germany) – here is a Capital "D" for something I cannot pronounce at the bottom of the page. And no English typist would type in the word "gez" and there is no German girl to do it there – "gez" meaning "signed" and then the signature in type-written characters. Quite in spite of the doubt thrown on it – quite obvious, was not it, really (you were only enquiring to see, I know) that this is the document that Oebsger-Roeder typed?

I put it to various witnesses who said so far as they knew it was, but Edmunds has told you it is one he knew, it comes from a file. And I do not imagine we shall hear from the prosecution, who jump about in the way they have done in this case, now that this is not an original document which they know perfectly well comes from a file.

COLONEL CAMPBELL: You will.

MR CURTIS-BENNETT: Thank you very much. Then I am astounded. If the prosecution are going to say that one of their documents they produce from a file in this case is not an original after Major Edmunds has sworn on oath that he never copied a statement of this sort, well, of course one's amazement goes beyond all bounds. But so many astounding things have happened in the case at the hands of the Judge Advocate General that I should not be surprised at anything. I am referring to that part of the department which is concerned with prosecuting. Because it is so difficult as things have been up to now, the Judge Advocate General prosecutes and judges and does everything. It will be changed, as we know, soon, to a more rational sounding place where there are judges and advocates are not both rolled up into one. But if the department who prosecute in this case have the effrontery to suggest this document is not original, then it is just in line with all that has happened in this case at their hands.

At this stage Curtis-Bennett was again showing the incompetence of the prosecution. Perhaps he went on a bit too long about it and might have lost the attention of the jury, so he summarises what he has somewhat tortiously (in my view) said and grabs the attention back with the following:

Well, here it is. The man who knows best has given evidence about it. The inset we have dealt with that in Germany; there is the man Oebsger-Roeder's handwriting upon it, and it is typewritten quite obviously, as I suggest, by Oebsger-Roeder who certainly did not deny having typed it – he was not sure about it – certainly did not deny it. And the various witnesses I put it to thought it was the original, and finally Edmunds says it is.

Well, all right, let Colonel Campbell say what he likes – I could not care less. You are the judges of the facts of this case ~ thank heaven and not he.

That, I put before you as original as I say, not that it matters a great deal. It does to this extent, that if Oebsger-Roeder were dripping with blood as he would have you believe, where is the blood on the document? Or, is Edmunds so wicked that having a document before him covered in blood, he has caused it to be typed out again with no blood on it in order to put it on the file in order to try and deceive Colonel Campbell when he comes on the scene?

I mean, there are limits to what people are entitled to suggest in these courts which are just the same (you will forgive me for saying so) – you are in exactly the same position as a special jury in the High Court; you are trying the case as a jury. Is there a jury alive which would convict him? Is there a jury born which would not by now know and believe that was an original document. Who on earth – and why is it typed out again? If the man has not got a pencil, it is quite obvious all he does is to type "gez Oebsger-Roeder".

Then you look at the form of it. It is under-lined, things are scratched out, and it is paragraphed, and it is not at all like a document signed by somebody who is suffering the agonies and tortures of the damned. But if it is a copy and if there is some extraordinary reason known only to my learned friend why it was copied of which there is not a shadow of evidence in my submission.

All the evidence is either indefinite or that it is an original. There it is. Where is the blood? Which merely shows that Oebsger-Roeder is what I have said all along he was, a liar, when he said he was dripping from the head and had been hit over the ear and all that stuff and nonsense yet that was mentioned, hit over the ear.

Well, before we move from the Mahnke/Oebsger-Roeder side the question I want to go to the hospitalisation of Mahnke now. He (my client) has got you see to deal with every single thing. It is quite right, that is what we are here for. But all these letters in the Mahnke file about the hospitalisation of Mahnke are matters which concern Edmunds and not concern Langham, and they are all being treated as if they concerned Langham. They do not. But as we have gone into them as it is quite as to whether Edmunds is a witness as to truth or to be believed or not, I will go into them.

The internee hospital at Rothenberg where Mr Mahnke – Dr Mahnke as my learned friend would keep on calling him (Mahnke, as I call him) – was taken on 22 April suffering according to the sick room book from something I cannot pronounce, lymphangitis – according to the evidence was suffering from not wounds at all but some disease, pleurisy. Well, how on earth is Captain Langham to know that pleurisy means an enlarging – that pleurisy means wounds? No burning wounds, no cigarette end wounds. Burn wounds are not so difficult to spot even by a German doctor. No burn wounds.

Off he goes to Rothenberg, we know to-day, that long ago, all arranged by the administration staff, all done between the administration staff and the hospital; but still the "I" officers are taking an interest in Mahnke. Oh, that was a terrible thing when that first came out. I remember almost shaking in my shoes, if that is possible. What? Taking an interest in Mahnke after 20 April? You know, these interrogators are not lunatics. Just because there is no uprising on 20 April it does not mean you throw Mahnke away and disregard him ever more.

Just look at the letters, 22 April – and here there was made another of those utterly astounding suggestions by Colonel Campbell which one can keep no track of or cannot even remember. "It is most essential that he be kept segregated and not allowed communication with any other internees whatsoever. We shall be much obliged therefore if you will take the necessary precautions in this respect". Letter written by Major Edmunds on behalf of the Colonel, Major Edmunds concerned in what Colonel Campbell quite erroneously calls a team, that "C" Section was a team. You have heard Edmunds say it was quite wrong: they were all individual officers.

Well, one has got beyond being surprised in this case, but really one thought one had not when my learned friend said, "I suggest that you had him segregated because you did not want people to know from him or him to talk about the way he was treated". You know, it is just like telling you when he opened this case on 2 March that the date the beating took place must have been 18 April, than which there was no greater nonsense as he could have seen quite plainly from his documents. He has not read his documents, or if he has I fear for his reason because – let us turn over the page. Letter written on 24 April to Captain – (I do not know whether the name is secret but you will see the name), I.B., the Investigation Bureau, this is being written to. No suggestion that I.B. knew that anyone had been beaten up. There was Captain Dawson of I.B. whom you have not seen and Squadron Leader Wigglesworth whom we have seen. This letter was written to I.B. (I only spotted this over the week-end):

"The above-named internee had to be evacuated hurriedly to Rothenberg Hospital. It was pointed out to the officer in charge at the hospital that it was essential that Mahnke should be kept segregated and not allowed to communicate with internees. We are asking O.C. Hospital today to notify us as soon as Mahnke is fit to be returned to so and so".

No suggestion is being made there that the hospital were being asked to segregate the man so that he should not talk to other people. It has got at the bottom Major for Colonel". Why is "Major" letting Intelligence Bureau know unless it is a perfectly ordinary thing to do; as Edmunds told you himself, it was a perfectly ordinary thing to do. If he has segregated somebody in hospital so that they shall not talk about the way in which they have been treated, why is he giving I.B. the chance to find out?

On my file there are two copies of the letter. The next letter is 24 April to the Hospital: "Will you please notify us as soon as Mahnke is fit to be returned to this centre". And the reply: "This patient is in a critical condition and will report if and when fit for return". Now, Edmunds is being criticised, as I reminded you, about that. Why? There may have been many other matters upon which they wanted to interrogate Mahnke. The 20 April is not the end of the world. They still have an interest in the interrogation of Mahnke and they let I.B. know that he is being segregated, and Edmunds has told you it was a perfectly normal thing to have people segregated in this way. What of it? Why are these criticisms being levelled at his head without, as I suggest, the slightest basis that they wished Mahnke to be segregated to avoid Mahnke talking about the way he had been treated? Mahnke talk about the way he had been treated! They neither of them complained to a soul about this treatment; they neither of them complained, and, I forget which one (it does not matter which one) but one of them, when I asked why: first of all he said it was futile and then he said later on when I asked the same question again (that unforgivable practice of barristers) gave a different answer and said he had not done it because he had no opportunity.

No opportunity that on these officer's rounds, the medical officer, the medical orderly, German doctor, prison control officials! Never one squeak by these people who are *supposed to have been so badly beaten up. That is another, surely is not it, quite incredible thing.*

Of course, as I say, it was not very difficult to resist because one has got a certain amount of training behind one, but if I could have agreed with Colonel Campbell's long thought out contention that this took place on 18 April, nothing would have pleased me more; because of course not only was Langham not on duty on that night at all but it was a day nearer the 20. But ordinary examination of facts made me say, "No, it cannot be that. It was the 17."

And again, before we leave Mahnke and Oebsger-Roeder, you will remember that I.B. wanted a report, a final report about this in by the 17, and that Dawson of I.B. went over to this Bad Nenndorf camp on the 17 and that by mistake he saw Major Rowe about something else. Then he went back again on the 18 and saw Edmunds. But the point is that the statement and the effect of it and what we found out, had to be discovered by the 17th so as information could be provided to I.B. by the 17 which means by the 16 they had to have it, Edmunds had to have it.

On the 15 at 5 a.m., Edmunds had made up his mind that these two people were washed-up so far as interrogation was concerned; nothing more could be done. What was the use of having them beaten up on the 17 in the evening, afternoon and night if Intelligence Bureau wanted the information by the 17?

This was a telling point.

Of course, that would not appear so in the eyes of the N.C.Os, Their one idea would be to beat up these people who they thought were going to be responsible for the death of British soldiers. But, in the eyes of the Intelligence Officers what do you say?

I submit that it is another nail in my learned friend's coffin or, rather, the coffin of my learned friend's case which has got so many nails in it that it is, in my submission, sealed right up; not that it has ever been anything more than partly sealed up; he simply has not got a case to stand on my submission here; because somebody has caused some investigations to take place this case has happened and you gentlemen are called together, through no fault of your own, to try this case and try it you will, according to the facts and on and on we go for twenty days.

Curtis-Bennett spoke uninterrupted, but at the risk of spoiling his flow I now interrupt him. He has scornfully but forensically dismantled the prosecution case which on any understanding cannot be proved beyond reasonable doubt, but he had not reviewed all of the evidence and not informed the jury of what they should think of the evidence of others, that Curtis-Bennett will now turn to.

CHAPTER 17
Curtis-Bennett's Closing Speech Concludes

Barristers make their closing speeches in these types of trial on their feet. It can be an exhausting process, to speak on your feet for hours, having to cover all of the evidence in a case that has spent twenty days hearing the evidence. A barrister must also pay attention to notes passed to him by his junior and by solicitors and in this case no doubt also by Frank. Curtis-Bennett would have discarded most of these notes but adapted what he was going to say on reading others. It is a strenuous thing to do, all the while retaining, he no doubt hoped, the rapt attention of the jury whom he hoped were hanging on his every word. He continued:

One thing that might not have been surprising on the part of the Department of the Judge Advocate General, who prosecutes, would have been that if, having found out their dreadful mistake, re Edmunds and prosecuting him, in ordinary fairness they had withdrawn the case against Langham; but they have not so we cannot deal with it. All of us, we have to go ploughing on and you are to hear another address from Colonel Campbell shortly, and on we shall go to the end.

What do you think of it? If you had been dressed in civilian clothes and sitting in a jury box and there had been five more added to your number making twelve, I suggest you would have flung this case out long age as being unworthy of your attention and quite unproved, and isolated, ludicrous case as I suggest it has become by now.

That is the hospitalisation of Mahnke and away he goes suffering from injuries which no one ever tells Langham about; no evidence that he ever knew about any of these; no evidence that Edmunds knew about these injuries.

Then you have the significant fact that Mathers has half confessed to Dawson about touching one of these people which is the least he could do to avoid trouble if it got out in the prison. Do you remember Mr. Timmerman? That very smart and, you may have thought, very capable Police Officer, whose superiors, seemed to have investigated the wrong end of the stick here. When I asked (and it is a cardinal rule never to ask a question in cross-examination unless you know the answer unless you have to, and there are times when one has to take that risk) – such was the case when I asked Mr. Timmerman whether he had ever heard anyone complain about any N.C.O's beating up a prisoner.

He said he could not remember a name, went away to think it over and look it up and (remember) next day came back and said that incident was about Christmas time. But the germ of the thing is that people were complaining that an N.C.O in a case at Christmas was beating up a prisoner of war; that is the germ. It is a thing quite unknown to Major Edmunds or Captain Langham. So, the germ is true; it is there. There was, apparently, an N.C.O who was beating up a prisoner at Christmas. Nobody suggests there is going to be an uprising at Christmas.

So the germ of this defence which has been put forward and which I shall continue to put forward strongly and, I hope, fairly and properly, it is true. There were complaints about it in one case at least and Timmerman was honest and fair not to say so at first.

Then we pass, I think, forever as far as I am concerned, away from Mahnke and Oebsger-Roeder personalities. Mahnke and Oebsger-Roeder must remain in the case because they are the people who were beaten up, but I have dealt with everything I am going to say about these two people and I have no hesitation in suggesting to a Court of British Officers and gentlemen, not only because they are Nazis but because they have been shown up over and over again as consummate liars and you should not believe one word they say.

I have dealt now with Mathers and I have dealt now with Thomas and I have dealt with these two statements of Mahnke and the statement of Oebsger-Roeder and I have dealt with a lot of the general background. We have got to go on just a little, I think, and see what it was said that the other N.C.Os said. There was not a great deal which they said which, perhaps, helped but they, in general, certainly did not incriminate Langham. That is to be noticed about them.

Thomas I have dealt with. Lewis was the next one. He said that he chased Oebsger-Roeder round the cell; that was all he said he did an entirely different story from the other people, of course, and did not incriminate Langham at all. Brant was saying, in part of his evidence that he did not think the Duty Officer could see anything odd, and Oebsger-Roeder had his clothes on at nine o'clock. Oebsger-Roeder had his clothes on at nine – that is frightfully important because these two persons have said they were naked all the time, and so has, certainly, Thomas and so has, I believe, Mathers, Brant "Oebsger-Roeder had his clothes on at nine."

That is one of the times when he has suggested he could see wounded naked men, exhausted naked men. "Had his clothes on at nine," That is a pretty good spike in the armour of my learned friend's case. That is what is extraordinary in this case, that the only case they can make out against Langham about violence at all was waving a stick at the interrogation; waving a baton at the interrogation, taking off his coat and all that ludicrous nonsense which these people expect us to believe, and which is not violence at all but is put up by the Department of the Judge Advocate General and is said to be wrong. No evidence of violence at the interrogation part at all. The only way he can be brought in is that he saw them naked at six and at nine he did not report it and he must have been acquiescing in what Edmunds instructed. That is as I see my learned friend was putting it forward.

Then you found Brant saying that Oebsger-Roeder was dressed at nine. Well, where are you really when you find a difference like that? That is not a trifling difference. Corporal Sore – I think he was (I will be corrected if I am wrong) – the man described as "Henry VIII" of course.

MR NORRIS: No.

MR CURTIS-BENNETT: It was Brant, "Henry VIII" says Oebsger-Roeder had his clothes at nine. Of course, these were the gentlemen pardoned by General MacGeagh and released from the terror of prosecution, and they come and why should they give favourable evidence to us? Why my learned friend went to all his trouble flying to Berlin or causing somebody else to, goodness knows but I am very glad he did. Look what Sore says, that Oebsger-Roeder put his clothes on between five and six. I have looked it up because that was evidence given when I was not there. Sore had left the prison, he said himself before this, Oebsger-Roeder put on his clothes between five and six. Bang goes that part of my learned friend's case when he says Langham saw him naked at six and must have known something improper was going on. I cannot dispute every single thing the Crown say; that would mean I would have to prove my client's innocence. It is a hackneyed phrase that the prosecution have to prove the guilt of the defendant but it is true and it means a frightful lot. Well, after Brant says Oebsger-Roeder was dressed at nine and after Sore says he was dressed at six, how on earth can Langham have seen anything about it when Oebsger-Roeder agrees with him – I am not saying something which is untrue?

COLONEL CAMPBELL: I do not think it is quite accurate. I shall deal with it, of course.

MR CURTIS-BENNETT: You were there, of course.[45]

THE JUDGE ADVOCATE: My note is: "Oebsger-Roeder said he would make a statement. This was between five and six p.m. The C.S.M. gave him back his clothes. They left cell 12 and he and Thomas went in the direction of corridor two."

MR CURTIS-BENNETT: It seems he was dressed between five and six.

THE JUDGE ADVOCATE: That is my note. You can submit what it means. I am only suggesting it is my note.

---

[45] Splendid sarcasm from Curtis-Bennett.

MR CURTIS-BENNETT: *The note which I have possession of says much the same, that is why I paraphrased it, that the evidence was Sore saw that Oebsger-Roeder had his clothes on before six o'clock and that is accurate and no one is going to drive me off that because you see the point which is that that is entirely against the case for the Crown which is that he was naked all the time so that he could see him at six. Well, after all, have I got to show any more doubt in a case than that because that is the whole case?*

You see, no one suggests that, supposing Edmunds was, say, for example (there is no reason to think he is – he is a high-minded person with a good character and a splendid record and plenty of experience in this sort of thing, intelligence work) – but supposing he was wicked enough to give these instructions.

There is not a shadow of evidence that he knew about it. So, you miss Edmunds out because he cannot be tried though he, himself, longs to be tried; you miss out Captain Van Rije and you descend on a man who has only been in the Camp from January and try him on these dreadful couple of charges without, I suggest, any real evidence, at all worthy of the name.

I think I would not have said "from January" because "twelve weeks" would have made a stronger point and not left it to the jury to calculate the time.

The only evidence, other than what I am saying, the inference to be drawn from what he saw at six, at nine, are the two Nazis and I dismiss that. That is the only other evidence, the two Nazis, and an inference which might be drawn when he went round at six if they were naked. When you find that two witnesses that, at two times, they went round, one of them was not naked; how are you to be sure of the matter? You see, gentlemen, imagine what Edmunds was doing if he was as wicked as the Crown say, and you do tell something from the demeanour of witnesses do not you, of witnesses, the way: they give their evidence?

I had not the privilege of hearing Captain Langham give his evidence, but you will know whether I am right or wrong if I submit to you on my instructions that he gave evidence admirably, that he withstood the onslaught of my learned friend (and a perfectly fair onslaught as I gather) without batting an eye lid or resigning from the position he had taken up.

You saw and I saw Dawson. Did he go back from what he had said in chief when attacked (I mean cross-examined) by my learned friend? No. Then you saw Edmunds and I saw him. You get something from his demeanour. Who would you rather accept the word of Edmunds, Dawson and Langham or a couple of Nazis and some N.C.Os who were trying to cover their tracks and put the blame other people? Who would you rather believe? That is putting the case in a nutshell. I dare not leave it like that or I should have said all at this stage and sat down. That is really what this case has become by now. Who would you rather believe?

Of course, to convict Langham you have got to disbelieve Edmunds, you have got to disbelieve Dawson, you have got to disbelieve Langham and you have got to disbelieve almost everything we have heard from the defence and you have got to think that Colonel Short is a pretty bad judge of character and all the rest of it. You have got to disregard the volumes of evidence which, in my submission, tend to show they knew nothing, these two, about this at all.

When dealing with a jury (or a judge for that matter) repetition is important. Curtis-Bennett had repeated this point many times and it did no harm to keep repeating the logic of it. He wanted to be sure that it was firmly in the minds of the jury.

You see, as I was just going on to say about Major Edmunds because one has to deal with him because he is, once Mathers said what he said, he is the foundation stone upon which my case is built indeed, he is the foundation stone upon which my learned friend's case must be built because his case must be that, prosecuted or not, Edmunds is the villain of the piece. That must be his case if he gave these orders.

Just imagine, quite away from intelligence, quite away from his training or anything else, just imagine in whose hands he was putting himself by ringing up Mathers and telling him all about this man and saying: "do what you like provided you get a statement." You will understand that better than I do because you know about these things but Mathers' duty, if he was told that, was to report it at once to Captain Dawson or Captain Bennett and Major Edmunds would have been on a charge and out of the Army very quickly; putting himself, forever, in the hands of Mathers. Do you think he would have done that? I just offer that out as a suggestion and away from the much more important thing of the training, of the spirit, of the appearance of the man here.

Notice the quiet and careful way he answered questions, thinking every time, looking at the documents; no witness ready to lie for the sake of lying but quiet and I suggest, honest witness endeavouring to tell you the truth after going through a pretty gruelling time, thinking he was going to be prosecuted, preparing his defence, the expense and worry of it going on for months. Finally, the day comes when he goes into the witness box and gives evidence. My learned friend cross-examined him very properly, but he got nothing out of him; I suggest absolutely nothing.

And the same with Langham; I suggest that when he was cross-examined absolutely nothing was got out of him which could pin anything guilty upon him.

Now, I have told you some time ago I was going to suggest to you what the times were in which Langham was conducting these interrogations on the question of food. If it is of any importance, as it has been raised, I am going to deal with it. In the Mahnke case on the 13 Langham was examining from 1.50 to 3.30. That is not a time when any food would be expected.

THE JUDGE ADVOCATE: On what date?

MR CURTIS-BENNETT: On the 13, the long interrogation on Mahnke, 13.50 to 15.30. I extracted it from my notes and I think it is right.

THE JUDGE ADVOCATE: That is right, yes.

MR CURTIS-BENNETT: Oebsger-Roeder the 15, 4.40 to 17.30 – no food then.

THE JUDGE ADVOCATE: Right.

MR CURTIS-BENNETT: So whether a complaint can properly be made with regard to Edmunds or not, no complaint can be made with regard to Captain Langham about food or no food and, of course, we did hear from the witnesses later on in the case of Oebsger-Roeder, he was taken out and given food in the next door cell, I was not aware that Mahnke mentioned anything about food in the interrogation at all, I do not think he did but he did say something about food during the beating up and he had not had food then. I do not think he said anything about food in the interrogation, but it does not matter because Langham was not there and cannot be responsible in any way. In any case the "I" Officers were not responsible for food; it was the "A" Officers who were. Of course, the instructions were that interrogations must not prevent a man from getting food; if other officers did not let the people have food in this particular case it can only be because of the urgency.

I do not know what value Major Edmunds, Captain Langham and Captain Van Rije ought to put on English lives; I do not know quite what this Court think as to how far they should have gone to protect British lives on the 20 April. I should imagine you would say: "anything short of physical violence". After all, there are limits to what we can stand in this country; there are limits to which we cannot let the Nazis go even now.

In 1946 it was not so far off from the time when Lieutenant Langham and Major Edmunds would have been entitled to drop bombs on their heads and kill them and get medals for doing so; but I am not suggesting that we can touch a hair of a prisoner of war's head.

One might add you know what people who you have got to disbelieve in order to find Langham guilty: Captain Van Rije, second of the C section against whom a summary was taken and no proceedings, very properly. Of course, if the Crown did not realise this beating up took place on the 17 heaven only knows the mental process which they went through to arrive at prosecuting him at all, because if he was not, because if it was not the 17 he was not the Duty Officer and you are left with the Nazis and I hesitate to think that even the Department of the Judge Advocate General prosecutes a British soldier upon the evidence of two Nazis. What their mental processes are I really cannot track down. If they had known it was the 17 well, then, of course, obviously their mental process was they went round at those times, and they may have seen them. One understands that.

Do you imagine for a moment (I do not know – I suppose Captain Langham might have changed over duties with somebody else if he had wanted) – that on the very afternoon this beating up was going to take place he would have allowed himself to put forever his own signature at the times which might incriminate him? When you know it is common ground, very largely so, that the beating up stopped before six o'clock then continued afterwards, and the evidence that one of them was dressed before nine o'clock and before six o'clock and I think that the beating up stopped before nine o'clock – just when he puts, in an appearance which is absolutely and only consistent with his innocence.

There was a witness called French who was called during my enforced absence to do some other work in this country, who said if my note is correct (and on all days when I was away during that evidence, I am subject to correction) that Oebsger-Roeder was dressed at tea, tea being served I suppose – he must have been dressed or he would have noticed it.

COLONEL CAMPBELL: Did not remember seeing Mahnke at all.

THE JUDGE ADVOCATE: My note is "I remember Captain Langham coming round at tea-time. There was nothing odd. Oebsger-Roeder was in cell 12 at that time. He was not naked."

MR CURTIS-BENNETT: That is what I mean by saying Oebsger-Roeder was dressed at tea.

THE JUDGE ADVOCATE: I think it bears you out.

MR CURTIS-BENNETT: It is a paraphrase. I am much obliged. I have not been guilty so far of a mis-statement of fact even if I was not there. He also said, if I am correctly informed that Captain Langham was a strict officer, that he (French) had never seen a naked man at the prison. You see, if a naked man was seen on the 17 or two naked men were seen at tea-time, everybody must have known of it and Langham could not help himself but report it, *because he would be playing into everyone's hands, to go away and not report it with all the N.C.Os and other ranks knowing about it – playing into their hands.*

And this beating up was so severe of these two people that, as you asked one of them or one of you gentlemen asked Mahnke it in Germany: whether he had false teeth and he said he had, but no damage was done to them. So you get this, the picture is this, on the one side (and I am dealing now entirely with the prosecution case) the Germans tell a story of complete horror so far as the 17 is concerned. The N.C.Os differ entirely. They tell a story between which you will find the truth somewhere between the two as I have said. But it is common ground (and this is vital) that if Oebsger-Roeder and Mahnke were dressed at six or nine, there was nothing he could ever tell by looking at them at all. Mathers' evidence – and there is considerable evidence of the various witnesses – that they were dressed at six or at nine and I really have not got to go on and prove it with regard to the others, have I – or else it – and I have to satisfy you of my client's innocence which can never be the duty of counsel in a case in a British court.

Now, this court returned to this country after the evidence that I have been describing now I say "returned" came to this country and you heard some more evidence for the defence. And we of the defence were very grateful that you agreed to take that course because of course we cannot behave like the Department of the Judge Advocate General and write deceitful letters to people telling them they have got to come over to Germany and they have not. When it comes to civilian solicitors, they do not trouble to write letters like that, and there is also the question of very considerable expenses involved in people travelling out there. And you have considered it in the only interests that matter, namely that of justice, and you have heard a number of witnesses here.

You have heard Hunt – I think he was the first one called. I do not think there was much I need refer you to in his evidence. He did refer to some telephone call (I am not plain in my own mind whether it was at six or at nine) but whenever it was it was long after the beating up started, which according to Oebsger-Roeder and co was two and was according to the .other N.C.Os somewhere round four o'clock; so whatever that telephone message was, it cannot have been instructions to beat up Mahnke and Oebsger-Roeder because the beating up started at four.

THE JUDGE ADVOCATE: *He put it as late as six. I believe.*

MR CURTIS-BENNETT: *Then you had Medcraft whose importance to us in evidence was that Thomas never told him anything as to what had happened on the night before or as Thomas said he had. Of course, Thomas had not. That was left in the dark very wisely, except* the precautionary semi-confession to Captain Dawson in case anything should happen; that was left in the dark that was a lie. Thomas is telling "Robert Taylor" – that is a lie to us.

Then you got Captain Teare and I heard a bit of what he said, but he told you that it was not at all unusual to have hysterical statements from prisoners of war. I daresay prisoners of war do get into a queer state of mind, for it must have been a very unpleasant state to be in, a prisoner of war, whether on one side or the other and you have not got to treat people exactly as normal, and they are used to hysterical statements. Therefore, one or more hysterical statements would not bear any weight one way or the other. Yes, before passing from Hunt, as I am reminded, he was not woken up until three-fifteen on the 18. That was Thomas' late night out, you know, with this trouble: it was very unusual and the only night that week that Thomas stayed up as late as that. And you will remember Teare's answer about an interrogation "I can get under somebody's skin" and produce a statement perhaps later on; he said, "I think the interrogation can get under a man's skin".

You see, those two documents, 2 and 3, were produced on the night of the 17 we know now how, being wise, listening to the evidence. But from Edmunds' point of view, I think I am right in saying the last time Mahnke was interrogated was on the 15, only two days previously.

THE JUDGE ADVOCATE: Yes.

MR CURTIS-BENNETT: The man had been shattered by interrogation according to him – shattered. Why is my client supposed to think, what a frightful thing, on the 17 "here are two ill-written documents – there must have been a beating up"? That only comes now through all of us being so frightfully wise after the events we now know happened which were hidden from Edmunds and which were hidden from Langham. That was Captain Teare.

Dawson, I have really dealt with. I have dealt with his evidence in dealing with the general case, but there is an observation which occurs to me about him or about that evidence. That is this. Dawson gave Mathers a "ticking off" or a dressing down; he did not think that it was fair to report him for this incident which apparently had taken place under the influence of alcohol after what Sergeant Jones has described as rather a drunken party, I think. Sergeant Jones said, "If this was the first unit dance" (was not quite sure whether it was) "it was a very drunken party". I think he used that expression. And Mathers, covering the ground covering himself very carefully in case of trouble, just lets out a little to Dawson and can you imagine Dawson dressing him down? Now, if Mathers had not been guilty of some conduct of a compromising nature, would he have accepted a dressing down from Captain Dawson? Quite obviously, in my submission, he would not.

And really the case could be decided on Dawson's evidence? I am not suggesting it will. You could say to yourselves and sometime there is a point in a ease which really blots out anything else and it is the advocate's difficulty sometimes in seeing which that point is and that is the difference between good and bad advocacy, (people who can spot a good point and people who cannot) but if I myself in my humble capacity for advocacy were to choose one point out of this ease, if I were given by you this sort of ultimatum (which you would not dream of giving) but if you did say I will give you five minutes to address us: for myself I should have chosen the evidence of Dawson and would have said, "here is something which can really decide the whole of this case, the question being not: 'Were Oebsger-Roeder and Mahnke beaten up? But did he cause it or was he a party to it?'"

I should say to you, "I have called before you an officer of character who has not been attacked as far as I knew, who has sworn to you that Mathers on 18 April mentioned that he had come back from a hectic party and had laid his hands on a prisoner. I should then have said that the case for the defence has always been that this was done off his own bat, and Dawson in his evidence said that is what he thought had happened about what he had been told. And I should say to you, "of course Mathers is not going to confess the whole thing to Dawson or Dawson could not merely dress him down: he would put him on a charge".

If that is so it is the defence proving its case going further, far further than we need – proving its case. And in what other respects and how much further are we expected to go than that one piece of evidence, because you can go on, and I am afraid I know I am taking up a time but I am deliberately doing it; and I can assure you that the result of the week-end has been that my address is much shorter than it would have been, having had time to eliminate certain things, but you can go on and on with nineteen days of evidence and you can go on for days dealing with it but that is a cardinal point.

And I know we shall hear and no doubt the ingenuity of the Judge Advocate General's Department will not be beyond dealing with that. I daresay we could prove that Langham was at Heligoland, but I suppose they would still go on with their case that he was at Bad Nenndorf. Nothing will stop them once they have started, not even a steam roller. There is Dawson.

You know, thinking back again (I cannot help thinking back again as things occur) it was untrue and a lie of Oebsger-Roeder to say, as he did, that it was generally Langham who interrogated him, when Edmunds has told you that out of fourteen hours interrogation Edmunds took nine hours himself personally. And this camp at Bad Nenndorf, you know, not just a camp where prisoners of war are kept, as they might be kept, harmless persons (some of them are more or less harmless persons) but a place where people of a subversive nature or who are thought to be of a subversive character are taken to be interrogated by specialists at the job; with the instructions given to them by the S.I.O. and the commanding officer, with the evidence before you that Langham was a person who stood in awe of Colonel Stevens, the commanding officer and quite right that he should stand in awe of his commanding officer.

Then you finally get to what may be the next most important evidence in the case; namely that of Major Edmunds. I do not need reminding you of his evidence because it is so recently in my mind and in your minds; but a complete and absolute denial of any sort of orders to Mathers of any sort or kind or description of this nature, which is foreign to his nature, foreign to his training, foreign to common sense and foreign to the preservation of his own good character as I have told you; he is playing straight into the hands of Mathers if what Mathers says about it is true.

Coupled of course with what must always be the most important evidence of all, that of the accused himself, which you heard in Germany and which I do not need to deal with except to say, as I have, that you may think it was evidence given in a first-class manner by a young man in terrible tribulation. I wonder if any of us knows what it is like to be in a dock charged by a court-martial with the whole of your future at stake. I wonder if we know what it is like when you are on a charge of this sort, to go in the witness box - which you need not do and which you choose to do on your own volition - and give your evidence; and then be cross-examined by one skilled at the art. How easily you might fall down on the job or be a bad witness, as it is called.

You were present. What did you think of the way Captain Langham gave evidence and what he said when he gave his evidence? And there it is. When you have heard Colonel Campbell untie the knots of which there are so many in this case (and if he can he will certainly try to), and when you have heard the learned Judge Advocate sum this case up to the extent that I know he will, fully and fairly, leaving the issues for you gentlemen to determine, whether it is proved beyond reasonable doubt that Captain Langham caused cruelty to be administered to either of these men realising the doubt which it is only my duty to raise if I can by proper means, seeing that this case in my respectful submission is simply riddled with doubt on the Crown Case. If you were to reverse the roles and if you were to make my client have to prove his case, have not we done so? Supposing it Langham's duty to prove that he did not know about this cruelty? What more could a defence do than call the evidence it has in this particular case? That is supposing it were their duty, which it is not. How many more people do you want? My own witnesses' testimony, Crown witnesses helping us, Colonel Short's wonderful evidence in our favour as to character and so forth did not believe that Langham was a man who would not report something unusual like he is supposed to have seen; Edmunds, his superior officer, who does not believe he is the sort of officer who would do that, who has been attacked himself by a man who is now out of the army and has been pardoned and is safe, because that man when not pardoned and not safe realised he had to throw the blame on to somebody or he might be in the dock himself.

This was an important point. The prosecution had to prove their case beyond a reasonable doubt. That famous phrase does not mean beyond any doubt, just beyond a reasonable doubt. Curtis-Bennett is pointing out that not only have they not proved the case beyond reasonable doubt, but he claims that the defence has done something it was not obliged to do. He says the defence have proved their defence.

When the investigation seems to have gone to the "I" officers instead of to the "A" officers, when it was a prison matter and "A" officers would know about it, why did not they start that end of the picture first? Why did not the police then start at the proper end and see the "A" branch of this prison, because if they had they would have met Dawson and if they had met Dawson he would have made his statement and if Dawson had made a statement Mathers would be there in. the dock – I do not know whether Mathers would be there; he is back in England, he would probably be illegally arrested by my learned friend and taken over to Germany where he could have been tried before the C.C.G.[46] courts wherever they are (heaven knows where they are – they spring up all over the place).

But at the time when he did not know he was safe and throws the blame on to Langham and chiefly on to Edmunds – when I say on to Langham, that is really wrong, I have led myself to a misstatement of fact. He does not: he throws the blame on Edmunds, not on Langham. He shirked, as I said, that final lie.

Well, they were all in the same position, all these officers from whom statements were taken and who were lured by deceit out of the country into Germany. Long before my friend got at them (I am not using that expression offensively[47]) saw them, long before that, they were trying to protect themselves. Mathers was by telling Dawson quietly what had happened.

Now, in all the long history of courts martial and all the long history of cases of people being prosecuted for anything, has there ever been a case which has ended up with such lack of proof as this? I hope I am not seeming to be light-hearted about it because

---

[46] Control Commission Germany.
[47] Of course, he was using that expression critically.

anything less light-hearted on a charge of this sort or charges of this sort, anything less light-hearted than the mass of evidence we have had to wade through, and anything less light-hearted than the way in which this interrogation matter has been brought forward at this court in spite of what was written and which I suggest and I have already said goes very near, if not over the border, of a breach of faith by the prosecution.

I cannot feel safe about that in my own mind, if I may be forgiven for representing my own mind for a moment. One has a feeling that there may be some members of this court who may say "that interrogation was cruel itself; there was in it a part of brutality. Therefore, we do not believe Major Edmunds when he says he is not a person who believes in brutality for this sort of case".

All I can say about this is to suggest to you that there is no hope of justice being done in a case if the authorities who make it plain to the defence that their case is one thing and then come forward and present another case and the court before whom it is tried take up that other case and say, "We do not care what the Crown think: we are going to take our line".

That seems to me, by far the most serious danger that I have to meet. It is a danger I never ought to have to meet; it is a danger against which I protest having to meet. I do not mind it but I protest against having to meet it, because the thing seemed so plain in black and white. But having protested and having met it, it has been dealt with I say is that justice will not be done in this case if anyone is going to have in the back of their minds that the nature of that interrogation is something which shows any sort of brutality. You have got to take the interrogation, have not you, on the background, of what was suspected was going to happen.

It does seem to me that that is, this thing I am talking about, is a danger which I have to meet. As I say, I ought not to have to meet it at all, but I have met it. Those instructing me have enabled me to meet it by their hard work. But our responsibility, mine, is very nearly over in this case. Colonel Campbell's will be over when he sits down after his speech. The learned Judge Advocate's responsibility will be over when he has finished his summing up and nobody who has not taken a case of this sort can know the responsibility and strain which a case of this sort imposes physically and mentally upon one, physically particularly.

Then all our serious responsibilities pass to you and you will go away and consider the evidence, remembering back to March 2 at 125 Transit Camp near Hanover and all that has passed from then to now, and all you are told about the law and that I know and you know you will take the law from him absolutely the Judge will assist you with regard to the facts, and he will be the last person to think I am being rude (which I am not intending to be) if I say that "assist" is the right word, not "direct" you as to the facts. What he thinks or what I think or what Colonel Campbell thinks about the facts do not matter to you a bit, but we are putting so far as we are concerned our cases and so far as the learned Judge Advocate is concerned, he is reminding you of the facts.

The facts of this case are for you, gentlemen, and for nobody else. You have taken him into your charge, and I put him in your charge with confidence in the system of justice which brings him for trial before a general court martial, before his brother and superior, senior officers. I ask you to say that there is one (as it has been described) golden thread running through the system of our justice (it is very often said one gets sick of saying it, but one ought not to): one golden thread running through the system of British justice that it is for the Crown to prove their case beyond reasonable doubt. And if ever there were a case which has been riddled with doubt from beginning to end, and I say that quite seriously, well conscious of my responsibility, well conscious of what I am saying, I suggest this is that case.

I venture to submit that if you were to convict this man upon the charges it would be to perpetrate a miscarriage of justice, which is the very last thing that you gentlemen intend to do. If you convict Captain Langham of these two charges, in my submission you are doing so on suspicion, not on proof. Therefore, I have absolutely no hesitation of any sort or kind, wash away all the improprieties that I suggest my learned friend and his department have been guilty of I do not care about them, nor do you. Wash aside all the protests I made – and they were numerous in Germany and I feel each one was justified; wash them aside. Forget all the acrimony, forget all the disputes about this and that and the other, forget my plea in bar (I have forgotten it myself, it was offered so long ago – I can hardly remember it) – a plea in bar based upon the fact that the conduct of the Crown here is such that it is inconsistent with even proceedings against him I made that as a hint, as you may have gathered, to my learned friend that perhaps his department might think it fair, as Edmunds was free not to offer any evidence against a junior officer who had only been in the camp three months and a bit. But you might as well prick an elephant with a pin as to expect anything to get home against the department I am battling against.

So I do now what I always wanted to do really, which is a short way out, to throw Captain Langham on your justice, as the people who stand between him and officials, as people who stand between him and outside people who talk, as people who stand between him and injustice. You are the people and the only people who can do justice in this, case, and I call upon you quite solemnly and quite respectfully, I hope, to say that when you have *gone through this with as many tooth combs as you like: there is only one verdict that can possibly be returned in justice to Captain Langham.*

It is always important to remind juries (and sometime judges) that they should do justice. In the complexity of the law this simple requirement of doing justice it seems to me is now these days more honoured in the breach than in the observance.

And remember, all the time you are trying him – and that even if you take the worst view of Edmunds which I do not suggest you should do for one moment, but I suggest you should take a favourable view you have got to go on from Edmunds and say whether Langham is guilty of causing this brutality. If it were possible for me properly to do so I should ask not only for a verdict of "not guilty" in respect of Langham but in respect of Edmunds, but I cannot. He is not before you. I ask you to say quite plainly here without any hesitation at all that Langham has proved his innocence of this charge. And if you do not agree with that, putting it at its lowest I invite you to say that the duty cast upon the Crown, which never moves from those shoulders (however many more stars appear on them) – never moves from them—that he has not discharged that onus and that my client must therefore as a right, as a British subject and an officer, that he should be found not guilty.

Curtis-Bennett's speech to the court martial ended on this crescendo. Every speech to a jury for the defence traditionally ends with the words "not guilty" but this speech was exceptional. He had explained the evidence and used all the rhetoric and persuasion that he knew. It was a good speech which charmed the jury and served the interest of his client well.

Chapter 18

The Prosecution's Closing Speech

Campbell started strongly. He said that the prosecution did not accept any of the defence's arguments and that the prosecution had an overwhelming case against Langham. He criticised the way in which Curtis-Bennett and Norris had attacked the Judge Advocate's organisation and said that they did so as a deliberate attempt to divert the court from the strength of the prosecution's case. The prosecution did not allege any impropriety or inappropriate behaviour up to the time when Mahnke and Oebsger-Roeder were beaten up.

The court had heard that threats were made; there was a thin line between making threats of violence and carrying them out. "*It is a matter of the greatest ease for a person to slip over and find himself putting into effect the threats that he had been offering only a short while before.*" The court had heard evidence that Michael was offered a beating up "*if you are accustomed to thinking in those terms, how much easier for you to translate or put those into action.*" Campbell conceded that if the court dismissed the evidence of the two Germans there was little strength in the prosecution's case, but the court could not "with an airy wave of the hand disregard everything that these men have told you." Campbell stood by what he said in his opening address; he did not suggest for one moment that the two Germans were men of good character:

I have little doubt that if the situation in April had been reversed and Mr Langham and perhaps Major Edmunds had been in the hands of Mahnke and Oebsger-Roeder they might have received the same or even worse treatment; but perhaps Mahnke and Oebsger-Roeder would have had the honesty to stand up and say "yes we did it, but why not? It was a matter of national importance."

I do not suggest therefore they are anything but men of bad character. They were, as Mr Curtis-Bennett remarked, Nazis, S.S. men. We know that and we know that Nazis and S.S. men are the most undesirable of persons you can meet. But does that mean that they will come before you and let loose a flood of lies regarding the events at Bad Nenndorf in which they were directly concerned? In my respectful submission it does not mean that for one moment.

I suggest to you it is absurd to suggest that these two witnesses, Mahnke and Oebsger-Roeder have no credibility. You know and you, as I say, can have no doubt that at least in the main what they have said is true. Why should they invent that last little bit, that Mr Langham came round when he was duty officer; that he came and saw them naked where they were and he spoke to them? And I would like to remind what it was that Langham was supposed to have said to these two men. It was not a matter touched upon by my learned friend during the course of his closing address.

You will remember that Mahnke said at six o'clock he went out of his cell to get his evening meal from the table that was in the corridor, he said that he was naked, he said when he got outside that Mr Langham said to him "well you are not dead yet. Do you now wish to make a confession?"

In effect Campbell was inviting the court to draw an inference from Langham's words that Langham was referring to the treatment Mahnke had received and would receive far worse treatment if he failed to confess. It was, in my view, a powerful point. A less powerful point was that even though Mahnke and Oebsger-Roeder were the most undesirable of characters you could meet they were credible witnesses. Campbell argued that they may have exaggerated or improved their story, but that was a natural human tendency.

Campbell then argued that there was no evidence to suggest that Mahnke and Oebsger-Roeder were confirmed liars. They should be believed. He went on to argue that Mathers had nothing to gain from lying, having been pardoned. Mathers may have minimised his role, but that was understandable with Mathers not having "the education that some of us have enjoyed". He also urged the court to accept the evidence of Thomas. It substantially supports the evidence of Mahnke and Oebsger-Roeder. "*The arrogance of these intelligence officers. they ask you to say, they ask you to accept that these are absolutely confirmed liars because Major Edmunds, Lieutenant Langham and Captain Van Rije say they are. Is that a valid reason for saying that they are such liars? I suggest it is not, not for a single moment.*"

It is a rule of advocacy that an advocate should not interrupt the closing address of his opponent. You will have observed that Colonel Campbell did not interrupt Mr Curtis-Bennett at all. Interruptions by the judge, in this case the Judge Advocate General, happened occasionally to clear up points of fact.

If an advocate interrupts another during a closing speech it will be extremely unusual and almost always because something unfair has been said or sprung upon the case which the other side have had no opportunity to answer. So you will see advocates up and down the courts of England and Wales (and no doubt in other lands too) patiently sitting on their hands (or as Curtis-Bennett may have put it, sitting impatiently on their hands) while the other side make a closing speech to influence judge or jury, but alert to establish that nothing is being said that was not in the case and which everyone has had an opportunity to deal with.

It is clear that Curtis-Bennett had severely damaged the prosecution case. Under the rules Curtis-Bennett had to make his speech before Colonel Campbell made his final closing speech. That would be followed by a summing up by the judge. Usually, it is an advantage to speak last but that advantage no longer existed after Curtis-Bennett devastated the prosecution's case, forensically and with spectacular advocacy and rhetoric. To help him in his final address, Colonel Campbell had to produce something more spectacular and Frank, who had been listening to Curtis-Bennett quite enthralled, thought it unsurprising that Campbell produced "something quite unfair, and unwarranted and newly concocted accusations".

In fact, that is what Colonel Campbell did. It was the last throw of the dice, and an obviously desperate throw. Colonel Campbell suggested in his closing speech that Captain Langham might have substituted the typed documents to hide bloodstains that appeared on them. It was an outrageous suggestion because no such suggestion had been put to Frank or to Captain Langham. If you do not put a suggestion that you intend to rely on to witnesses and then coming as it did after Curtis-Bennett had made his closing speech was highly improper.

Mr Curtis-Bennett protested vigorously; I would expect no less from him.

This was one of the highest profile trials of the day and had such a suggestion been made in front of a jury today there would be calls for a retrial and the advocate might well have been severely censured. Instead, the Judge Advocate General said that the point could be now put to a witness and Mr Curtis-Bennett, not wanting the jury of senior officers to feel that the defendant was hiding something and having no real choice in the matter, acquiesced and recalled Frank to give evidence on the point. A stronger judge would have refused to permit Colonel Campbell to make the suggestion and directed the jury to ignore that suggestion.

JUDGE ADVOCATE GENERAL: *If you wish to put it to him, let's get on with it.*

CURTIS-BENNETT: *Let's get on with it by all means but let's get on properly.*

This exchange prompted the headline, "Get on with it says the K.C. – clash at 'beating up' trial", which I suppose had the virtue of being mysterious, uninformative, inaccurate and spectacular, qualities which seem a prerequisite for newspaper headlines then and now. It is unusual for an advocate to be rude to a judge in a trial, but sometimes it is necessary, and this was a rare occasion when it was necessary. It takes great courage to put a judge firmly in his place and courage was a quality that Curtis-Bennett was not lacking.

This was the final extraordinary development in an extraordinary trial. Charges had been dropped against two defendants, a key witness had run away and had to be recaptured, and another insisting on getting a pardon before giving evidence were simply some of the highlights of the trial.

Curtis-Bennett recalled Frank, who calmly denied retyping any documents or giving any instructions that documents be retyped. He also denied that Langham would ever retype such a document; they were always kept in their original condition, no matter how bad that condition was.

Frank could go further than that; he pointed out that Oebsger-Roeder freely admitted having typed the document itself and that he had admitted that the document contained his (Oebsger-Roeder's) handwriting on part of it, and therefore could not have been a substitute of the original.

I have not heard of a case where a witness was interposed in the middle of the prosecution's closing speech. Perhaps it may have happened before, but it was, in this case, just another extraordinary turn of events which made this case so spectacular.

Frank was released from the witness box and Campbell ploughed on with his speech. He did not have the turn of phrase of Curtis-Bennett; he did not have the charisma of Curtis-Bennett and so in an unspectacular fashion he went over the facts picking on minor inconsistencies in evidence. He spoke, for example, about Langham seeing Mahnke and Oebsger-Roeder after they had been beaten up and claiming that he saw nothing unusual.

"You are men of the world. You must know what you look like, what any man would look like even after a hard afternoon's exercise on a football field or any other sort of field. One does not come back looking normal. Is it not apparent at once, straightaway, to the casual observer that you have been engaged in some physical and violent pursuit? If that is the case how much more would it be the position in regard to Mahnke and Oebsger-Roeder?"

Compared with Curtis-Bennett, Campbell's advocacy was pedestrian and uninspiring. Cases are not meant to be decided on which lawyer talks best, but often are. Campbell also advanced the argument that if Mathers had done the beatings up "off his own bat" he would have taken these men into a cell and given them the thrashing of their lives. He suggested that the only way that Mathers could have got to know that these men had not given up important information was from Frank Edmunds. Frank himself had given evidence that nothing further could be got from these men by interrogation, but these men were still of intelligence interest.

Accordingly, Campbell argued that Edmunds had authorised violence in a last desperate attempt to get something: *"the last despairing attempt to break these men down completely."*

He went on to criticise Dawson and pointed out that the dressing down he gave Mathers did not show Dawson as an efficient, responsible second-in-command of the prison. Dawson instituted no enquiries about Mathers striking Mahnke. He accepted what Mathers told him. He went through the other defence witnesses, claiming that they supported the prosecution theory of the case.

"Last of all, there was Major Edmunds. What was the impression you got of Major Edmunds? He too, I agree with Mr Curtis-Bennett, maintained his story under cross examination but there were curious things about it."

He said that the wording of Frank's report was curious.

"Perhaps when he used the word 'interrogations' he was merely using it as a cover for 'intensive investigations' meaning physical violence which he had applied to these men in a final and despairing attempt to get some admission from them which would clear up the case."

Campbell finally submitted that Mathers' evidence that Frank had authorised Mathers to use violence over the telephone was true.

"Now, I do not think I have any more to say to you about the defence. The problem is, as Mr Curtis-Bennett has said, is with you. I want to conclude by saying this. Even though you may have to find the accused guilty of the charges, you may feel the utmost sympathy for him. Consider his position. He does a fortnight's intelligence course and when that is concluded he finds his way to ... DIC. You may well feel, having heard what you have heard about it, that it was an evil and wicked place. You may feel that rapidly he rapidly assimilated the atmosphere of this place and there he was a young officer, two weeks' training only – and there he is. He assimilates the atmosphere: hence these things that happen.

For that reason, you may feel considerable sympathy for him. But even if you do, might I respectfully be permitted to point out that is not a matter that is to be taken into account when you are determining whether or not Mr Langham is guilty of the charges before you. At this stage it is not relevant. It might be later on, but that is a different matter. That is all."

Those final words were the cleverest that Campbell had said in his closing speech. He was trying to show the court 'the way home' or the reasons why a nice young man had done these things – in effect he was claiming that Langham had been corrupted by Frank and that if Langham was found guilty, the jury might expect the court to show leniency, but that was not a matter for the court at this stage.

Chapter 18

The Summing up

In a normal English criminal trial, the judge sums up and the jury, being twelve ordinary people, carefully listen to what the judge says. In some countries, like in many American states, the judge does not sum up the facts at all, but simply gives directions on points of law. England does things differently. By summing up the facts the judge can (and regrettable sometimes does) put a spin on things favouring one side or another. Of course, it is perfectly proper for a judge to point out logical inconsistencies in the case, but they often go further than they need to.

In this court martial the Judge Advocate General had the conflicted role of both prosecutor and judge of law. The jury comprised officers of field rank and were judges of fact and as such could be expected to approach the facts more robustly perhaps and with more confidence than a lay jury. However, Mr Curtis-Bennett had, I am sure, virtually persuaded the jury of Captain Langham's innocence, which meant that to get a conviction the Deputy Judge Advocate Colonel Campbell would have the almost impossible task of persuading the jury that Captain Langham was guilty.

Campbell would have to discredit Frank. Campbell would have to argue that Frank escaped prosecution on a mere technicality, which was in fact the case. Campbell would try to exploit the fact that Frank was not being prosecuted and that Curtis-Bennett's protestations that Frank would like nothing better than to be prosecuted were not true.

In this court martial the Judge Advocate General was Mr G L Stirling, one of His Majesty's Counsel. Mr Stirling's King's Counsel duty was to sum up impartially; Frank thought that he was extremely biased towards the prosecution, but I disagree.

THE JUDGE ADVOCATE: *May it please the Court. This is a grave and serious charge. For many days you have been listening to the evidence, and the prosecution allege, and it is for them to prove beyond reasonable doubt to your satisfaction, the charges which are shown in the charge sheet before you. You know that there is no duty upon the accused to come here and prove his innocence.*

The case for the prosecution is briefly that on the 17 of April, 1946 (and I think we can accept that as the agreed date, though that is not the date mentioned in the charge sheet) the accused before you, Richard Oliver Langham, together with Frank Edward Edmunds, were together concerned in the matters which you have been investigating for so long. To use the words of the charge sheet "when acting as interrogators at (the) Detailed Interrogation

Centre, caused (in the one charge) Horst Mahnke, internee at the said centre, to be subjected to brutal treatment", and (in the other) a similar charge in relation to Rudolf Oebsger-Roeder.

Now, as I told you, it is for the prosecution to prove those charges beyond all reasonable doubt, and if when you come to your finding you have a reasonable doubt, then it is your duty to acquit the accused.

Now, gentlemen, only Langham is before you, and it is only in respect of him that you are to arrive at a finding in this case; but you will realise that the case for the prosecution is that he was combining with Edmunds, who is not before you on trial today. I think first of all I would remind you of what Major Edmunds said in his statement that he made in this case. It would be altogether wrong to imagine that the particular interrogations of Oebsger-Roeder and Mahnke were in any way typical of the intelligence work of the section or indeed of the formation concerned. They were, in fact, exceptional cases owing to the security implications, the information at our disposal, and the type of prisoners involved. An entirely false picture of the conditions would be created if a very special case of this nature and urgency were thought to be a typical occurrence at my section or at the formation concerned.[48]

Now, I think you will agree with Major Edmunds, who was speaking of it from the interrogation point of view, and you may think from the evidence you have heard that what he says is quite true, and I suggest that in your deliberations you will probably keep before you that the matters you have to consider are exceptional for Bad Nenndorf according to the evidence you have heard. Now I would, if I may, deal with the case rather as if there were milestones along the road of evidence you have to travel. I shall not make many milestones, but I would ask you, when I arrive at each one, to pause, look back, and then decide there and then how far you have got and where exactly you are.

Now, the first milestone I would invite you to consider would be from the commencement of relevant matters until the 11 April, 1946. Bad Nenndorf was a small spa in Germany, and you will appreciate that we are sitting here nearly two years after these events happened. The evidence therefore is stale and provides ample ground for honest witnesses to make genuine mistakes. It also affords ample opportunity for dishonest witnesses to come and mislead you in this case, because it is difficult after that lapse of time to check up and find who is telling the truth, the whole truth and nothing but the truth.

---

[48] This seems to be the judge giving evidence of something was not touched upon in the trial, which is quite wrong of the judge.

Now, it seems quite clear that the authorities believed that these two Germans Oebsger-Roeder and Mahnke were concerned in a plot for an uprising on Hitler's birthday on the 20 April 1946. I think you will be satisfied that they were being brought to Bad Nenndorf with a view to getting interrogations administered to them which would produce information primarily on that aspect of the case.

Gentlemen, it may be that you will agree that there were proper grounds for holding that belief that these men were concerned in that uprising. On the other hand, you may take the view that there was no great substance upon which these people were working. That is entirely a matter for you. You have heard the grounds put forward upon which they were acting, but I feel it would be wrong, as Judge Advocate in this case, not to express the view that even if you did not think the grounds were substantial in the sense that you would have liked them (the grounds) yourselves before you took these very drastic interrogations.[49]

I think it only fair to say that the evidence does not establish in any way that there was not complete bona-fide belief by these interrogations officers that they were genuinely carrying out a proper duty as was required from them and I would be the last to put to this Court that there was any suggestion that Captain Langham, Major Edmunds or anybody else was doing these matters other than in a sense of duty and with no sadistical motive.

Now, gentlemen, these two Germans are brought to Bad Nenndorf. I think Oebsger-Roeder came there on the 25 March and I think that Mahnke came there about the evening of the 11 April. And that, gentlemen, is why I have fixed the first milestone at that date, because on the evening of 11 April I think you will be satisfied that these two men had been brought there for the purpose of being interrogated. It is true that earlier than this date Oebsger-Roeder had been interrogated, and it is true, I think, to say that he had had certain matters put to him which resulted in him writing that document. I think it was on 3 April, which has been put before you as an instance of an hysterical document. Now gentlemen, I do not propose to deal with the organisation of Bad Nenndorf. You have heard it at great length. You know all about the division between "A" and "I"; you know how the prison was run and you know how the interrogation sections were run. You are soldiers, you have heard it all and you have had a plan or chart put in by the defence.

I propose very shortly at this stage to refer briefly to the more important characters who will come into the picture as we travel along the story. You know that there was a

---

[49] That strikes me as an odd statement by the judge; there was no examination of the evidence as to why the authorities had sent the two Nazis for interrogation, and indeed whether there were good or bad reasons for this was entirely beyond the control of Frank Edmunds and Oliver Langham.

Commanding Officer, Colonel Stephens. We have heard very little about him. We know he was acting in the absence of Lieutenant Colonel Short as the Chief Intelligence Officer. We have heard about a British doctor but really nothing to help in this case at all. We have heard a great deal about this interrogation section C which was commanded by Major Edmunds, who had under him Van Rije, Langham and Teare.

I am not going to say very much about Edmunds. He clearly a very intelligent man and he was obviously a very excellent interrogating officer. Langham is a man who comes before you with a most excellent character. Nobody can say a word against his character or his integrity. He was not a very experienced officer at this time, but you may believe that under tutorship of Edmunds and Van Rije he was rapidly becoming an efficient and able interrogating officer.

Now sir, a point was made that the prosecution said that Langham had been born in Munich. Gentlemen, Langham quite frankly, said so in the statement he made. It is right, gentlemen in a case of this kind where you have to consider the credibility of every witness before you that you should know the full facts, and I myself see nothing wrong in the fact that the accused, Langham comes before you as having been born in Munich. I would, however, add this for you who know perfectly well how difficult it is to become a citizen by naturalisation of this country that it rebounds entirely to his credit that he has been able to pass through those portals and become a British Subject. It indicates that the closest enquiries have been made into his life and his work and that he is found fully proper to become a citizen of the country to which you and I belong.[50]

Now, gentlemen, I have very little to say about Van Rije and very little or nothing to say about Teare. They were in that organisation, but I should like to put this point, that while it is not right to describe these interrogating officers as a team, you may think it right to say that when it came to dealing with the specific case of Mahnke and Oebsger-Roeder, they were acting as a combination. That is shown by the interrogations which were being carried out. And you may think, and you have been told that these three, Edmunds, Van Rije and Langham, were conversant with what was going on in these cases that they had been selected because of their ability to handle a difficult case which had to be dealt with quickly and expeditiously, and that they all three were in their own way and in their own time taking part in these investigations in regard to the activities of these two particular Germans.

---

[50] I cannot add a comment beyond an exclamation mark; this was of the times.

Now, sir, a word about the prison staff: I am not going to say very much about Dawson for the moment. You know that he was the second-in-command of the prison under Bennett. Bennett has been attacked. We have not heard him. It is suggested he was not efficient and that the state of discipline under him at the prison was poor. Dawson was his second-in-command and you have seen and heard him. Now, there are two important members of that prison staff that I would just like to recall to you – Mathers and Thomas.

Mathers is a man who received rapid promotion. There seems to be a good deal of evidence that he was rather inclined to be a bully, that he was inclined to try and dominate the prisoners, and that the prisoners were more afraid of him than of anybody else. On the other hand, you have had evidence from Dawson, who should know, who says he was a perfectly proper person to be in charge of a prison. These are all matters for you to decide but I think you must decide, when you come to deal with the story later on, what kind of man Mather really was.

Thomas – he becomes important because he was the sergeant in charge of the warders on the night in question. You have heard the various opinions about him. It is for you to decide and later in your own good time you will decide as to the credibility of these witnesses and whether they have told the truth and whether you are going to act upon it.

But you will realise perfectly well that you cannot believe them. There are fundamental contradictions which you cannot escape and which I will come to later on and on which you will have to say that one or other of these people are not telling the truth. Now, gentlemen, I now come to deal with the two Germans. I do not think, after the care that has been taken in analysing the make-up of these two men, that I need detain you very long.

Taking Mahnke first. Mahnke is about 34 years of age, and he was what he called himself, an assistant professor at Berlin and an adviser to the Foreign Office for two years, in the Cultural Political Department. In. 1937 he became a member of the S.D. He is a Nazi, and he is an SS man. Oebsger-Roeder is a Doctor of Philosophy of Leipzig. He is about 35 years, of age. He has detailed his antecedents and again I think we can sum it up; he is a Nazi and an SS man.

Now it is for you later to later assess the credibility of these two most important witnesses. I know of no rule of law or even of fair play that a man who is a German or is a Nazi or is an SS man must never be believed. If there was any such doctrine as that and if it were binding on a court such as yourselves it would be idle to call such witnesses before you, and therefore I do not propose to give you any advice in regard to these two men. Just treat them like any other witnesses. Hear the good, hear the bad use your knowledge of the world;

look upon what Nazis do, look upon what SS men do. Take it all into account, be fair, be just and be very searching.

If in the result you do not believe them or you do not accept that they are telling the truth, you will reject them. On the other hand, if they do satisfy you that they have told the truth, then I cannot advise you that you should not act upon their evidence merely because they are Nazis and SS men. But I agree with Mr. Curtis-Bennett that you should be very searching, and you should put their evidence very critically through almost a legal microscope to make sure that you can act upon their evidence with safety.

Now I do not really feel that there is much more I need draw your attention to up to the first milestone, except that I think should remind you of one or two matters which appear in the documents I would remind you first of all that when these men were coming or at any rate when Mahnke was coming after Oebsger-Roeder had been there for some little time, a plan of action was drawn up which is before you in the exhibits. It is dated 10th April 1946 and it was a plan which was to be put in operation and operated, I think I may fairly say, by the joint efforts of Major Edmunds, Captain Van Rije and Captain Langham.

I do not propose to read that plan to you. You can do that in closed court. But I think you will accept that the evidence appears to conform very generally with that plan. Some point has been made that it says in paragraph 6. "If nothing comes of it" (that is, the interrogation) "the interrogation of Mahnke will be continued until Mahnke breaks". Now, gentlemen, I am going to tell you that you will be wise in this case not to throwaway the hard-headed common sense of the reasonable man. When you are dealing with experts and especially dealing with matters of MI5, all these kinds of secret enquiry agencies, one is always being told that you must be an expert to understand it; it is all too complicated for the ordinary man. Now, gentlemen, you are ordinary men, and you are reasonable men, who generally sit upon courts martial to decide matters of fact. Use your common sense. Listen to what the experts have to say, but you are entitled to form your own common-sense views when you have done that.

Now, gentlemen, the interrogating side has been put to you, I am sure quite fairly, by the witnesses. But it is for you to decide what all these matters mean. Now, I do not propose to say anything about that paragraph "until Mahnke breaks". You will have to consider that. You have had the explanation from the interrogation side. I myself am not suggesting that it has any sinister meaning, but you will consider that in due course. Now I would only like to mention at this stage of the case one other matter and that is, for what it is worth, that the two Germans seem to have come to Bad Nenndorf with a kind of report. Apparently, those who saw Oebsger-Roeder before, Smith I think it was, put in a report that Oebsger-Roeder would be likely to be a useful tool for the "political education of the German nation". That is emphatically denied by the interrogating officers at Bad Nenndorf and they say it was fallacious and quite wrong as a result of what they themselves discovered. In the case of Mahnke it was I think again by Smith in a report which is to be found eventually in the papers, that he was a man who felt it dishonourable to lie. That account is profoundly disagreed with by the interrogators at Bad Nenndorf. In the result they say both men were deceitful and both men were liars.

Now, gentlemen, shall we just for one moment pause at the first milestone? I think you have got a fair picture. Two Germans under suspicion being brought to Bad Nenndorf for interrogation. Nothing very difficult in this part of the case and I think there is really almost a common agreement between the prosecution and the defence and there I propose to leave this part of the case with the two men in custody at Bad Nenndorf on the evening of 11 April 1946.

Now, gentlemen, I want you to come with me and proceed to the second milestone, which I think might be taken as five o'clock on the morning of 16 April. This is a rather more difficult piece of the case but not the most difficult. And now I propose to deal briefly, shortly, with the evidence which relates to that time.

First of all, I would remind you of what Mahnke told us, very shortly. He said that he was first questioned in the interrogation cell by three officers one of whom was Captain Langham, on the night of 11 April, when he arrived. I do not think anything turned upon that interrogation. On the 12 April, the next day, he was interrogated by Langham, and certain matters occurred which I am not going into at this moment. And then, gentlemen, we come, according to Mahnke, to the long interrogation of 13 April, which started about two o'clock in the afternoon. I do not propose to go into it as far as the evidence of Mahnke is concerned. The only thing he said, which affected Captain Langham, if you believe it, is that Captain Langham' stood in front of him, took off his coat, used a sort of boxing stance but did not hit him. I think, gentlemen, also I should remind you that after this long interrogation of the 13 Mahnke was interrogated by, I think it was Captain Van Rije, on the 15 April from 10.30 in the morning until 12.30 and again in the afternoon from 2.15 to 4.30.

Now Mahnke was dealt with, as I say, in a long interrogation on 13 April. Oebsger-Roeder's version is that he was interrogated at one time by Major Edmunds. This was earlier on when he came to Bad Nenndorf and then Edmunds said to him "Your life must be ended and you are going to be hanged. You have only the chance of easing that by making a full *confession. You must give us all particulars of the so-called Frei Battalion. You are now in the hands of the British Secret Service. You know what that means." And then he pointed to a thick file, the confessions of his accomplices, and showed him certain sentences.*

He said that Captain Langham was present and he used the words "he was very annoyed and he said we have all the necessary means to break your silence." He said that at that time or later Captain Langham warned him that his wife and child were in prison and that something would happen to them if he did not tell what was wanted. He was questioned and he denied knowing anything about it.

Then, I think, gentlemen, we can come to the long interrogation which took place on the 15 April. We now come to what we call the long interrogation which lasted for a matter of 14 hours. In the case of Mahnke we know that it was 9 hours. I do not propose to deal with that interrogation in its details because you will find they are all shown very fully in the files of Oebsger-Roeder and Mahnke; but it is common ground that they were very severe interrogations, that they were prolonged and they were intended to be, and their object was: to get out from these men as quickly as possible and as soon as possible information in regard to this (up)rising.

Now, gentlemen, you have been accustomed to deal with confessions at courts martial, and you know how that is hedged round and you never hear of one unless it is proved that it was a voluntary confession. Now please do not be led away by that in this case. I think you will accept that these officers were entitled, and it was their duty, to put severe pressure on these two men to get interrogation information. They were going, you may think perhaps, to the extreme limits of what they were allowed to do by carrying on interrogations in relays for 9 or 14 hours, but, gentlemen, I think you will take the view that they were entitled to use severe methods but not to use physical violence, which was absolutely prohibited according to the rules and regulations at Bad Nenndorf, and no violence of a physical nature was used in these interrogations at all by Captain Langham, by Major Edmunds or by Captain Van Rije.

Some little criticism has been made by one or two witnesses about these interrogations. But it is accepted by the prosecution that what was done was not wrong in the sense that it could be made the subject of any criminal charge; it is accepted by the prosecution that nothing that was done there was wrong in the sense that it should be punished in any criminal court, and no charge whatsoever has been made in respect of that and you know that.[51]

At one time it seemed to me that an objection was being made by the defence to the admissibility of what was going on during these long and severe interrogations. I myself did not quite understand that because it seemed to me essential for the defence, for their own defence, to show that there was a long and severe interrogation because on that many other matters were founded which are very necessary for the defence.

It was because there was this long and severe interrogation that the defence largely say there were hysterical notes later. It was largely because of this that you get references into S.I.R. 29 that you have heard. And in my view, there can be no question at all that justice in this case could never have been administered unless you had the whole picture and dealt with it not from the point of view of convicting Langham or using it as a lever to say that he was a cruel and ruthless man on these occasions, therefore that adds weight to what may have happened on the 17. Not for that purpose at all and I know you will not use it for that purpose. But, gentlemen, it seems to me you must have it to understand the story; the defence must have it for the purposes that I have outlined to you.

Now, gentlemen, there were these long and severe interrogations, and they produced no results, no results from the point of view of the interrogation section, and I think it is true to say that Major Edmunds was taking the view (and after all he was in command of this section) that at the end of the interrogation of Oebsger-Roeder at the end of 14 hours and at the end of 9 hours of Mahnke, they had used all legitimate methods and had failed from the interrogation point of view. And therefore at 5 o'clock on the morning of the 16 April they were arriving at the view that from the interrogation point of view there was nothing more that could be done in regard to this matter of the alleged uprising on the 20 April.

Now we seem to be approaching what I have called the second milestone. Is it fair and is it right to say that by the morning of the 16 April Mahnke and Oebsger-Roeder were perfectly fit and well, that they had been severely interrogated and that they had made no statements of any use so far as the matter with which they were alleged to be concerned; that the section as accepting that point of view and did not want to have any more to do with them unless they were prepared to come forward with some more specific information on this point?

Now, gentlemen, let me make it quite clear that nobody suggests, nor is there a scrap of evidence to show, that up to that time any violence of any sort had been used either with or

---

[51] The implication must be that the interrogation was morally wrong.

without the connivance of Major Edmunds or Captain Langham in respect of either of these two Germans.

Gentlemen, that seems to me to have got us to about 16 April with a reasonably clear picture of what the position was, and now we come to travel along to what I call the third milestone, and, gentlemen, this is the really difficult stretch that you have go along. It is controversial, there are absolutely flat contradictions between witnesses, there is a good deal of confused evidence, and you may think there is a good deal of lying. The stretch between the second and third milestones is of vital importance in deciding this case. And I will take that stretch to be up to the morning of 18 April.

Now, it is difficult really to decide where to start, but I think perhaps it would be simplest to start with the story told by Mathers, because that seems to me to be rather the point at which this story starts.

He says he saw Major Edmunds on this day, and he had a conversation. He then said that about 4 o'clock in the afternoon he was in the prison and he was telephoned by Major Edmunds. Gentlemen, this is a question of fact. He says that Major Edmunds told him that he had tried to get information from these people that he had not got it, and that he (Edmunds) told Mathers to try and see what he could do, and that he could do whatever he liked provided he got the necessary information.

Now, gentlemen, that means, does it not, if you should accept it, very clearly that Edmunds is telling Mathers to use violence, not by way of revenge but for the specific purpose of getting information from these two people, and you know what it is. Mathers swears that to be true. On the other hand, Major Edmunds says it's quite untrue. And there you have the conflict between the two witnesses.

Now, sir, I want to say here and now that because a witness gives evidence for the prosecution that does not mean he is a better witness or to be more relied on than a witness for the defence, and equally, gentlemen, you should not disbelieve Captain Langham merely because he is the accused in this case. He is entitled to have the same careful, fair appraisement of his evidence like anybody else.

Well, now, did that happen or not, is for you to say. There, does not seem to be any other evidence, direct evidence bearing on the point. We know that there were some curious moves taking place from cell to cell on this date. I use the word "curious" because we have never been able to get any very satisfactory explanation of why they occurred. The Court later on can consider, and they may be able to find a solution. We have been told by Captain Dawson that moves might be approved before they took place in view of a certain eventuality.

We have also been told that it is a prison matter to make these moves and not one for the "I" though the "I" people are consulted.

Now, you remember, that in the guard-book there was a move of Oebsger-Roeder, I think it was at 2.40 in the afternoon, into cell 12. That is rather earlier, as you see, than four o'clock, but if you believe Mathers as the result of this telephone conversation with Edmunds he said that he went to cell 37 with Thomas, that they stripped Mahnke naked and they doubled him round the cell and they slapped him and they then went to cell 12 where Oebsger-Roeder was and ill-treated him; so if that is right it was after the move that is shown in the book of Oebsger-Roeder.

Mathers then says, "About five or five thirty after tea I saw Mahnke in cell 37" and they ill-treated him again. Then he says he thinks he probably went to see Oebsger-Roeder and then he goes home to his billet. He claims to have returned to the prison again about seven or seven-thirty, and that he went to cell 37 where there was more ill-treatment of Mahnke. Then he thinks that they probably ill-treated Oebsger-Roeder again: then he had a discussion with Thomas about the case; and then he says he left the prison to go to this camp dance.

Now, the camp dance has been described, if it is the one, as rather a drunken one, and the suggestion is that Mathers may have taken too much to drink and came back in rather a fighting mood. He comes back (according to Mathers) to the prison about midnight or half past twelve and he goes to cell 37 in which Oebsger-Roeder has now been moved, because you know according to the guard-book at nine fifteen there had been this switch-over between the two Germans. He says that when he went to cell 31 Oebsger-Roeder was sitting in the cell fully dressed, typing. Then he goes to cell 12 where Mahnke is naked - and then I think perhaps I should read to you what he says:

"I first spoke to Mahnke and he replied. After the conversation was over we took Mahnke into the corridor. There was a table in the centre of the corridor, a dinner table. Mahnke was naked in the corridor and we doubled him up and down the corridor. I was in the centre by the table; Thomas was at one end, someone else at the other end; and we ran him from end to end. I pushed him but did not use the table so far as I can remember. Mahnke collapsed and fell down; he tripped over a chair; I pushed the chair in his way and he fell over. I and someone else pushed him under the shower in the corner. We carried him there. I put him in the sink. The water was turned on, a few seconds. I saw brushes and mops. I put one of the mops in the water and put water over Mahnke. I deny that the mops were used in any other way".

Then he took Mahnke back to the cell. Mahnke then wrote out a statement. He probably gave him paper and pencil:

> "I think he was still in the cell naked. I cannot remember whether he was on the floor or not. I probably took the paper from him. I looked at it. I thought that Mahnke was still withholding the necessary evidence. I could not read German, but I thought the statement was too short. I then spoke to Mahnke and he wrote out another statement.
>
> He probably had several pieces of paper. I think I and Thomas took this first piece of paper to the guard commander's room and put it on the table. I went back to the cell after this and spoke to Mahnke and gave him more paper and he wrote another statement. Mahnke was still naked.
>
> I cannot swear if Exhibit 3 is the paper. I took the paper from Mahnke and looked at it. I was still dissatisfied and so more was written on the paper. I stayed there and Mahnke was given back his clothing. I then took the paper to the guard commander's room and left the building.
>
> I left the papers, the two papers, together as far as I can recollect. I left Thomas in the guardroom with these papers and I only remember two statements, and I never saw the documents after that time."

Now, gentlemen, it seems to me quite clear that Mathers is telling you a story of how he was trying by force to obtain statements from both Mahnke and Oebsger-Roeder. Now, what had Captain Langham to do with it according to Mathers? He says as far as he can recollect Mahnke was naked when he was getting his food at six o'clock, but he said that the duty officer, he thought, was not present at that time. He says that he (Mathers) did not see Oebsger-Roeder get food on the occasion at six o'clock, and I think he also (to sum up his evidence) was saying that on this occasion he never saw the duty officer at all.

Now, that very shortly is Mather's version of what was happening so far as he can tell you on the afternoon and evening of 17 April. It does not in my view go any further to show that the crime alleged in the charge sheet was committed. It does not seem to me, Mathers' evidence as I have detailed it, to implicate Captain Langham by showing that at this time he was there having an opportunity to see Oebsger-Roeder and Mahnke in a naked condition.

Let me deal now (and it was very long) with the evidence of Sergeant Thomas. He was the sergeant in charge of the warders at Bad Nenndorf from, I think, nine o'clock in the morning of 17 April until nine o'clock in the morning of 18 April. He says that he was in the prison about four o'clock and he says that Company Sergeant Major Mathers came to him and spoke to him. Gentlemen, I think you are entitled so far as the case for the prosecution is concerned to say that presumably he is representing that after the Company Sergeant Major had had his talk with Major Edmunds, he came to him (Thomas) and spoke to him.

And he says that they went to cell 37 where Mahnke was, about four-thirty and they ill-treated him, and that he was naked; that they then visited cell 12 and stripped Oebsger-Roeder. Then he says he went back to Mahnke to see if he had written anything, and found him sitting naked on the floor, and he started slapping him again. It is clear, is it not, gentlemen, that a certain amount of violence (and it is for you to decide) had been administered to both Oebsger-Roeder and Mahnke between four o'clock and six o'clock, and that the object of that violence, if you believe it, was to try and get statements out of these two men.

The next thing that happens so far as Thomas is concerned is the arrival of the duty officer to supervise the meals about six o'clock. Now, it was the duty of Thomas to go round with the duty officer, and I am not going to detail exactly what the duties of the duty officer were. You have heard them. But Thomas's version of what happened is this: I met the duty officer, and we went to corridor 1, and we supervised the distribution of the food. Then we went to corridor 5 and 6, then to corridor 2, and then to corridor 3, where Mahnke was. He says that Mahnke had his evening meal either in the corridor or the cell and he says he saw Mahnke with food in his cell but could not say where he got it. He thinks that at that time Mahnke was naked, and he says the duty officer was with him when they left corridor 3.

They then went to corridor 1, as I have said, where Oebsger-Roeder was in cell 12. He says he cannot tell you how Oebsger-Roeder got his food, but he is quite positive that at this time Oebsger-Roeder was naked.

Now, that is Thomas's version of what happened at the evening meal about six o'clock. It is common ground that Captain Langham was the duty officer and that he must have been there. It is for you to decide on the evidence what Langham saw and what he did; but it is accepted by the defence, although Langham has no recollection specifically about this particular six o'clock meal in the case of either man, that he must have been there and that he must have supervised.

But Langham on his oath says that at this time, looking back, there was nothing of any shape or kind which occurred to cause him to be curious in any way. He tells you quite frankly that he would not have tolerated any violence, that if he had seen any violence or sign of violence it would have been his duty to report it and he would have to report it; that if he had seen people running about naked, he would have at once said to Thomas "What is the meaning of this? Have that man clothed at once" and probably considered whether he would put him on a charge or report him to prison control.

Well, gentlemen, that is the defence of Captain Langham so far as part of the prosecution case is concerned: that he was there and he denies that any of these matters about which Thomas speaks, occurred to his knowledge, and therefore he cannot remember anything about them. He is quite positive that be saw no ill-treatment and that he saw no naked person.

Now, apparently after this Thomas goes without Mathers back to Oebsger-Roeder, and he ill-treated him again until he was exhausted, but Oebsger-Roeder wrote nothing in the form of a statement. Then went back to Mahnke, he says, who was naked and he ill-treated him again. Now, I would like to read at this point part of the evidence he gave:

"I went on to Mahnke with the same people. Mahnke was still naked. We pushed him around the cell making him run; we slapped him to get up and down on the floor for fifteen minutes. He was panting a bit; he did not look so bad as Oebsger-Roeder. I had to return to my normal duties, so I stopped this. I left the cell and Mahnke was still in it naked. I went to see Corporal Brant in the guardroom at the end of the corridor. I spoke to him and then I went to cell 12 with a warder I think. Oebsger-Roeder was standing in his cell. Mathers was not there. He was naked and was standing to attention. I spoke to Oebsger-Roeder and he replied. I then started slapping him again and this went on for about ten minutes." (He puts this time at somewhere about seven o'clock)

"We tried to make him exhausted and we kept on giving him kidney punches. I left Lewis in the doorway. I went back to my office leaving Oebsger-Roeder naked. The Company Sergeant Major came back some time before eight o'clock and we went together to cell 37. Mahnke was there naked, standing to attention, and there was no sign of his clothes. We spoke to him, made him run round the cell, slapped him on the back, pushed him, stood him against the wall, knocked his chin with my hand underneath, questioned him but he would not answer.

I went on slapping him. He seemed a bit fatigued; he was dishevelled, and his hair was all over his face, but he was not bleeding and I did not notice any scratches. I left Mahnke with a warder to whom I gave instructions, and Mahnke was still left naked.

About eight o'clock I went to cell 12. Oebsger-Roeder was there still naked with no clothes still standing against the wall with his hands up. The warder was watching him, the warder was off duty. We questioned him and then started slapping him again. He was against the wall; he ran round. We slapped him again and he fell down (and so on). He became so exhausted he fell down, and we pulled him up. He was dishevelled, dirty and his hair all over the place.

I then went to cell 37" (he puts this at about 8.30 or 8.35) "Mahnke was still there naked. I was alone. I went in. Mahnke was standing to attention by himself. I spoke to him and then started slapping him, pushed him around, and when I left the cell, he was still naked."

Now, sir, there can be no doubt, I should have thought that both these men had been subjected to a certain amount of violence between four o'clock and six o'clock, and then very much more considerable violence between six o'clock and nine o'clock. And one of the matters you will have to consider is whether Thomas and Mathers are telling the truth.

They have made statements as you know, regarding these matters long before this case came to trial, long before Major Edmunds dropped out; and they have certainly incriminated themselves by showing a course of conduct which they agree they committed, and which surely is cruel and disgraceful. It is surely disgraceful and surely it is cruel, even in the case of another rank.

And I think, gentlemen, your task on this part of the case should be a simple one. Having heard (and I have only got as far as nine o'clock on the night of the 17 April), having heard this long and horrible story of what was happening to these two men, are you not satisfied, if you believe that it is substantially true, that there was brutality of a kind which was absolutely forbidden to be used at Bad Nenndorf, that it was something which can properly be described as brutal, disgraceful and cruel, that its object was to force these people to make a statement in regard to the uprising and that there can be no doubt at all that these N.C.O.s have been guilty of a very brutal course of conduct lasting over a long period?

Now, gentlemen, it would be opportune perhaps at this moment to remind you that the charge against Captain Langham is that he was guilty of disgraceful conduct of a cruel kind, and I think we may very well dispose of that. I think Captain Langham and his learned counsel would not contest for one moment that if this was going on and he was a party to it, in the position of an officer who was there on duty with the power to step it, that that could properly be called disgraceful conduct of a cruel kind. But, gentlemen, that is a military charge, and it is for you later on to decide whether or not it comes within that description.

Now you will ask yourselves, gentlemen, (and this is one important question in the case): Why should these N.C.O.s take part in this beating up?[52] I am going to deal with it later when I have completed what happened later on in the evening but that is one of the important questions which you will have to consider in this case. If you do not believe that substantially what they say occurred, then, gentlemen, of course you will act accordingly; but as reasonable men—and I think we who have been engaged in this case are all well aware that there must undoubtedly have been this savage cruel and long sustained beating up occurring in fact at Bad Nenndorf between roughly four o'clock and midnight of 17 April.

Gentlemen, you have in addition to the story of the warder the evidence of Mahnke; you have the evidence of Oebsger-Roeder covering these same periods. And I think perhaps before I deal with that it would be better to dispose entirely of the evidence of Thomas. Now, what inference are you going to draw about the visit of Captain Langham at six o'clock? You have heard what Thomas has to say. There is the conflict which I pointed out between Langham and Thomas.

The next time we have to consider so far as Captain Langham is concerned is nine o'clock. Thomas says he waited for the duty officer who came before nine O' clock. This time they went to corridor 1. The door of cell 12 was open.

"The duty officer and I stood in the doorway. Oebsger-Roeder answered his name. The lights were on. Oebsger-Roeder was sitting on the floor. He got up: he was dirty, with matted hair, he looked tired and he was naked. I cannot remember if the duty officer said anything about this. I went to corridor 3 with the duty officer to cell 37. The door was opened by a warder. The duty officer and I stood in the doorway. Mahnke stood to attention; he answered his name. He was dirty, he was dishevelled and in much the same state as Oebsger-Roeder. We stood there for a few seconds. I think there was a conversation between Mahnke and the duty officer or with me about a statement just as we were leaving the cell, and then the duty officer left about nine o'clock."

Now, gentlemen, again I think I can be quite fair to Captain Langham if I remind you that his answer to this is, as it was at six o'clock: "This was a routine going round. I saw nothing of this kind at all. If I did, I would have taken action, and I cannot do any more than come along and go in the witness box and deny that I saw that Thomas says." Gentlemen, there is a matter of great importance in your deliberation. Thomas is picturing a story of a

---

[52] The inference here seems to be that the NCOs would only act in this way if ordered to do so.

man naked, two men, dirty and dishevelled, tired, and so on. If you believe that, then clearly Captain Langham was seeing a picture which should have caused him to take immediate action if he were performing his duty in a proper way and there was no ulterior reason for him doing otherwise. Those are your responsibilities, gentlemen.

Nobody can help you about that, Mr. Curtis-Bennett, the Prosecutor or myself. You have to shoulder the responsibility for these decisions, you and you alone. But there you have a conflict of fact which is of great importance to Captain Langham. Now, let us go on with the story of Thomas. We get (all this, gentlemen, I have been speaking about seems to have occurred before nine o'clock on the evening of 17 April) - then we get this rather puzzling and in some ways intriguing matter of the entry in the book which we have all accepted apparently as being an accurate entry, the switch-over at nine-fifteen of Oebsger-Roeder and Mahnke.

Now, it is quite clear, gentlemen, that this switch-over took place with the knowledge and on the instructions of Sergeant Thomas, if you believe him. He says, "I gave orders for it. I do not really remember whether I supervised it, but I gave orders for it, and as I was performing (as I thought) a perfectly proper authorised duty I entered it in the book and I entered it at the time."

And there is the book, gentlemen is that entry by Thomas which he claims to have been making at the proper time. It is a record made at the time and it is a record which shows exactly what was happening. It is placing on record a matter which you may think had it been observed by Captain Dawson at the time might have produced important results. But there was no secrecy apparently by Thomas or no attempt not to put it into the official record and then if it was found out say "Oh, I forgot".

Well, gentlemen, we were all interested in why Thomas did this and we asked him. "Why did you make this switch-over when you were on duty? What was your authority for it"; and rightly or wrongly he says. "I got instructions to change over these men from the duty officer after he had left. I believe on the telephone. I satisfied myself at the time that it was the duty officer speaking and because I thought it was a proper order coming to me from an officer, I carried it out".

Gentlemen whether he got that as he says or not, I do not know; but the defence have tried to show (and I think, with considerable force) that it would be impossible or next to impossible for you to decide that a telephone call came in that way from outside once the switchboard had ceased to be manned at seven o'clock – or whenever the time was but in any event this is much later than that time. Having got this order, as he says, he then made the switch in the cells.

Now I think perhaps I should once again read a little more, and I shall not read much more after this, of the evidence of Thomas:

"I think I went to cell 12 alone. I questioned Mahnke in the cell. He was naked. I ran him round. He did not seem exhausted but then he did fall down and I assisted him up. I still left him naked standing to attention. The warder may have been left with him. I went to cell 37. Oebsger-Roeder was now in it. He was standing up naked. There were three of us in the cell. We started slapping him again and running him round, all over his face and body. He was very dirty and dishevelled and tired. I left the cell. Oebsger-Roeder was still naked. A warder was left watching him. I went to the guard office. I took a foolscap paper and pencil to cell 37 to Oebsger-Roeder. He was standing shivering in the cell watched by a warder. I spoke to Oebsger-Roeder and gave him paper and pencil and left the cell. I left the warder in the cell and I left him a chair so that he could write on. I then went to cell 12 to Mahnke with the warder. Mahnke was standing up with no clothes, I spoke to him; he replied. We started slapping him again. He was dirty and dishevelled, and I left the cell, and I cannot remember seeing Mahnke's clothing. I went to the guardroom and made out a report. Then the company sergeant-major came in just about midnight or just after. We proceeded to cell 12. I spoke to Corporal Brant who went away. The Company Sergeant Major and I entered the cell. Mahnke was still naked. We started hitting and slapping him. He collapsed on the floor after twenty minutes. We dragged him under the shower next door. We pulled him by the arms, put him in the sink turned on the water just to make him wet. Nothing happened then other than that water was on him. We made him run up and down the corridor, I at one end and the C.S.M. at the other. He fell over several times. He was tripped up on several occasions by the Company Sergeant Major and myself. We ran with him, pushing him; we tripped him up in the centre two or three times. The C.S.M. placed a chair in front of him, the chair by the table, and on several occasions he pushed it at him. Each time he collapsed we put him under the shower. We put him under some three or four times. We kept him under the shower until he was freezing for about four minutes. The company sergeant major took a wet mop in front of his face. Mahnke did not like being under the shower and kept on calling out. We ran him up and down the corridor and he collapsed. We turned the water off eventually and he spoke to us. We took him back to his cell and gave him a pencil and paper with a carbon. Mahnke was very exhausted and naked. He wrote on the floor on the rubber matting. I watched him. He wrote three or four lines. It was not enough. I took this piece of paper back to the office. I cannot say who took it. We ran him up and down for a quarter of an hour or so and he collapsed again and we had to put him under the shower. He could not stand on his feet, so we took him into the cell and we left him in the cell. I believe I had paper and pencil placed in the cell, I or another warder. I then went back to 37 where Mahnke was and spoke to him. I then went to Oebsger-Roeder's cell with the company sergeant-major. Oebsger-Roeder was writing on foolscap paper on a chair alone, still naked. I spoke to him. He replied and I left him writing. He had several pieces of paper and we took nothing out of his cell."

To go on, he said:

"I waited for the duty officer. We left together to go to corridor 1 to cell 12. The door was open. The duty officer and I stood in the doorway. Mahnke was naked, almost unconscious. He could not stand up. We were about two minutes at the door.
I believe Mahnke spoke. I think I gave Exhibit 2 to the duty officer. I had got it from the guardroom. I believe the duty officer asked me what had happened to Mahnke and I said he had been run up and down. We closed the door leaving Mahnke lying naked on the floor. When I gave the duty officer the statement the duty officer read it, but I cannot say what he did with it.
We went to corridor 3, opened cell 37, and the duty officer and I went in. Oebsger-Roeder stood to attention and handed statement he was writing to the duty officer. The duty officer spoke to him in German. Oebsger-Roeder was naked. The duty officer took the written statement away and told me to give back the blankets to cells 12 and 37. I think that the duty officer signed the book at (he said I think) one o'clock. When doing a routine check in cell 12 I spoke to Mahnke and I believe he gave me the paper then about three o'clock. I cannot identify Exhibit 3 as the document. I took it to my office, gave it to the orderly on duty to take it to the duty officer, and then went to bed. After this, Mahnke was always lying on his bed. Oebsger-Roeder appeared to be all right."

He denies the allegations of Mahnke that the duty officer looked in several times when this ill-treatment was going on. He says the duty officer did not look in as is alleged by Mahnke. He says that he did tell Medcraft what happened verbally next day, and he says that these men were beaten up before the duty officer came round, the bad beating up occurred before the duty officer came round about midnight. He denies any allegation that at the teatime he had these men dressed so as to deceive the duty officer, and he says that he did think he spoke to Dawson the next day about the beating and he says that Dawson may have asked him if he had got a statement. Everyone knew of these beatings, he said, in the prison; and he says that he told the people concerned in these affairs that he had been instructed to make these people talk.

At 11.35 the court was adjourned until 11.45 when the summing up continued.

Well, sir, I had just dealt with in brief the evidence of Sergeant Thomas and, leaving it there for the time being there can be no doubt at all that he is incriminating Captain Langham in the evidence that he is giving. What bearing that has on the case will be of course for you to consider later.

Now, sir, I would like shortly to deal with the evidence of Mahnke and Oebsger-Roeder in regard to this part of the, case, and I think you appreciate that it is my duty to try and discriminate between the cases as they are separate charges, but we all found it quite impossible to do that and I am afraid they are so inextricably mixed up together that I cannot really take the case of Mahnke separate from Oebsger-Roeder; but you will appreciate when you do come to your finding that you must consider each charge separately.

Now, Mahnke's version is that at about two o'clock on the 17 the Company Sergeant Major and sentries came to his cell, and that they started turning him round and punching him; that they pulled out a mop a bucket of water was put over him. This is before the interval. He then says that at six o'clock Captain Langham came to supervise the food. "I left the cell and stood before Langham, I was naked; I was bleeding at various places, and I had the appearance of being knocked about. Langham said, 'Well, you are not dead. Do you wish to make a confession?' I said, 'I have nothing to confess' and then Langham made a gesture indicating that I should go back to my cell. Langham remained standing by the door of the cell. I was forced to eat the food by the sentry and in fact I walked some three to four metres from my cell to the table."

Then he agrees that he was ill-treated between six o'clock and nine o'clock, and then he says that Captain Langham came on his round between nine and nine forty-five p.m. He said that in the meanwhile he had been struck in the sexual organs, that sentries had held cigarettes to his body and that he had lost consciousness and had water poured over him.

He says at nine o'clock Langham came round and came to his cell door. "I could not stand erect through weariness and I was bleeding at several points. Langham said, 'would you now like to make a confession?' I said, 'I have nothing to confess. I cannot add to my statement but would have to incriminate myself with untruths if I wish to put an end to this treatment.' Langham made no reply and left."

Then he says he was ill-treated in cell 12, that he was taken out of the cell by Thomas and "Henry the VIII" and two sentries. He was run up and down the corridor. He lost consciousness and he was put under a shower in the next room to revive him, and water was put on him and he was beaten by mops and brooms. He was taken back to the corridor and collapsed, was under the shower again, brought back, struck specifically on the sore parts. He was brought back in front of cell 12, was leaning on the wall and then he was given a pencil and paper, and something was said to him. He said he lay on the ground and wrote, and he says he wrote Exhibit 2 and that he gave it to a soldier, and he does not know what the soldier did with it.

Three or five minutes later he wrote, he thinks, Exhibit 3 on another bit of paper and gave it to a soldier, and then there was a third piece of paper which he gave to a soldier, and he says this was about one or two o'clock in the morning. Then he says he was put back in cell 12, that the clothes were given to him, and that was the end of the events of the night of 17 April.

Now, Oebsger-Roeder says that after he had been put in cell 2 with no furniture, he was stripped naked, and that the company sergeant major was in the cell. He says that he was ill-treated and collapsed, and that he heard the evening meal and that he had to go naked to the table to get his food. He swears that he was still naked, that he was in a very bad condition, that he was dirty, with skin abrasions.

He says he got the food from the table himself. He saw Captain Langham was there standing about three paces away looking at him, and that he said nothing, and then he said something about him having an ironical look. After this he says he was taken to the bath-house, put under a shower but not struck. Then he went to the bath-house in corridor 4 next to cell 40; then he was put in cell 37 or 38, run round in circles, struck again, lost consciousness, had his hair pulled, cigarettes was extinguished on his upper arm, and he was hit in the sexual organs.

He then says that after this (this is about the last visit of Captain Langham) he says that Captain Langham stood in the doorway and that Oebsger-Roeder turned towards him. "I was a naked wreck bleeding and knocked about, practically finished. Langham said 'Now I suppose you have had enough. Now make a full confession', I cannot remember what else he said, and I may have said to him to put an end to my life." Langham then spoke to the sentry and left shortly (he says) before eleven o'clock.

They started running him round and punching him; that they pulled his hair, and a bucket of water was put over him. This is before the tea interval. He then says that at six o'clock Captain Langham came to supervise the food.

"I left the cell and stood before Langham. I was naked; I was bleeding at various places, and I had the appearance of being knocked about. Langham said, 'Well, you are not dead. Do you wish to make a confession?' I said, 'I have nothing to confess' and then Langham made a gesture indicating that I should go back to my cell. Langham remained standing by the door of the cell. I was forced to eat the food by the sentry and in fact I walked some three to four metres from my cell to the table."

Then he agrees that he was ill-treated between six o'clock and nine o'clock, and then he says that Captain Langham came on his round between nine and nine forty-five p.m. He said that in the meanwhile he had been struck in the sexual organs, that sentries had held cigarettes to his body and that he had lost consciousness and had water poured over him.

He says at nine o'clock Langham came round and came to his cell door. "I could not stand erect through weariness and I was bleeding at several points. Langham said, 'Would you now like to make a confession?' I said, 'I have nothing to confess. I cannot add to my statement but would have to incriminate myself with untruths if I wish to put an end to this treatment'." Langham made no reply and left.

Then he says he was ill-treated in cell 12, that he was taken out of the cell by Thomas and Henry the VIII and two sentries. He was run up and down the corridor. He lost consciousness and he was put under a shower in the next room to revive him, and water was put on him and he was beaten by mops and brooms. He was taken back to the corridor and collapsed, was under the shower again, brought back, struck specifically-on the sore parts. He was brought back in front of cell 12, was leaning on the wall and then he was given a pencil and paper and something was said to him. He said he lay on the ground and wrote, and he says he wrote Exhibit 2 and that he gave it to a soldier and he does not know what the soldier did with it.

Three or five minutes later he wrote, he thinks, Exhibit 3 on another bit of paper and gave it to a soldier, and then there was a third piece of paper which he gave to a soldier, and he says this was about one or two o'clock in the morning. Then he says he was put back in cell 12, that the clothes were given to him, and that was the end of the events of the night of 17 April.

Now, Oebsger-Roeder says that after he had been put in cell 2 with no furniture, he was stripped naked, and that the company sergeant major was in the cell. He says that he was ill-treated and collapsed, and that he heard the evening meal and that he had to go naked to the table to get his food. He swears that he was still naked, that he was in a very bad condition, that he was dirty, with skin abrasions.

He says he got the food from the table himself. He saw Captain Langham was there standing about 'three paces away looking at him, and that he said nothing, and then he said something about him having an ironical look. After this he says he was taken to the bath-house, put under a shower but not struck. Then he went to the bath-house in corridor 4 next to cell 40; then he was put in cell 37 or 38, run round in circles, struck again, lost consciousness, had his hair pulled, cigarette was extinguished on his upper arm, and he was hit in the sexual organs.

He then says that after this (this is about the last visit of Captain Langham) he says that Captain Langham stood in the doorway and that Oebsger-Roeder turned towards him. "I was a naked wreck, bleeding and knocked about, practically finished. Langham said, 'Now I suppose you have had enough. Now make a full confession'. I cannot remember what else he said, and I may have said to him to put an end to my life."

Langham then spoke to the sentry and left shortly (he says) before eleven o'clock. He swears that Langham made two or three visits when he was being run round in circles in cell 37 or 38, that he just took a step over the threshold and looked in. (You will of course remember that I pointed out to you that Thomas does not agree with that allegation at all.) He says that about eleven o'clock he puts it, he went into an adjoining cell where there was a table and a typewriter. This was about half an hour after Langham had left, that he was given tea and his clothes and a cigarette, and that after he had rested, he wrote the report on the typewriter when he was alone. He gave it to a lance corporal who took it away. He slept until seven in the morning, and he did not see Langham again.

Next day he says he went in cell 37 or 38 for a short time (this is the 18*th*) where there was a table and a typewriter. He really has nothing more to say about the case, and I think that completes it so far as Oebsger-Roeder's statement of facts is concerned. He agrees that he never complained to anyone about his treatment at Bad Nenndorf.

Now, gentlemen, there you have in short form, because I know you have your own notes, the evidence of the four main witnesses in regard to the ill-treatment taking place before we reach the third milestone. Summing it up, it seems to me that Mathers is establishing that the crime in the charge sheet was committed but does not implicate Langham. Equally it seems to me, if you accept the evidence of Thomas that he establishes the crime was committed but implicates Langham very strongly. Equally in the case of the two Germans, if you accept their evidence, that it is not lies or is not exaggerated, they prove that the crimes were committed and implicate Langham.

Now, gentlemen there is only one legal direction which I have to give you in this case, and I am now going to give it to you. There is no doubt at all that Thomas and Mathers (and probably some of the other N.C.O.s that I am going to deal with later) are what we call in the law accomplices. They were clearly present, aiding and abetting, taking part with one another in the crime set out in the charge sheet. And of an accomplice the law says this. You should not act upon the uncorroborated testimony of an accomplice alone. You should only act upon it if there is some corroboration of the kind laid down by law. The kind of corroboration required is not confirmation by independent evidence of everything the accomplice relates, as his evidence would be unnecessary if that were so. What is required is some independent testimony which affects the prisoner by tending to connect him with the crime, that is evidence direct or circumstantial which implicates the prisoner, which confirms in some material particular not only the evidence given by the accomplice that the crime has been committed but also the evidence that the prisoner committed it.

Now, gentlemen that is a warning which I am called upon to give you, but at the same time I have to point out that it is not a question of all these witnesses being accomplices. It is these British witnesses who have come and clearly demonstrated to you that they are accomplices. The German witnesses are not accomplices, and of course if you accept them as witnesses of truth and credibility, then they would corroborate the story of Thomas if you accept it, not only that the crime was committed but that the accused committed it.

Now, that is the only legal direction I am going to give you, because after all what you have to decide in this case are questions of fact. But just in passing, you do find here the situation of the lion and the lamb rather lying down together. You find a great deal of corroboration between Thomas and the German witnesses. The question of injuries, the question of the visits of Langham, what he saw, and the question of whether they were naked or not: there is a good deal of common ground between these people[53]. Why that should be, I do not know. It is for you to decide and I am only here to point out the evidence and it is for you to weigh it up and decide what view you take of it; but it is quite clear that there is a considerable amount of common ground between the account of Thomas and that of the two Germans in regard to Captain Langham.

---

[53] There is very little common ground of evidence corroborating the perpetrator of the crime, rather than the crime itself.

At the same time, you will appreciate that there are divergences, that they are not on all fours, and you will have to consider that in your own good time later on. Now, sir, I have really dealt with the witnesses of great substance – I do not mean necessarily in weight but I mean in view of the amount of testimony they have given; and I think perhaps you will be a little relieved to appreciate that I am now going to deal with some of the other witnesses whom I can take quite shortly.

First of all, there is Lewis of the warder company, and you know he was working, I think, as a Lance Corporal under Corporal Brant on this evening. He was on from nine o'clock on the 17th to nine o'clock on the 18th. He says that he thinks Mathers and Thomas came along about four o'clock into the prison in his view. He says: "I saw Thomas come across the landing" (you will remember the little landing where they were stationed) "about seven or eight p.m. to corridor 1"; that he went to cell 12 and that he heard shouting and bangs.

Then Lewis goes in to the cell of Oebsger-Roeder. (This is somewhere, as I say, about seven or eight o'clock). "Oebsger-Roeder looked a bit worn and he was completely naked and I was alone with him. I ran him round the room put him against the wall with his knees bent for five minutes, and Oebsger-Roeder fell down more than once. I dragged him to his feet again. I then threw water over him to revive him, a half bucket of water. I was in the cell inside about half an hour. I gave him a rabbit punch below his neck and made him jerk a bit, and then I left the cell."

Now, the extraordinary thing about Lewis is that apparently he did this off his own bat, according to him. He just seemed to have taken part in this beating up because he felt like it, so he steps into the cell and according to what he says, off his own bat and he administers this further punishment to Oebsger-Roeder. It is a curious performance, and later on I may have some comment to make about it.

What else he said was that he was in bed at eight o'clock until two o'clock, and he did not see the duty officer at six o'clock. He could not have seen him at nine o'clock and he could not have seen him at twelve o'clock; and therefore it seems to me that Lewis, apart from establishing this curious onslaught of his own on Oebsger-Roeder, is unable to incriminate in any way Captain Langham either at six o'clock because he did not see him or at nine o'clock or at twelve o'clock because he was in bed.

The next witness was Brant, "Henry the VIII". You remember he was on from nine o'clock to nine o'clock in charge with Lewis under him. He says he remembers the switch from cell at nine-fifteen. He says at some time before nine-fifteen Mathers, Thomas and he went into cell 12, that Oebsger-Roeder was stripped and his clothes were outside the door, and he said he thought they were put in a corner next door.

He says that Oebsger-Roeder was run up and down the corridor and then in the cell, and that he saw his clothing in a corner in the next room. He says at nine fifteen Oebsger-Roeder may have had his clothes. I think he said he gave orders to a warder to give back the clothes, but he did not actually see him give them back. He says (whether he is speaking the truth or not I do not know) that he does not remember seeing the duty officer on that night at all. He says that he must have ordered his clothes to be given back to Oebsger-Roeder on the orders of his superiors.

Now, gentlemen, if you accept the evidence of Brant and you work out his times, I think you will come to the conclusion that the move at nine-fifteen, the switch, must have occurred after the duty officer had left the precincts of the prison.

Now, Sore, he was in the warder company, and he says he came into the prison between 1530 and 1600 hours; that he and the sergeant major and Thomas went to cell 12; that Oebsger-Roeder was stripped, and the clothes were put outside. And he is the man (and the only man I think) who spoke about a radiator being put on.

"The Company Sergeant Major left us and for one and a half hours or two hours. Thomas and I were chasing the prisoner around in the cell. There were relays and there were two at a time, and he was naked."

"About five or six" (I think he puts it) "Oebsger-Roeder said he would make a statement and the company sergeant-major gave him back his clothes."

That was dealing with Oebsger-Roeder. He says that at nine-fifteen he saw Mahnke being escorted by a sentry, that there was nothing odd about him, and that he was fully clothed. He says he left the prison before 1800 hours, before the duty officer came round. He speaks of seeing Mahnke on the 19th with Mathers under a shower and of some red marks, but I think he must have got confused about that.

Also, he says that on the 19th Mahnke was given a pencil and paper and he wrote out a statement. Well, gentlemen, you saw Sore. It is for you to decide. You may think he got confused on some of the things he was saying, but it is my duty to point out that he does not as far as I can see in any way incriminate Captain Langham in regard to these events.

Now, the next witness I have a few words to say about is Corporal French, also of the warder company. He was on block 1, corridor 1. You remember how he says that he was sleeping in a room in No.3 corridor and that he heard shouting coming at 2 p.m. from cell 12. He says he remembers Captain Langham coming round about tea time but that he saw nothing odd at all and that Oebsger-Roeder was in cell 12 and that he was naked. He says he never saw the company sergeant major on this night at all and he never heard any rumours about what had been happening to Oebsger-Roeder or Mahnke.

You will probably think that Corporal French does not help you very much, but it is entirely for you to decide. He is the man who, as you will remember, talked about the condemned accommodation, when he must be wrong. At any rate, that very briefly sums up the substance of the evidence given by Corporal French.

The next witness was Hunt who speaks about the telephone call about six o'clock (that clearly is not a telephone call of any importance in this case) and then he said: "I saw Thomas pushing a prisoner around in cell 36 in corridor 3." Then he takes a hand too, "I helped to push that man around with Thomas for twenty minutes, but I cannot say which man it was". He says he cannot remember who was the duty officer and he cannot say anything about what happened at nine o'clock.

He usually went to sleep until two o'clock but he relieved Thomas later on this morning at 3.15 a.m. The defence make some comment on that in regard to the late time at which he was relieved. He was the man who made the entry of the removal of Oebsger-Roeder from cell 2 to cell 12 at, I think, two-ten on the afternoon of the 17th. He is also the man who says he put in the entry, 0020 or 0030 hours, which is crossed out in the guard-book. He says he did not cross it out, and that is the move that is set out there which I think was from cell 37 to cell 1.

Now, he was a man who gave evidence that a great number of people were involved in this ill-treatment. He says at one time there were half a dozen warders, and I think he said something like eighteen people must have known of this ill-treatment he was speaking about.

Now, Medcraft, I think I will deal with him later when I come to the fourth milestone. Dawson I will deal with later. The only other witness I think that I want to deal with on this part of the case is to remind you of the evidence of Scholes. He says that he heard about the beating up about two days after the long interrogation of Mahnke. He said there were general rumours about the prison that he had heard about Mahnke being beaten up in the early hours of the morning after the officer had come round and that he had heard that Company Sergeant Major Mathers was the instigator. Then I think he made it clear that he really had heard about the beating up on the morning after it had taken place.

Now, I am afraid that is rather a mass of evidence which will have to be carefully sorted out by you later on, because we are all in this difficulty, not being the judges in the case and not knowing what points appeal to you and which do not; and therefore it will be *your duty with your members, sir, later on to go into such parts of the evidence as you consider to be material, and decide what is right and what is wrong. For the moment let us revert again to the third milestone.*

Where have we got now? What is the position at Bad Nenndorf by the early morning of 18 April? The case for the prosecution is quite a simple one, but they have to prove it, and that is that these undoubted beatings up were instigated and authorised in the first instance by Major Edmunds, that the order went to Mathers and that he in turn passed it on to the others under the guise that they were orders from an officer, that these N.C.O.s were doing what was wrong and what was illegal but that they were doing it because they received orders so do it.

Now, gentlemen, it seems only common sense, does it not, that if the prosecution are right and you accept the evidence of Mathers that Major Edmunds was issuing this order or giving this authority that the accused Captain Langham who was the orderly officer must necessarily have been made a party to it. I think that is why Mr. Curtis-Bennett very properly put to you that it would be difficult to convict Langham unless you were satisfied that Edmunds was guilty.

Now, let us see. Supposing Major Edmunds had given this order to Mathers and had not arranged with Mathers that this should be a knocking about in secret, hidden from the eyes of almost everybody, but had left it, as Mathers says, for him to do what he liked. It would surely have been obvious that if a duty officer comes round and he has not been told of this, supposing it happened, and he sees the N.C.O.s going on in this way, he is going to intervene and the plan of Major Edmunds to get the evidence would become useless.

Therefore, the prosecution (and it is entirely for you to say whether they are right) are saying that if you accept the evidence that Major Edmunds was doing what Mathers says, you ought to find that that could only be done provided Captain Langham, the duty officer, was also brought into the picture. And they ask you to say that if you accept the evidence of Mathers and the Germans, that is borne out up to the hilt. They say that these witnesses (entirely again a matter for you) are saying that not only was Langham there, not only was he seeing what was going on, but he was asking for statements.

Well, gentlemen, that is really the case for the prosecution on that point. The defence say it is quite untrue. Major Edmunds says: "I never gave any order. I was no party to this; I saw nothing wrong". It is a complete denial by Major Edmunds, by Captain Langham and by all those surrounding matters which have a bearing on it from the interrogation point of view. Now, sir, another point that you will have to consider. They are all points that seem to me very reasonable, very simple, but ones you will have to apply your minds to very carefully.

The evidence as I have told it to you may seem to you overwhelming, that this was a long, drawn-out affair and that all kinds of violence were being used over a long period, that it was being used indiscriminately by quite large number of people, for instance, as I have told you, Lewis who comes in and does it off his own bat. There were, I am sure, very large eyewitnesses. No attempt seems to have been made as far as I can see to hide this.

You are told that Mahnke yelled, that there were noises going on all over the place, some (but not really of course so severe) as early as four o'clock in the afternoon when the prison control is functioning. And the prosecution rightly or wrongly asks you to most carefully consider what inference you are going to draw from this. They ask you to say, as reasonable men there is only one sensible inference that can be drawn, and that is that if you take the story of orders by an officer they are carrying out, flagrantly and openly, that is all in keeping; but if you take the other story of the defence which is that they were doing this on their own, then you get what you may perhaps think is one of the most flagrant bare-faced flouting of discipline you ever had in your career.[54]

For N.C.O.s – even the N.C.O. in charge – to do these things in a prison such as Bad Nenndorf and for it to go on for hours and hours and hours in such a way which you would have thought would be bound to be found out with everybody talking about it, warders looking on, everybody presumably seeing—how is this being allowed? All this, the prosecution say, points to one conclusion only.

Well, gentlemen, that is one of the major issues in this case. Do you believe that it is possible at all that these men Mathers and Thomas and the others were all taking part in this because it was based entirely on Mathers' idea either to punish these men or to obtain statements from them? Or do you think that the reasonable, fair and sensible inference is that Mathers had been told, as he says, to try and get the statements, given carte blanche, and this was his method of doing it?

Gentlemen, there is the issue as I see it in regard to the third milestone. That is the difficult part of the case; what happened during that time is the controversial part of the case. That is the one I would ask you in closed court to give your most anxious consideration to. When you have done it, whichever way you decide, I think you will have a pretty clear picture

---

[54] This is a rather strong direction that presumably builds on a point made by the prosecution, but would it really constitute the most flagrant flouting of discipline that the jury had ever seen as the judge makes out?

according as you find the evidence to be to your satisfaction or not, what the position was at the time when these two men, Mahnke was proceeding to make the statements Exhibits 2 and 3 and Oebsger-Roeder was making the statement of the 17 April as amplified by further statement of 18 April.

Now, I am very anxious not to labour this part of the case. I do not want in any way to suggest any of my views or how I feel about these important matters. If I have, although I have tried not to give any indication of what I myself feel about them, I want to tell you that you are in no way bound by them. I do not think I have; but if I have, gentlemen, remember that what I say really carries no more weight, except upon a point of law, than you should pay in attention to Mr Curtis-Bennett or the prosecutor.

Now, gentlemen, there it is. With that mass of evidence, confused, as it often is, contradicted as it is, that of an accomplice in some cases: you have to decide not really whether on 17 April there was violence of a brutal kind to both these men (that seems to me very simple[55]) but whether the evidence brings conviction to your minds to establish with judicial certainty to the exclusion of a reasonable doubt that the picture you have left when you have sorted out the evidence of that night, clearly implicates Captain Langham.

That, gentlemen, in this case seems to me the real issue – the two issues you have always got in cases of this kind: one, was the crime set out in the charge sheet committed and, two, if it was did the accused commit it?

Now, gentlemen, it is for the prosecution to satisfy you beyond reasonable doubt that this evidence you have got up to the third milestone is clear and cogent and conclusive. If you are satisfied that it is quite impossible to accept that these N.C.O.s in the way they did it were participating in this flagrant disobedience of discipline and orders (because the one thing Mathers must have known was that violence could not be tolerated in any shape or kind), if you are satisfied that that is not possible at all, as reasonable men, to take the view that they were doing this on their own and you are satisfied that the prosecution have proved to your satisfaction that they were doing it upon orders then, gentlemen, you would be entitled to draw inference which would be very adverse to Captain Langham.

One the other hand, if you say that this is possible, they may have done it on their own gentlemen, then that finding of fact is in my view sufficient in itself to acquit Captain Langham.

---

[55] Hint, hint!

Now, I want to pass on and deal with the last and final milestone which I call number four. In that I would include from the end of the beating up when the statements are being made until the end of the story of Bad Nenndorf.

Gentlemen, there can be no doubt at all that on the morning of 18 April Mahnke, apparently physically fit and well on the evening of the 17 was in a somewhat battered condition. His version is (and it is for you to say whether it is a right one) that he was bleeding with skin abrasions all over his body, that he had a wound in the shoulder, one on the right elbow, one on the right knee, one on the right ankle and the right shin bone; and he had high fever and ague. This is the condition which was working up until he was removed to Rothenberg Hospital, I think on 22 April.

Now, the evidence of Dabritz, just to remind you of it, who was the German who saw him before he went to hospital: "He was lying on a stretcher. I took off his clothing and put him to bed. He could not be spoken to and he had a wound on the right arm that was swollen, one on the right leg (the tissue was filled with blood); his right leg was deformed by swelling and he had some teeth missing" – I do not think there is anything in that because he told us that he had false teeth.

The physical state was also deposed to on his removal to hospital by Dr Buttner, and he says on his first examination that the overall condition was bad, and that the patient might have died, that he seemed to have had nourishment and that his physical condition in that respect was comparatively good. He had a temperature, was delirious, and part of the time was inarticulate. His right leg and upper thigh was badly swollen, the skin was livid and red; the right knee had a little suppuration – the area of the knee was very painful when touched and he could not move his knee joint. "Small wound on the fore-arm, similar wound above the right shoulder blade, discoloration of skin in the abdomen and neighbourhood". It is not quite the same as a bruise and we had some difficulty in understanding what he was trying to convey.

Now, gentlemen, what was the condition in fact on the morning of 18 April? It is for you to decide on the evidence and in that connection I perhaps ought to remind you of the evidence of Medcraft. Now, Medcraft was the N.C.O. who relieved Thomas on the morning of 18th April, and besides telling you that he never saw any signs of ill-treatment and that he was not told about any when he was relieved by Sergeant Thomas, he told you the story about seeing Mahnke in the cell - he speaks about Mahnke in cell 12 in the morning of 18th April when he was going round to see what the position was. He said, "I had a special look at Mahnke just after 9 a.m. The prisoner was trying to stand to attention and I waved him thus" *(and he indicated). "He was lying on the floor with blankets which I assumed he had got back in the night. He still had these blankets at nine o'clock and this was unusual."*

Well, gentlemen, you heard his evidence, he was cross-examined, and it is for you to say whether he was trying to say or not that at that morning Mahnke was being left his blankets because he was a sick man or whether there was just a dereliction of duty, as he was told on the part of an earlier N.C.O. At any rate he tells you how he found Mahnke on the morning of 18th April.

Now there was at one time some suggestion (I do not think it was followed up) that Mahnke was limping before he ever came to Bad Nenndorf, and some allegations have been made about his bona fides in using a stick to impress the court and others. That was investigated and if you think there is anything in it, well, you will take such note of it as you wish.

Now, on the morning of 18 April something appears to have occurred which you may or may not think is of importance. You have got to go back to five o'clock on the morning of 16 April. As far as I know, with the exception of the letter to his wife, there is no suggestion that Oebsger-Roeder or Mahnke had been writing hysterical notes. Gentlemen, the defence have not produced any hysterical notes in this case from prisoners, and you have not seen any, but it is fair to say that there is a bit of testimony from the interrogation section which says that that was quite a common thing.

It will not have escaped your notice that on this night, the night of the 17/18 April, Mahnke is according to the view you take of it writing Exhibit 2. Then he writes (it is for you to decide in what circumstances) Exhibit 3. And Exhibit 3 is in two parts. He signs his name three times. You may think from the context (and it is difficult, I think, to believe that this was a document which was compelled to deceive somebody at some future date), it is entirely for you gentlemen, but you may think that it is a genuine document compiled by a man who now at any rate quite clearly was in pain and suffering and was protesting and asking for protection.[56]

Now, gentlemen, there are three statements there. Equally Oebsger-Roeder produces two, two typewritten documents. So you get although this case was supposed to have ended from the interrogation point of view at 5 a.m. on 16th April no less than what one might call

---

[56] Technically it was of course a matter for the jury, but the judge was leading the jury to find that Mahnke was in pain and was suffering greatly. It does not assist the jury to connect that up to Langham or Frank.

five statements coming from these two men which are not the result at all of interrogations being made to them by officers.

Whether there is any significance in that or not I do not know. You have seen Exhibits 2 and 3. They were undoubtedly written by Mahnke. How they got from the cell to the case file is for you to decide. You have had the somewhat confused story from the prosecution, and you have had the story from the defence that they must have come in to Major Edmunds and then been passed out and eventually got on the file. Mahnke must have written these. In the case of the other two documents, whether they are original or not, by Oebsger-Roeder, is a matter for you to decide. I rather agree with the learned counsel for the defence that whether it is original or not, it would be a safe assumption that what is now in that document is that he did write in the first instance.

And therefore Mr. Curtis-Bennett (and I think this is the only purpose for which it was being used by the defence) says "Look at it. It is a coherent statement, and it should induce you to say that Oebsger-Roeder was not in a bad condition when he made it, and that therefore he has been exaggerating to you." But there it is, gentlemen. There was coming in to Major Edmunds, and I think to Section "C", no less than five documents, from these two men.

And the prosecution say again, as reasonable men, such as you are on the court, is that not significant? You cannot treat Major Edmunds and Captain Langham and Captain Van Rije as intellects of an inferior order. They are astute, they are capable men." And the prosecution challenge the defence rightly or wrongly (it is for you to say) that this was significant and that if they got these statements and they did not make any enquiries about them, you should infer that they were expected, that they were a party to the obtaining of them and that they therefore knew all about and instigated this crime.

Whether that is sound reasoning is for the court to decide. There is some confusion about these documents of Mahnke. Whether Captain Langham saw Exhibit 2 and 3, he is not very sure. Major Edmunds thinks that he must have seen both. Captain Van Rije, he is not very clear. But it seems to be the case for the defence that all these documents were on the file and properly there, and that it would be madness to put them on the file if they had been obtained by a beating up.

Now, gentlemen, I am not going to read these documents to you again. They are before you; they have been read innumerable times; but that is the issue between the prosecution and the defence. The prosecution argue that no reasonable man, no man so astute as these officers, knowing what had gone on, knowing the importance of any information which might be got from these men in regard to the uprising – that they must have known that these had been obtained by violence and therefore they were a party to the bringing of it about.

Now, gentlemen, there is another matter which seems to me (though it is entirely for you) of great importance, and that is that on the morning of 18 April when the Mahnke statement came to Major Edmunds he apparently wanted it looked into and he passed it to Captain Langham and, I think, Captain Van Rije. Now, Captain Van Rije was leaving Bad Nenndorf about noon on 18 April, and therefore this incident which I am going to refer to must have occurred before noon on 18 April. Van Rije says he is quite confident that he did not see Mahnke, but Captain Langham has admitted quite freely that on the morning of 18 April (and there seems to be some agreement between him and Mahnke) Mahnke was sent for to the interrogation cell somewhere about ten or eleven o'clock, and that he was questioned by Langham in regard to these statements.

Now, Langham says, "On the morning of 17 or 18 Major Edmunds gave me this" (and by 'this' he meant Exhibit 3) and he said,

"This statement came in from Mahnke. I cannot read it and he told me and Van Rije to go through it and see Mahnke and if there was anything important, I was to take it up with him. I went to see Mahnke in the interrogation room. He was brought there, and I saw him there for a very short time. I asked him what was the meaning of the statement. He said, 'It is all a pack of lies'. I said, 'Why did you write it in the first instance?' and he answered, 'I wrote it because I could not stand the place any longer'. I took the view that it was written under mental stress or hysteria. I said, 'if there is any trouble on the 20th you have not seen anything'. I left him then and I did not know that Mahnke had been subject to violence and it never crossed my mind. I thought that he was really referring to the long interrogation and I had no idea that the document came into existence in some wrong way."

Now, gentlemen, the importance of this meeting, if you think it important, is surely this – Captain Langham agrees that between six o'clock on the 17 April and, let us say, noon on the 18 April, he had an opportunity of seeing Mahnke on no less than four occasions. If the case for the prosecution is right, at six o'clock there had been a certain amount of violence. (I do not put it any higher than that). That he should have had a good opportunity to beat Mahnke there can be no doubt. I think it is fair to say that at nine o'clock he also would have a fair opportunity to see Mahnke, and that between six and nine there had been a good deal of violence going on.

I do not think it would be fair to say that at midnight he had an equal opportunity because the evidence seems to be there that a man might be laid in his blankets and as long as he moved you would not take much notice. But it is for you to say: on the morning when he is investigating this document, would he not have a reasonable opportunity of seeing the then condition of Mahnke?

Now, gentlemen, I read to you, because I thought it was only right I should do so, those horrible accounts from the witnesses of how Mahnke was treated, and if you accept that evidence as being reasonably accurate at all Mahnke must have been dirty (not on the morning of the 18, I agree), he must have been dishevelled, he must have received innumerable blows around his stomach; he had been tripped up going at full speed and crashed down in the corridor.

And, gentlemen, here you must be on sound ground: you have had experience of physical exercises and physical violence. Is it possible for a man of the physique of Mahnke on the morning of 18 April before twelve o'clock – or put it at twelve o'clock – to be in a condition that the eyes of any ordinary intelligent person must not have noticed that he was in a serious condition?

It is not necessary of course to see cuts and bruises, but do you think or not (it is entirely for you) that the man on that morning could hardly move without the greatest pain and discomfort, even only from bruises or from these innumerable slappings and punches which had been administered to his body these few hours before?

Now, gentlemen, these are grave and serious issues; they are grave and serious issues for Captain Langham, and I know you will not rush them. You will consider them carefully from every point of view when you come to close the court. If I have said something which you think is unduly oppressive to Captain Langham, disregard it; but what I have tried to do for your benefit is to pick out what would appear to be very salient matters of fact which it should well be within the compass of reasonable minds to find the right answer.

And so the prosecution ask you to say it is not reasonable that Captain Langham could have seen Mahnke four times in the circumstances which were detailed by the prosecution, if you believe it, without knowing he was being beaten up and had been beaten up. Whether that is right or wrong is, as I say, entirely a matter for you.

Captain Langham, I think it is quite fair to say, was a reasonable intelligent witness, and he attempted to answer every question quite frankly; and what he says to-day at any rate in regard to Mahnke is substantially what he said in his statement. He has not mentioned

Oebsger-Roeder in his statement but that is for the very good reason that he was not asked apparently do deal with it.

Now, gentlemen, you have his statement. There is one phrase in it which may or may not be significant. I would not advise you to attach much importance to it. He has already been allowed to give his explanation and you will consider it. At one time he said: "Although I do not recall visiting Mahnke whilst he was undergoing punishment, it is quite possible that I did so whilst duty officer and asked him if he was not prepared to tell the truth". I personally do not attach any importance to that, gentlemen, but it has been mentioned and you no doubt will put it in its proper position.

Now, the 18 April still has matters which I am going to deal with, and before I adjourn, I would like to dispose of the evidence of Captain Dawson. Now, I feel that you will be able to deal fully and fairly with the evidence of Captain Dawson. It is a military matter and a matter which you will consider in its proper light, but Dawson came here, and he gave evidence on oath.

He told you that he remembered the names of Mahnke and Oebsger-Roeder but had not got any very clear picture of the men, and he says that in the mid-morning (and I think it was accepted that he was speaking about 18th April) Mathers came to him when Captain Bennett was on leave. It was a general conversation at first and then Mathers said that on the previous night he had returned to the prison after a hectic party and that he had found the prisoner Mahnke had fainted. Mahnke was taken to the ablution room by himself and Sergeant Thomas, he thought, and they tried to revive him with splashing water on him, and for this purpose they used a mop.

"I placed my hand against the prisoner and I hit my hand. I did not mark or injure the prisoner in any way."

Dawson says he got the impression that Mathers was telling his everything that had happened. Well, gentlemen you remember how Dawson told you what he did. In other words without any reference to his own C.O., without any reference to Colonel Stephens, he decided to do nothing about it. He then "ticked off" or rebuked Mathers, so he says. There is a complete denial by Mathers that this ever happened, and it is for you to decide what view you take of this incident. The prosecution roundly criticise Dawson and ask you to say that he is lying, that no person in his position would act in such a way. Whether you think there is any substance in Mr Curtis-Bennett's point or not, I do not know, but I think he was suggesting that Mathers was being rather clever in mentioning this matter and that it would then come to the notice of Dawson and if Dawson dropped it that would be the end of the matter.

Well, gentlemen, do you believe for one moment that Mathers' brain acted that way?[57] *It would not matter in the slightest if Dawson were to say, "I will take no action against you, Mathers, because you were a little drunk and you hit a man so that you did not mark him" but it would make all the difference if this story once opened up, the real conduct of Mathers came into the picture. Then there is no doubt that Mathers would have been on a court martial, and it would not have mattered in the least what view Dawson had taken about this incident. Well, there it is. I do not want to labour it. It is a military matter. Do you believe Dawson when he says that this happened in the way he says? If these N.C.O.s were doing it surreptitiously in breach of discipline (and once this was opened up it would have been a fearful breach of discipline, being discovered) do you think that he would tell Dawson? On the other hand, if he was doing it on the orders of an officer then there would be no reason why he should mention it to Dawson. But any rate there you have one of those numerous conflicts of fact that Dawson swears that this happened and Mathers swears that it did not.*

At 1300 hours the court is adjourned until 14.15 when the summing up resumed.

I have already given you the version of Captain Langham about the interview with Mahnke on the morning of 18th April. Mahnke's version of the same thing was that he was taken before Captain Langham as Langham says and that Langham was alone, and he thinks that what he was asked to read was Exhibit 2 which he did; and that Langham after reading it said, "I have heard that on Hitler's birthday, 20 April, there is to be a rising against the British in the British Zone. If on that day a hair of the head of a single British soldier is hurt, that which you have experienced will be as child's play compared to that which you will experience in the future". So much for the incident on the morning of 18 April.

Now, I do not propose to take up your time in dealing with whether these documents emanating from Mahnke were hysterical documents or not. You have heard the evidence of Major Edmunds, Captain Van Rije, Captain Langham, and they all assure you on their oath that at that time they were fully satisfied they were hysterical documents. That again is a matter which you will have to consider in the light of all the evidence you have heard. That is what the defence say, that "we did not consider that there was anything in these documents to put us on our guard and you should not draw any adverse inferences from them."

Now, gentlemen, we have travelled during the morning this somewhat lengthy road, and now I would like in concluding my remarks to put certain matters very shortly before you.

---

[57] The phrase "for one moment" is telling and highly prejudicial to the defence.

The case for the prosecution as it now appears to me to be is a simple one. The case that they submit for your approval and ask you to say has been proved is apparently this, that all legitimate methods for obtaining information from Mahnke and Oebsger-Roeder having proved futile, Major Edmunds and, in concert with him, Captain Langham, decided to try methods of violence which were quite unauthorised and which the prosecution say amount to disgraceful conduct of a cruel kind; that each of these officers had his particular part to play and it does not really very much matter what part they played individually if you are satisfied that they were acting together in concert. They say that the order came from Edmunds and that it was necessary for the duty officer, Captain Langham, to play his part; that these N.C.O.s through Mather were told to go ahead and use violence, and it is obvious they would not have done that unless they were fully satisfied they would be protested by those in authority above; that as the result of this evidence occurred in the way that has been described, public flagrant violence extending over a long period – not the result of a drunken trick to get revenge but a systematic course of conduct with a view to obtaining statements, statements having a bearing on this rising on 20 April that these N.C.O.s carried it out; that they could only do it with the connivance of the duty officer because if the duty officer was performing his duties this would never have happened. Therefore the prosecution claim that you should find that Captain Langham was a necessary cog in this plan; that it was he who was to keep an eye on this, not very obtrusively but quietly, and that he was not to stop it, and that he was to try and get statements through these N.C.O.s; that as the result of this Mahnke was considerably knocked about, knocked about in such a way that any reasonable man seeing him at any rate between twelve o'clock midnight and noon the next day must have known what had happened. They claim that if you look at this in a reasonable sensible way it is the only possible explanation of what happened.

They also claim in aid the fact that these four documents, five documents (whatever you like to call them) were being produced after this violence; that they were all handed in or got into the case file. And they say (whether there is any substance in it if for you to decide) that these documents are not properly reflected in SIR 29 that that is a bowdlerised version which has got into it.

Gentlemen, they also say it would be quite impossible not to have discovered the injuries which had been inflicted upon Mahnke, whether he was fully dressed or whether he was not. They also suggest that it is quite impossible to believe that murmurings of this must not have come to the intelligence staff who were so intimately connected with these two particular men.

And they ask you to say that you should disregard the sworn evidence of Captain Langham, Major Edmunds, Van Rije, and all those others who have laid this foundation that Captain Langham and Major Edmunds by their training, by their experience could never have been a party to such an affair; to throw that on one side and find that what they submit is the reasonable and only explanation which the evidence put before you can bear.

Now, sir, I am not saying that the evidence has established that. Please do not think I am saying that. That is the case for the prosecution, and I think I can say that on these points there is some evidence to support that case wherever you look at it; but of course, gentlemen, it is for you to say whether that evidence is such that you are going to act upon it. That gentlemen, very shortly and very briefly is the case for the prosecution.

On the other hand, the defence and I think there is no doubt about it that the learned solicitor who has been instructing in this case has been at great pains to do everything possible to put every point through learned counsel for the defence of Langham. What are they saying? (Though they have to prove nothing, you have to appreciate that). They are saying: – We offer you evidence and we offer another explanation. We say these are men of integrity, men of honour they know they may not use violence. They may use hard methods; they must use hard methods. They interrogated these men severely. But they did nothing which went beyond the code which was permitted at Bad Nenndorf.

That they are men brought up not to talk, that they are people who realise that you will not get much out of a man if you knock him about. They say that they failed admittedly to get anything out of these people, and they left it there. They were prepared to put into the report, and they had prepared the report on the 16 or 17 that they had failed, and that they had placed on record that the position as regards these two men was not clear at all. They say that they did that in the ordinary course of duty and they say that is what happened on the 17 and after was entirely the idea of Mathers, and others if you like, but nothing to do with any officer who was employed in "C" Section; and then ask you to say that what happened was the act of these N.C.Os; that Major Edmunds knew nothing about it, that Captain Langham knew nothing about it and that you should accept from them that what occurred was an unauthorised application of violence by these N.C.O.s and others acting entirely on their own responsibility with no authority and no cover of any shape or kind from Captain Langham, or Major Edmunds.

They have dealt with the documents, the hysterical documents; they have dealt with these suggestions of what inference they should draw from certain happenings. They are all before you and you consider them.

Now, gentlemen, put very widely and very briefly, those are the cases which have been put before you. Now let me remind you once again. It is not for the defence to prove their case is right: it is for the prosecution to prove that their case is right and that their case is the only reasonable possible case there can be on the facts. If you have a reasonable doubt, if you think the defence put forward creates a doubt (although they have not got to do it) naturally you would not convict the accused.

Now, gentlemen, before you go into closed court to consider your finding, I would just like to say a word on the charges. They are both the same and they allege that Captain Langham when acting as an interrogator together with Major Edmunds caused one Horst Mahnke or one Rudolf Oebsger-Roeder, an internee in the said centre, to be subjected to brutal treatment.

Now sir, in my view the words "caused to be subjected to brutal treatment" are not words of art, they are not legal words, they are not words which have any particular significance. In my view you must give to these words the ordinary reasonable meaning which should be given to such words, and it is not for me to define the ordinary meaning of words. I should assist you on technical terms such as an intent to defraud or something of that kind, but on this matter where you need no assistance from me it is for you to give the ordinary accepted meaning to these words. But it does seem that you will probably say in the terms of this case that you will have to be satisfied beyond reasonable doubt that Langham when acting as duty officer and having a duty to stop violence or take steps to prohibit anything which was irregular, was deliberately assisting to bring this matter to a successful conclusion by intervening and taking steps to make it successful.

You must be satisfied in view that Langham was well aware of what it is alleged Major Edmunds had done, that he agreed with it and that although he had a minor role, if you like, he was taking part in bringing that about, in causing this brutal treatment, and by the way he acted as orderly officer or duty officer on that night; that he was without any question in your view deliberately trying to make it successful in the sense that the brutality was being allowed to go on, being seen, being assisted; that he was taking part in asking, as is alleged by the prosecution, for statements, and that he was doing so knowingly and deliberately.

Gentlemen, if you believe for one moment, if you think it possible at all, that he knew nothing about this, that he had never entered into any agreement whatsoever with Edmunds, that he was an honest decent duty officer performing his functions properly; that these N.C.O.s were deliberately deceiving him, that they were arranging to have these men dressed on every occasion when he had an opportunity of seeing them and that he was at worst only to be criticised for not having been perhaps as observant as he might have been; gentlemen, if you think he was a man that night who was nothing to do with it, saw nothing unusual then of course the case for the prosecution must fail and Langham must be acquitted. Now, gentlemen, I have had to line in a gigantic canvas and I am fully aware that I may have emphasised one matter and not emphasised another; there are some matters I may not have mentioned and others perhaps I have mentioned too strongly. But it is a gigantic canvas and it is for you to say and you alone, how you are going to paint the picture when it eventually emerges.

Very shortly Mr Curtis-Bennett, Colonel Campbell and myself will leave you to your own devices. This is a case, gentlemen which in my view rather lends itself to rhetoric and a forensic approach. Perhaps quite properly learned counsel and the prosecutor have availed themselves of their right to so approach it. But I felt, gentlemen, you have a difficult task and a responsible task and therefore I hoped that I gave you what I conceived to be my duty to give, a plain straightforward statement of the facts, such little law as there is, putting it as far as I can in the cold plain fair language of the world and making it crystal clear to you that you are the judges of any matter in this court – that that would be the most fair way and most helpful way to put it.

Now, gentlemen, as I say, lawyers have finished in this case. We have all done our best to put the matters, before you fairly and justly. Very soon, sir, you with your members will decide this case. It is, as I began a serious and grave case; it is a case which has caused a great deal of interest. It has raised matters which perhaps from the British prestige point of view we are not altogether proud of; but, gentlemen, do not let that bar you in the least from doing your duty to Captain Langham.

If you feel he is guilty and that this is proper verdict after you have examined the whole of this evidence, convict him; equally if you are satisfied that conviction has not been brought to your minds, that there is a genuine reasonable doubt, then, gentlemen, it is your duty to acquit him and you will pay no attention to what the great big world outside may think or say when you have arrived at your verdict.

Now, sir, I really do not think there is anything more that I feel I should say to you in this case. As I said before, I see no question of law at all. They are questions of fact entirely for you and feel now that I have done my duty as far as being Judge Advocate of this case, if I ask you, sir, with your members to close the Court and decide whether the prosecution have made out this case beyond reasonable doubt.

It can be sometimes hard to realise what is missing from a speech. In the case of Curtis-Bennett's speech he did not refer to the evidence of Scholes. I think that was important and the jury should have been reminded of it. I can understand why Campbell did not refer to it, but I am at a loss to understand why the Judge Advocate General did not mention it, having mentioned the evidence of virtually every other witness in the trial.

CHAPTER 19
The Verdict

Those were the last words the court martial officers comprising the jury heard before a verdict was given. I personally do not agree with Frank that the summing up was biased. I think it was largely fair, and it was now left with the seven senior officers and their prejudices and life experiences to retire (without the Judge Advocate General) to consider their verdict.

Frank must have been very worried waiting for his brother officers to deliver their verdict. He thought that the Judge Advocate General's summing up was biased against him and he feared such bias might cause the jury to find a guilty verdict. Certainly, the Judge Advocate General did spend more time reminding the jury of brother officers of the salient points of the prosecution's case, and offering various suggestions as to how the jury might treat the prosecution's evidence.

But bias is not measured in minutes. On paper it looks like a fair summing up, but I was not there and do not know if the summing up was accompanied by gestures, faces of disdain or by a certain tone, all of which can show bias but such bias will not be apparent in the printed word.

Also, we must remember that Frank had been elated by Curtis-Bennett's speech and he saw no error in it. To have to listen to the other side of the story would have been a worrying experience. He would have gone from a high, made probably higher by Campbell's somewhat ineffectual speech, to a low caused by the Judge Advocate General pointing out there were possible interpretations of the facts which differed from those set out by Curtis-Bennett.

It took the jury an hour and ten minutes to conclude their deliberations, a fraction of the time that either advocate spent in their closing speeches and the summing up.

I have no way of knowing what the jury discussed. The fact that it only took them an hour and ten minutes means that most of them had probably made up their minds well before the summing up finished. Ultimately it would be decided on whether they believed Frank, Langham and Van Rije.

When the jury walked back into court the seven officers of field rank comprising the jury were asked whether they found the defendant Oliver Langham guilty or not guilty. These are the moments that make the heart beat faster for the accused and also the lawyer for the accused. Curtis-Bennett, Norris and Goy had become close to the case, close to their clients and despite what lawyers may claim, they actually believed in their innocence. They had to try to maintain impassive features as the jury trooped back into court, looking at their faces for a hint of the verdict, all the while their hearts beating faster. Soon Curtis-Bennett, Norris and Goy would see the result of their hard work on the case. Soon Langham would know his fate and soon Frank, who had worked the hardest on the case and financed all of it except Curtis-Bennett's fees, would know whether he had been convicted as a shadow defendant of being cruel to the Nazis.

The Judge Advocate General asked the seven officers of field rank, "How do you find the accused, Oliver Langham, guilty or not guilty?"

The foreman of the jury replied, "Not Guilty, and that is the verdict of us all." Langham was acquitted and Frank, by association, was acquitted.

Curtis-Bennett stood up and invited the court to honourably acquit Langham of the charges; the court retired, but after another short break the officers comprising the jury simply acquitted Langham and ordered him to be released. In acquitting Langham, they also in reality acquitted Frank Edmunds. Frank was a shadow defendant in the case; he too had been found not guilty.

In Frank's own words:

"The court retired and came back with their clear verdict of AQUITTAL." It must have given Frank as much pleasure to type that phrase years later as it did to hear the verdict of acquittal years earlier in 1948.

I am puzzled by the failure to honourably acquit Langham. It reflects that the officers did feel that Langham performed some act which reflected upon his honour and therefore did not leave the court with his character entirely untouched. But these are nuances; in most criminal trials in England the jury returns a verdict of guilty or not guilty. Questions of honour seem to be for certain members of the military, not for ordinary folk, and not for the likes of Jewish Munich-born Dick Langham who had served his adopted country so honourably.

Frank had been too dazed and too stunned for months at the extraordinary injustice and the warped manner of the so-called investigation and prosecution to be bitter. He had concentrated his mind on what was needed to be done to obtain an acquittal, rather than ruminating on the injustice of the prosecution.

Deep down, he wrote, that he knew that all the vile methods employed by the prosecution could not adversely influence the honesty and decency of the military jury comprising seven senior British brother officers under the presidency of Brigadier W. E. Underhill. British justice ultimately did prevail.

Dick Langham and Frank first went off to a press conference in Fleet Street. Frank was very outspoken and was later glad in a way that he was not quoted verbatim, but it was a relief to him to say what he had to say.

Frank and Dick both went to their homes from there. Frank was quite shattered, but relieved that it was all over. His parents were anxiously awaiting him and then congratulatory telegrams began arriving and letters from friends and other officers and this made Frank very happy. He was glad that he was strong enough to stand up to it all and see it through.

Frank's parents were not untouched by the trial; during the course of the trial, sensationally and often inaccurate reported in the press every day, they had received many ugly, anonymous and threatening letters and phone calls at their home in Wembley following some of the adverse publicity given in the press.

There was still work to be done by Frank before he could forget this whole, nasty business.

First, it was necessary for him to do battle with the War Office, to recover the costs Frank had laid out for the defence. Secondly, he felt that he had to do all he could – based on all the unpleasant experiences he had been through – to assist his Commanding Officer Colonel Stephens in his predicament and give advice regarding his forthcoming court martial.

Frank had already promised Kees Van Rije and Dick Langham whilst they were all under arrest in Bielefeld between 3 and 17 November 1947 that he would do all he could within his means and help from friends to take care of the joint defence costs.

Having only just restarted a business career from scratch, after an interruption of over six years of war service, it was not an easy matter to undertake. However, matters were made easier for him *"because friends offered their help in this respect and our not only brilliant, but quite extraordinary, human and generous Kings Counsel, Derek Curtis-Bennett had not only turned down other profitable briefs, in order to be able to devote himself fully to the twenty-two days' Court Martial, but he also waived his fees. Nevertheless, it was essential for me to get the War Office to at least reimburse most of the expenses incurred in our defence."*

Frank's solicitors issued writs against the War Office and several individual officers and they wanted him to go through with the necessary legal proceedings, in order to obtain proper compensation. However, when the War Office came forward after months of negotiations which were to Frank "not unacceptable proposals", Frank decided to come to an amicable compromise agreement with them.

The Treasury solicitor, who acted on behalf of the War Office, offered a certain lump sum payment, on condition that Frank would withdraw all claims completely. He accepted the terms of the agreement and payment in full and final settlement of "*all claims by me for wrongful arrest, false imprisonment or detention whether such claims lay against the War Office or any other defendant named in the Writ.*"

In view of Derek Curtis-Bennett's generosity, Markby Stewart & Wadeson's reasonableness with their charges, the fact that practically all of the travelling charges and other expenses of military and even ex-military defence witnesses had been met by the War Office, the War Office's four figure compensation offer was not far short of actual costs incurred including the fees of Malcom Norris, Frank's junior counsel.

Frank decided that an amicable agreement with the War Office was a far better solution for him to accept than to indulge in expensive and distracting litigation. Also, quite honestly, he had had enough and was relieved that it was all over. His legal advisers were very disappointed about his decision as they would have liked – at no cost to themselves – to have fought the War Office and obtained a large sum in compensation for Frank and Langham. Not a bad thing for them from a publicity point of view, thought Frank.

CHAPTER 20

What Happened to the People Involved

It had been agreed between the solicitors that the respective courts martial of Langham and Colonel Stephens would be kept quite separate and that they would not join together in respect of witnesses common to both courts martial. Since, however, some of the charges levelled against Colonel Stephens overlapped with this court martial, Frank volunteered to assist Colonel Stephens in providing him with much useful information for his defence. They spent many hours together in Stephens' room at the Grosvenor Hotel, Victoria Station, London, where the Colonel had been detained and later on at his hide-out at Bourne End in Cambridgeshire.

The charges against Colonel Stephens did not include mental cruelty to the detainees, but exclusively dealt with violence carried out by N.C.O.s and warders in the prison and also the prison conditions: mainly there was no heating at the time and the prison experienced temperatures of minus 10° Fahrenheit in the prison, due to the boilers' breakdown as a result of lack or absence of coal. Seven blankets were issued to the prisoners at the time to alleviate their hardship. It transpired that violence in the prison, committed by N.C.O.s and warders was not restricted to Oebsger-Roeder and Mahnke, which Frank had thought to have been isolated cases, but it was also meted out to other prisoners, who subsequently complained – months later – to Mr R.R. Stokes M.P.

The 'star' witnesses for the prosecution in Colonel Stephens' court martial were principally Nazis and SS men Dieter Albrecht of Lueneburg; Menzel of Hamburg; Graf Buttlar-Brandefels, alias Hermann.

Colonel Stephens' principal defence witnesses included Sergeant Jones and Sergeant Brant and a numbers of warders, who had also figured in Frank's court martial. His principal defence witness was the adjutant, Captain MacKean, who was able to confirm that everything possible was done to obtain coal supplies for the prison, but without success, and that everything was done to alleviate the hardship suffered by prisoners.

It was almost a foregone conclusion that Colonel Stephens would be acquitted, because his case should not have even started once Langham had been acquitted.

It was a great relief when Colonel Stephens, demoted for his court martial was acquitted of all charges. He was promoted to Brigadier a few months later. His defence costs, I was informed, were fully borne by MI5. Frank wrote, intriguingly:

"There were two highly top-secret matters – of which I had full knowledge in Colonel Stephens case, which he had been requested by highest authority not to divulge under any

circumstances. These matters, which I am not allowed to mention, were such that it was surprising that the Colonel's Court Martial was allowed to take place at all, because if the Colonel had convicted I could in extremis to bring the matters to light, some very top-ranking officers would have been implicated."

Captain J.S. Smith, R.A.M.C's[58] court martial ended on an unhappy note in June 1948. He was found to have been negligent in his duties and he was dismissed from the army.

His case had absolutely nothing to do with either of the other courts martial, nor with any matter concerning the intelligence side at the Bad Nenndorf Camp. There was nothing that his defence counsel Mr Gerald Slade K.C. could have done to prevent the outcome. Whilst it was an unhappy ending to Captain Smith's military career, he was due for demobilisation and imminent return to civilian life anyway.

Frank went back to Manchester where he developed his business in Manchester with some moderate, but not spectacular success. He retired to the South of France and bought a flat in Nice where his homosexuality was not offensive. He developed happy relationships and played tennis well into his eighties and tended the gardens of the block of apartments where he lived for the sheer joy of it. He then moved to Mougins, as many older people do, high above Cannes where he lived and enjoyed his old life. Later he developed dementia and had to be hospitalised. He died in hospital.

Of the other people who figured in this extraordinary court martial, Oliver 'Dick' Langham left the army and went to America, where he disappeared from sight. You could hardly blame him, not wanting to stay in the United Kingdom. Frank completely lost touch with him. David Goy immigrated to Tasmania.

Frederick Henry ('Derek') Curtis-Bennett went on to defend John Christie, Klaus Fuchs and many others. He died in 1954, some three months after his young second wife committed suicide.

Oebsger-Roeder did not remain in prison for long. He was released and lived for a while in Munich and then went to Indonesia where he worked for the Indonesian Federal Intelligence Service and had enough access to President Suharto to be his biographer and consultant. He returned to Munich where he died in 1992, at the age of eighty.

Horst Mahnke went into journalism and worked for Der Spiegel. He was presumed to be the weaker of the two. He rose to be Chairman of Axel Springer and Chief Executive of the Association of German Publishers.

---

[58] Royal Army Medical Corps.

As for the rest I do not know what happened to them. I can only guess that they eventually returned to normal peacetime life and like most soldiers wanted to forget the war by immersing themselves in what became the new normality.

The interrogations that resulted in this extraordinary court martial were intended to discover whether there would be a terrorist uprising or plot on the first anniversary of Hitler's birth, after the end of the war. At that time Germany was a beaten nation, enduring hardship, and almost famine conditions. Several million Germans had perished in the war and the defeat, which Oebsger-Roeder described as the "capitulation" of Germany resulted in many high office, privileged people, especially in the SS who were lauded and respected when Hitler was alive, being treated as criminals, to be hunted down, caught, tried and from time to time executed.

The conditions for terrorist activity were there and, in my view, Oebsger-Roeder had been trying to foment this activity. The Soviet Union were mischievous enough to encourage any failure by the British authorities in the British Zone of Germany. The fact that Frank and his team had information from two separate sources corroborated by senior allied military people raised a probability, but not proof, that Oebsger-Roeder was involved in the kind of plot that the Allies feared.

In October 1949, just over a year after the end of Frank's trial, the Federal Republic of Germany known as West Germany was formed and the British, French and Americans handed over their authority to the new West German government under the leadership of Chancellor Konrad Adenauer. East Germany had been formed as a state a few days earlier.

Germans, by their nature, are well organised people and Oebsger-Roeder and Mahnke, in my view, were probably arrested before they had completed their plans for the uprising. It was this arrest, I suspect, that stopped the plotters in their tracks, and their imprisonment left their sympathisers without a leader and without a plan. Without leaders the other Germans who would have involved themselves in the plot simply did nothing, they had simply run out of steam and like the rest of the German nation tried to put the war and Adolf Hitler as far behind them as possible into the darkest depths of history, so that they could get on with the rest of their lives in peace and to develop prosperity for themselves and for Germany.

Ultimately the trial determined the issues, as trials do, not absolutely and unconditionally, but on the basis that the prosecution had failed to prove its case beyond reasonable doubt. Innocence and guilt are, as far as the law is concerned, relative terms, not absolute ones. A trial is an attempt to reach the truth, but in human affairs truth is an elusive concept and once found has many facets and complexities, most of which are beyond human understanding.

THE END

Glossary

ADC	Aide de Camp
BAOR	British Army of the Rhine
BLA	Office of Bilateral Affairs
CCG	Control Commission Germany
CSDIC	Combined Services Detailed Interrogation Centre
CSDIC(BLA)	Combined Services Detailed Interrogation British Liberation Army
CSDIC(WEA)	Combined Services Detailed Interrogation Centre Western European Area
CSM	Company Sergeant Major
DDMI	Deputy Director Military Intelligence
DIC	Detailed Interrogation Centre
Freiheit Bewegung	Freedom Movement
HQ	Headquarters
KC	King's Counsel – the highest grade of barrister or advocate at the English bar, now known as Queen's Counsel
MI6	A name used for part of the UK's Secret Intelligence Service
NCO	Non-Commissioned Officer
NSDAP	Nazi Party
RAMC	Royal Army Medical Corps
RHSA	Reich Security Main Office
RSM	Regimental Sergeant Major
SIO	Senior Intelligence Officer
SIO	Senior Intelligence Officer
SIR29	Special Interrogation Report no 29
SS	Schutzstaffel
USFET	US Forces European High Command

Printed in Great Britain
by Amazon